FIGHTIN' WORDS

FIGHTIN' WORDS

25 Years
of
Provocative Poetry and Prose
from
"The Blue Collar PEN"

Edited by Judith Cody, Kim McMillon and Claire Ortalda

PEN Oakland Publications
Oakland, California

Heyday
Berkeley, California

© 2014 by PEN Oakland

All rights reserved. No portion of this work may be reproduced or transmitted in any form or by any means, electronic or mechanical, including photocopying and recording, or by any information storage or retrieval system, without permission in writing from PEN Oakland, Box 71268, Oakland, CA 94612.

Publisher's Cataloging-In-Publication Data
(Prepared by The Donohue Group, Inc.)

Fightin' words : 25 years of provocative poetry and prose from "The Blue Collar PEN" / edited by Judith Cody, Kim McMillon and Claire Ortalda.

   pages ; cm

   ISBN: 978-0-615-96797-4

   1. Protest literature, American. 2. American literature--Minority authors. 3. Cultural pluralism in literature. 4. Social problems in literature. 5. Minorities in literature. I. Cody, Judith. II. McMillon, Kim. III. Ortalda, Claire. IV. P.E.N. Centre for Writers in Exile. American branch. Oakland Chapter. V. Title: Fighting words

PS509.P73 F54 2014
810.8/0355   2014912601

Cover Art: Pomegranate Design
Cover Design: Pomegranate Design
Interior Design/Typesetting: Pomegranate Design
Printing and Binding: Thomson-Shore, Dexter, MI

Orders should be addressed to the distributor:
         Heyday
         P.O. Box 9145, Berkeley, CA 94709
         (510) 549-3564, Fax (510) 549-1889
         www.heydaybooks.com

10 9 8 7 6 5 4 3 2 1

This book is
dedicated to

Reginald Lockett

"Yes"

Table of Contents

	xi	A Note from the Editors
Ishmael Reed	xii	Introduction
Elmaz Abinader	1	Poetry, Politics and How Tyranny Changes the P to a p and the p to a P, *essay*
Opal Palmer Adisa	3	Urban Death Altars, *poem*
Francisco X. Alarcón	4	Manifiesto Poética, Poetic Manifesto, *poem*
	5	In Ixtli In Yollotl, Rostro y Corazón, Face and Heart, *poem*
Mimi Albert	6	I Never Thanked My Father, *essay*
Karla Andersdatter	8	A Poet in the Third World, *poem*
Avotcja	10	Cosmic Soul Mates, *poem*
	11	Blue To The Bone, *poem*
Devereaux Baker	12	Reunion, *poem*
Marsha Lee Berkman	13	Words That Transformed the World, *essay*
Christopher Bernard	14	Is There a Nazi in Your Future? *poem*
Carla Blank	15	A New New Deal for the Arts, *essay*
Abby Lynn Bogomolny	16	the bus station, *poem*
	17	natural law, *poem*
Marek Breiger	18	Who We Are, *essay*
Cecil Brown	19	MC Cyrano, *play*
Janine Canan	21	We Are the Women, *poem*
	22	Blessed, *poem*
Neeli Cherkovski	23	At the Caffé Trieste, *poem*
Judith Cody	25	Truth. All of it at Once. *poem*
	25	Going Home, *poem*
	26	Did You Shoot Anyone, Daddy? *poem*
Gillian Conoley	27	occupied, *poem*
Lucha Corpi	28	Berkeley Blues, *poem*, translated by Catherine Rodríguez-Nieto
John Curl	30	O Columbia, *poem*
Steve Dalachinsky	32	the snake reborn, *poem*
J.P. Dancing Bear	34	Independence Day, *poem*
Lucille Lang Day	36	The People Versus Oscar Cole, *poem*
Kathleen de Azevedo	37	Before the Ship Sailed, *short story*
Wendy Doniger	39	You Can't Make an Omelette, *essay*
Sharon Doubiago	41	Maybe The Revolution, *poem*
Camille T. Dungy	43	Daisy Cutter, *poem*
Margarita Engle	44	The Observer, *poem*

Maria Espinosa	45	Dying Unfinished, *novel excerpt*
Adelle Foley	47	60 Years Later /After the Camps, *poem*
Jack Foley	48	H.D. Moe (1937-2013): Fluxional, Vehicular and Transitive, *essay*
	51	"The Name is Popularly Interpreted to Mean 'Wanderer,'" *poem*
CB Follett	53	Words to the Mother Whose Son Killed My Son, *poem*
	54	The Jackdaws Come at Noon, *poem*
Joan Gelfand	55	Good Morning America, Where Are You? *poem*
Herbert Gold	56	Cri de Coeur – Cri de Spleen, *essay*
Rafael Jesús González	57	*Al fin de la Cuenta Larga*, poem
	58	At the End of the Long Count, *poem*
Ray Gonzalez	59	A Judge Orders the Opening of Federico Garcia Lorca's Grave, *poem*
	60	They Call the Mountain Carlos, *poem*
Nathalie Handal	61	On the Way to Jerez de la Frontera
Peter J. Harris	62	American Man, *poem*
Gerald Haslam	63	The Great Biblical Colloquy, *fiction*
Juan Felipe Herrera	66	Photograph with Tony, Francisco & Jorge Outside Brava Theatre, San Francisco, 9/15/12, *poem*
	67	The More You (Hotel Realization Poem #1. 9/22/13, Washington D.C.), *poem*
Jack Hirschman	68	The *Da-Sein* Arcane, *poem*
Mitch Horowitz	70	Black Moses: The Radical Metaphysics of Marcus Garvey, *essay*
Doug Metapoet Howerton	72	Fighters Fight the Wars, *poem*
Kitty Kelley	73	Unauthorized, But Not Untrue, *essay*
Vandana Khanna	76	Echo, *poem*
Paul Krassner	77	Remembering Kesey, essay
Michael Lally	79	Fighting Words, *poem*
Nhuan Xuan Le (Thanh-Thanh)	80	Just Cause, *poem*
Rabbi Michael Lerner	81	Loving Words To Heal and Transform the World, *essay*
Leza Lowitz	83	Stop the Bullet, *poem*
Kirk Lumpkin	85	Occupy Poem, *poem*
	86	Two Poems for My Father, *poem*
Alison Luterman	87	Day's News: Oakland, *poem*
Mary Mackey	88	Walking Upside Down on the Other Side of the World, *poem*

Mike Madison	89	Polite Fighting Words, *essay*
Tony R. Rodriguez	90	Preface to the excerpt from "The Meaning of 'Western Defense'"
Norman Mailer	91	The Meaning of "Western Defense," *essay excerpt*
devorah major	93	political poem, *poem*
Clive Matson	94	Thank You, *poem*
Michael McClure	96	Solstice Thumbprint, *poem*
Colleen J. McElroy	97	The Tongue, *poem*
Kim McMillon	98	Pele and Yemaja, The Goddesses, *poem*
	98	Excitement Junkie, *poem*
	99	Cosmopolitans and Passion, *poem*
	99	A Hatful of Butterflies, *poem*
Adam David Miller	100	My Nisei Friends are Dying, a Colloquy, *poem*
E. Ethelbert Miller	101	Wounded by Words, *essay*
Yasmin Mogul	102	It Was the Feast of Purima, *novel excerpt*
Jefferson Morley	104	Unspeakable: My JFK Lawsuit, *essay*
Jill Nelson	106	Old Dog, Old Tricks, *essay*
Gerald Nicosia	107	The Greeks Who Stole Kerouac, *essay*
A.L. Nielsen	109	Technology Transfer 41, *poem*
Elizabeth Nunez	110	Boundaries, *novel excerpt*
Peter Orner	112	Plaza Revolución, Mexico City, 6 A.M., *fiction*
Claire Ortalda	113	NO-Body, *flash fiction*
Sandra Park	115	If You Live in a Small House, *novel excerpt*
Margo Perin	116	Entropy, *poem*
Richard Prince	118	Interview by Ishmael Reed
Jerry Ratch	123	Unemployment, *poem*
Ishmael Reed	125	Why I Will Never Write A Sonnet, *poem*
Tennessee Reed	126	The Mid-Afternoon Brain Freeze, *poem*
Fred Reiss	127	Fightin' Cancer: Space Walking in the Outer Big C Galaxy, *essay*
Doren Robbins	128	Vet Ode, *poem*
Tony R. Rodriguez	129	"I'd Rather Smile With You," *poem*
Andy Ross	130	Becoming a Bookseller, *essay*
Clifton Ross	132	Night in the New World Order, *poem*
	132	The Proud Sinner's Prayer, *poem*
	133	Once It's All Lost, *poem*
Suhayl Saadi	134	The Oracle of Easter Monday: For Murdered Writers, *poem*
Floyd Salas	136	The Politics of Poetry, *poem*

Mona Lisa Saloy	138	September 2005, New Orleans, *poem*
	138	New Orleans, a Neighborhood Nation, *poem*
	139	When I saw bodies in Post-Katrina New Orleans, *poem*
Richard Silberg	140	George Hackett Simpson and the Three Sad Cigarettes, *poem*
Leslie Simon	141	Authorship, *poem*
Jarmila Marie Skalna	142	Laura, *fiction*
Rebecca Solnit	144	Oakland's Beautiful Nonviolence, *essay*
Barry Spector	146	What Will the New Myths Be? How Will We Create Them? *essay*
Jayne Lyn Stahl	148	Did Someone Order Fireworks? *poem*
Doreen Stock	149	The Oil Poem, *poem*
Susan Suntree	150	Lineage, *poem*
Susan Terris	151	Bald Eagle on Potato Lake, *poem*
Clifford E. Trafzer	152	Never Enough, *essay*
Alma Luz Villanueva	154	Breathing While Brown, *poem*
Gerald Vizenor	156	Blue Ravens: Native American Indians in the First World War, *novel excerpt*
Michael Warr	158	Hallucinating at the Velvet Lounge, *poem*
Harriet A. Washington	159	Thalidomide Redux: Prudence and the Pill, *essay*
Eric Miles Williamson	161	Back to Oakland, *essay*
A.D. Winans	163	Dancing with Words, *poem*
Koon Woon	165	The Phantom of the Opera, *poem*
	166	The high walls I cannot scale, *poem*
	166	A Smoke Break at the Nuclear Command, *poem*
Sue Owens Wright	167	Homed for the Holidays: A Christmas Wish for Homeless Pets, *essay*
Al Young	169	Four Septembers, *poem*
	170	One August Summary, *poem*
Andrena Zawinski	171	What About a Fight? *poem*
Claire Ortalda	172	Appendix A: The History of PEN Oakland
Ishmael Reed	174	Appendix B: The United States Needs a New PEN Center
Floyd Salas	176	Appendix C: PEN 55th World Congress—Funchal, Madeira, Portugal
Acknowledgements	178	
Contributors	182	
Our Thanks	200	

A Note from the Editors

Fightin' Words began with the notion of chronicling the literary legacy of PEN Oakland, which, in the words of former board member Jack Foley, was founded with the "unique purpose to promote works of excellence by writers of all cultural and racial backgrounds and to educate both the public and the media as to the nature of multicultural work."

To achieve this mission, beginning in 1990, PEN Oakland hosted a series of symposia on issues of freedom of expression affecting marginalized groups within our society including minority representation in the media and inequalities within our justice system. We also instituted the PEN Oakland Josephine Miles Literary Awards and, a few years later, the PEN Oakland Censorship Award and the Lifetime Achievement Award.

Included among our winners and panelists were such notable figures as Iris Chang, the late author of *The Rape of Nanking*, Daniel Ellsberg, Paul Krassner, Bill Moyers, Norman Mailer, Greg Palast, Kitty Kelley, Barbara Lee, and Gary Webb, who died tragically in what many believe was in direct response to his exposé, *Dark Alliance: The CIA, the Contras, and the Crack Cocaine Explosion*, honored by PEN Oakland with a Censorship Award in 1999.

Yet many of our speakers and award-winners did not and do not enjoy the name recognition of the writers cited above. Though their works are published, many of these writers — chroniclers of communities outside the mainstream and of unreported societal injustices — remain largely invisible to the public consciousness. This is the reason why the publication of *Fightin' Words* is so important — because it acknowledges those writers who have helped PEN Oakland make a difference in the struggle for social and economic justice for the past twenty-five years.

With the assistance of a Zellerbach Family Foundation grant, we assembled the work of as many past winners and symposia speakers as possible, as well as that of members of PEN Oakland, in a book of writings chronicling our legacy of activism via the written word.

Our history is one of celebrating the underdog — the writer who may or may not become a household name, but is often the heart of his or her community, writers that honor culture, humanity, life, family and community. *Fightin' Words* offers a form of immortality — through the written word — to those that have been part of PEN Oakland's twenty-five years of fighting, celebrating, and honoring multicultural literature.

INTRODUCTION

Pulling Marginalized Literature To The Center: The Origin of "The Blue Collar PEN"

Although I'd written poetry and nonfiction and maybe some fiction before entering college, it was at the University of Buffalo, which was a private university at the time, that I became inspired by cultural nationalism and multiculturalism in literature, particularly the cultural nationalism of W.B. Yeats and the Celtic Revival, which challenged the culture of the British Occupation, which like all Occupations require that the Occupied assimilate to the culture of the conqueror. I was also influenced by Ezra Pound, who explored Chinese culture and even tried his hand at writing in Kanji and reported in a letter his awareness of the "Nigerian god of thunder," which those in Nigeria and the Yoruba Diaspora in South and Central America and elsewhere identify as Shango.

So that was the origin of my mixing and sampling of cultures, and a quest to find my roots instead of imitating a European model, slavishly. When I went to New York in 1962, I came in contact with a group of cultural nationalists at *Umbra* magazine, an important contributor to the quest for a sovereign approach to creating art. We met at the late Tom Dent's apartment on The Lower East Side. *Umbra*'s contribution was overshadowed by the tendency to feature white male art by the uptown publicity machine. (Ed Sanders has done a good job in capturing the white male domination of Lower East Side culture in his fascinating memoir *Fug Me*.) Women were there to provide pleasure and blacks and Puerto Rican writers and artists were left out in favor of people like Andy Warhol with whom my partner Carla Blank and I used to have long conversations, sitting with him and Gerald Malanga at Max's Kansas City, where he held court.

Though it was a fight between black poets and some private security guards, hired by the owner of a poetry cafe called Le Metro, that led to the founding of St. Mark's Poetry Project, the website of the Project neglects this history, another example of the white counter culture refusing to give credit to blacks who participate in the founding of important artistic institutions. Ted Joans complained until his death about his being disappeared in the history of The Beats. Blacks, Iranians and others contributed to *The East Village Other* founded by Walter Bowart and me, yet they were omitted in a recent retrospective about this newspaper, which I had named.

In 1964, I was introduced to Carla Blank by the late poet N.H. Pritchard, now the subject of an almost cult like retrospective. Carla, a star at the Judson Church avant garde dance scene whose masterpiece, a performance called *The Wall Street Journal*, was revived in 2009 by Robert Wilson, was in contact with the Japanese avant garde, among whom was the great Japanese dancer and choreographer Suzushi Hanayagi. After my first novel, *The Free Lance Pallbearers*, our circle expanded to include a variety of artists of different backgrounds.

After the publication of *Pallbearers* in 1967, I approached Doubleday about publishing an anthology of black writers. As I was compiling the anthology, someone told me about an eighteen year old poet named Victor Hernandez Cruz. I included Victor, now a Chancellor of the Academy of American Poets, but who, at the time, was flunking Spanish at Benjamin Franklin High School. While teaching at the University of Washington at Seattle in 1969, I read Frank Chin's *A Chinese Lady Dies* in an underground newspaper called *The Great Speckled Bird*. I included Frank. *19 Necromancers From Now* thus became one of the first multicultural anthologies and the primitive ancestor of this PEN Oakland anthology *Fightin' Words*. At the party for *19 Necromancers From Now*, held at the Oakland home of Luther Nichols, west coast representative for Doubleday, Frank Chin, Lawson Inada, Shawn Wong and Jeff Chang met for the first time. Shawn traces the beginning of the Asian American Renaissance to this meeting. Al Young and I began *The Yardbird Reader*. *Yardbird Reader 3* was edited by Frank, Lawson and Shawn.

In the mid seventies, I became a director and later Chairperson of the Coordinating Council of Literary Magazines, which, at that time, was run by William Phillips, a survivor of the old left wing literary wars and editor of *The Partisan Review*. Rudy Anaya and I replaced the old leadership and opened it up to Asian American, African American and Hispanic writers. This included bringing Leslie Silko and Toni Cade Bambara onto the board. With a grant from the Ford Foundation, Victor and I began the Before Columbus Foundation in 1976. We decided that instead of waiting around to be accepted as tokens by existing white nationalist institutions like the National Book Awards, or awaiting an invitation by the segregated counter culture, we would begin our own book awards program, one that would be inclusive. The American Book Awards were begun in 1980. We started at The West Side Community Center, but by the next year Joe Papp hosted us at New York's Public Theater. Among the presenters were Toni Morrison and the late Donald Barthelme. The M.C. was former California Poet Laureate, Quincy Troupe.

In the mid seventies, I was hired as director of The San Francisco State Poetry Center. Uproar occurred. Some of the white poets feared a black uprising that would eliminate their participation. I met Floyd Salas. Floyd became my ally to reform what I was calling at the time "the AT&T of the poetry world," which at that time was dominated by The Beat Generation and its acolytes. I wrote an essay about this monopoly, which incurred the wrath of Allen Ginsberg, who bawled me out during a luncheon at Enrico's. I held my ground and Bob Callahan pointed out to Ginsberg about the Beat Generation's reputation as misogynist and exclusional, racially. Ginsberg saw the light and toward the end of his life taught a course in African American literature at Brooklyn College. I was one of his guest lecturers. All one has to do is read *Poets & Writers* to see that the American literary scene is still a white chauvinist scene. The possible exception is the Naropa Institute, which, under the leadership of Anne Waldman is a model of diversity. The mainstream? Forget it. With the exception of a few tokens, it remains one in which multicultural poets are marginalized. An example occurred recently, in *The New York Times Book Review*, in which one of the tokens wrote about politics and contemporary culture. Not a single Black American, Native American, Hispanic, or Asian American was mentioned. Floyd had shown his mettle when a movement to make San Francisco State more diverse was met by strong-armed resistance. Al Young and I published his novel, *Lay My Body on the Line,* about the drive for an inclusive Ethnic Studies Department. He is probably the best Oakland novelist since Jack London. Floyd Salas was the perfect ally in our attempt to build institutions that would support diversity.

In keeping with our philosophy of building our own institutions instead of waiting around to be selected as a token by the establishment, like the dog who showed up every night at the train station to greet his master, not realizing that his master was dead, Floyd, Claire Ortalda and I founded PEN Oakland. We have become known as "The Blue Collar PEN" by *The New York Times*, which is appropriate since most of us are of working class origin, and often our discussions take the form of a Pier 6 brawl. Ultimately, we have survived these decades intact because none of us has forgotten where we came from.

It's been twenty five years since Claire, Floyd, the late Reginald Lockett and I met at Asmara, an Eritrean restaurant in Oakland, to establish another institution for the purpose of pulling the marginalized literature into the center. The resistance continues as a No Nothing Tea Party mentality sweeps not only politics but culture. In Arizona, they are raiding schools and removing books by Chicano and Chicana authors from the shelves. In the same state, Ethnic Studies has been banned. The Tennessee Tea Party wants to ban any reference to slavery in text books.

We are in for a long twilight struggle, but in the end, our country will be in better shape than the one we found. We will have helped to create not an exclusive City on the Hill, but the inclusive Rainbow City in the Valley.

-Ishmael Reed, Chairman of the Board, PEN Oakland

FIGHTIN' WORDS

ELMAZ ABINADER

Poetry, Politics and How Tyranny Changes the P to a p and the p to a P

Two poetic practices moved side-by-side in my coming up. The one I inherited as an Arab daughter lives on the ground. The events of the day were often transformed into poems—about everything—from how ripe the fruit was to a cautionary tale to hide possessions from invaders. The tradition that engaged me the most was the oral poetry duel called a *Zajal*—partially sung, partially spoken with a specific metrical form, oral and improvised by maybe two men in an outdoor setting. In the case of my family, the two poets stand on the *roojme*, a terrace behind our house. One starts a poem about truth and justice. The other answers, challenging his perspective, fueling the battle with his own. The duel goes on until the enthusiasm turns to warfare and competition, the action gets hot and sometimes chairs are thrown. Rarely are these poems written down. But reputations grew on them.

My father, who is a poet, told me these stories, while my US education was presenting poetry with a capital P. Lofty work of sophisticated language that praised aspects of nature. We focused on British works because they used the Queen's English, *Come Live with me and be my love/ and we will all the pleasures prove...* Marlowe. They had recognizable rhyme and unapologetic romanticism. The pastoral poems were often memorized without our even recognizing their content: *Under the spreading Chestnut tree, the village smithy stands...* Longfellow

If the poems contained something other than rhyme that needed scanning, symbols that needed interpreting, literary devices that needed recognizing, lines that needed counting, and author's lives that needed learning, my education forgot to point them out.
So the world seemed to divide into two: those who thought poetry had nothing to do with them and those who yearned to mimic those elegant and sophisticated phrases. I won a poetry contest in fifth grade for writing a sonnet about the pain of Jesus on the cross. The poetry world at school seemed polar opposite of the poetic tradition I inherited.

By the time I finished my MFA at Columbia in poetry in the late seventies, poetry still smacked of exclusivity in the US. My workshops had criticized my work for too much cultural content, i.e., sentimentality, or too political and so my poem won't live beyond the moment. Simultaneously I was learning about Ernesto Cardenal in Nicaragua, a minister in the government, who was also a famous poet. *The Triumph of the Revolution is the Triumph of Poetry.* All the manicuring of my poetic sensibilities collapsed after seeing that banner in the newspaper and poets gathering together to make a revolution.

Like writers-of-color of my generation, I had to create my own education—I went to Whitman, read the Beats, who were dismissed in my scholarly life, pumped in the Black Arts Movement like elixir. I read South American poets from Neruda to Andrade, and shifted to Europe, starting with Garcia-Lorca, moved further East until I landed back in Lebanon with Nizar Qabani. And my ship kept sailing until I discovered worlds where poetry was part of everyday life, the political scene, of writing history, of literature.

Suddenly for me, the capital P, became a small p—poetry began to live on the ground again. This understanding was happening all around me. Particularly as writers-of-color had some minor presence in the poetry scene. I watched a new political sensibility unfold. And while some people write and read only the poetry of language or the poetry of still waters, they probably know that, in the continuum of poetry, "others" are there and they are being read and listened to.

All this is a long way to get to my moment of the day and to Facebook which, as a rule, can be a writer's enemy. However, I dropped in occasionally to see what my friends were reading and displaying. Last year, in every visit, I saw postings called *Poets responding to SB 1070* (the law in the state of Arizona criminalizing undocumented residents—police are directed to stop and demand "papers" from someone of "reasonable suspicion."). Poem after poem, poet after poet, put their voice against this law.

I have been heartened in the last twenty years by poets, famous and otherwise, on the issues that are threatening our freedoms and well-being, from Homeland Security, to the invasion of Iraq, to the ICE raids, to poisonings of all kinds, environmental and informational, to Abu Gharib, to SB 1070. We have taken the poetry from the ground and given it a capital P.

Poets protesting a bill may have little or no effect on what happens to it. But a rallying point makes us more a community. We can sit on our separate mountaintops writing about our own visions, but when pushed by the sense of violation, we unite, if just for a moment.

Last summer Seni Senerivatne a Sri Lankan, British, South African writer, read a poem about the Israeli Drones and the new capabilities of this destructive fleet (wingspan of 86 feet). The poem was beautiful and clearly pointed out how much terror can be developed legally, and how it will become a fact of our lives. Chills—writers from different places, of varying styles rallied around this poem emotionally, as well as poetically. We experienced this poem with a small p and a large P.

It's a (re)-new(ed) world where poetry has its say. Truth to power in verse. I'm home again. Where I started, sitting on the *roojme* with poetry in my head. I am ready for praise-song, I am ready for homage, I am ready for protests; I am ready for a fight.

OPAL PALMER ADISA

Urban Death Altars

at certain street corners
on some dilapidated blocks
by liquor-lined stores intersections
amidst broken fences
houses with paint peeling
windows with broken blinds askew
and hard brown dirt
instead of lawns or patches of grass
you will find
flowers   balloons   stuffed animals
cards   footballs   notes
tee-shirts   candles   poster note-boards
and other paraphernalia declarations of love

for the one hundred and twenty-two people
murdered in   oakland
i was the first in 2007
wanted others to   see me   all my life
but not this way   shot and dumped
on 98th Ave   do you even know
my name   yeah curtis twiggs
aka verdair laroy mosley
what's that you leaving there
did you know me when i was alive
and prowled these streets seeking
anything to keep my feet on the ground
did you look me in the eyes
asked how i was getting on
called me homey affectionately
when i passed you on the sidewalk
or did you avert your eyes
fold in on yourself   thinking
i wasn't shit   in my four size too large jeans
almost to my knees white tee-shirt well
below my waist   did you ever bring me
flowers or any of that shit you leaving
on the side walk   did you ever stop
to buy me lunch   write me a note
of encouragement   tell me you
love me and had my back
shit   i'm dead   so none of that
means anything   but you still have a chance
you can still make it right for the next brother
or sister before they die
you can turn it around
yes   you   can

FRANCISCO X. ALARCÓN

Manifiesto Poético
*a los Poetas Respondiendo
a la Ley SB 1070 de Arizona*

cada poema
es un acto de fe

en el poder
de la Palabra

una flor cedida
de mano a mano

y enraizada
en el corazón

una oración/canto
iluminando la noche

una canción
entre tanto ruido

un murmullo
de ramas de árbol

al mero filo
del gran desierto

rompiendo las fronteras
de la desesperanza

plantando las semillas
de la renovada esperanza

cada poema
es un llamado a la acción

es decir "sí"
al régimen del "no"

un desafío   a
al silencio social

construyendo confianza
en respuesta al temor

un testimonio
del alma humana

reconociendo
que a pesar de todas

nuestras diferencias
y peculiaridades

todos respiramos
amamos y soñamos

celebramos y sufrimos
bajo un mismo Sol

Poetic Manifesto
*to the Poets Responding
to Arizona Law SB 1070*

each poem
is an act of faith

in the power
of the Word

a flower passed
hand to hand

and rooted
in the heart

a prayer/chant
lighting the night

a song amidst
so much noise

a murmur
of tree branches

at the very edge
of the big desert

breaking down
the borders of despair

sowing the seeds
of renewed hope

each poem is
a call for action

is saying "yes"
to the rule of "no"

defiance
to social silence

building trust
in response to fear

a testimony
of the human soul

recognizing
that in spite all

our differences
and peculiarities

we all breathe
love and dream

celebrate and suffer
under the same one Sun

In Ixtli In Yollotl *
Rostro y Corazón

que nuestros oídos
oigan
lo que nadie
quiere oír

que nuestros ojos
vean
lo que todos
quieren ocultar

que nuestras bocas
digan la verdad
de nuestros rostros
y corazones

que nuestros brazos
sean ramas
que den sombra
y alegría

seamos llovizna
tormenta inesperada
mojémonos
en la lluvia

seamos la llave
la mano la puerta
el pie la pelota
el camino

lleguemos
como niños
a este inmenso
parque de juegos:

¡el universo!

Face and Heart

may our ears
hear
what nobody
wants to hear

may our eyes
see
what everyone
wants to hide

may our mouths
speak up
our true faces
and hearts

may our arms
be branches
that give shade
and joy

let us be a drizzle
a sudden storm
let us get wet
in the rain

let us be the key
the hand the door
the kick the ball
the road

let us arrive
as children
to this huge
playground:

the universe!

---

* *Ixtli* in Nahuatl, the language of the Aztecs, means *face*, and *yollotl* means *heart*. When your face reflects your heart that is how you say *truth* in Nahuatl.

MIMI ALBERT

I Never Thanked My Father

As a child, I wasn't very happy with my father. After I was adopted, when I was 6 months old, he went into a recording booth and made a little record for the express purpose of informing me that I was going be the first person in his family to earn a Ph.D. But when I grew up and it was clear that I really could accomplish such a thing, he made me turn down a major scholarship from a fine college, Bard, which certainly could have made it easier.

"You'll stay at home with us," he yelled, "and go to Brooklyn College like I did. That's it!"

My father yelled a lot, probably because of the way he himself had grown up. He had wanted only to study botany at Cornell University, but his own father, a self-made millionaire immigrant (before the Stock Market crash of 1929), had refused; he wanted my father to become a rabbi, or at least a lawyer. Ironically, my father never went into a synagogue after he got married. And the Law was out; he couldn't pass the Bar Exam.

Crushed by his family and the Depression, he earned his living by taking care of other people's gardens and by teaching sixth grade in an inner-city school. He wasn't happy, nor were the people around him. I fell in love with Beethoven when I found out that he was deaf because his father had punished him by boxing his ears repeatedly throughout his childhood. It was a pretty safe assumption that this was similar to getting beaten with a strap (as my father beat me), or dashed across a room by one of my father's slaps. So at the age of 10, I could identify with one of the world's great geniuses – because like him, I had been abused.

The idea of living with my father for four more years after I graduated from high school scared me into the streets. At 17, I fled to a tiny bug-infested apartment on the Lower East Side of New York. By the time I was 20 I was what was called "a bad girl." I hung out in Greenwich Village, especially after I got a role in an off-Broadway play. I dressed in black and sandals at a time when girls were supposed to wear twin sets and little pearl necklaces. I smoked and talked a gritty New Yorkese.

It took a long time for me to realize that my father was not entirely to blame for his treatment of me. Oddly, when my mother was away—frequently escaping to "rest homes" to calm her nerves and "get herself together," as she put it—he and I maintained a kind of frozen truce, which sometimes felt almost like affection.

In place of the extravagant meals my mother cooked, we'd share containers of deli and potato salad. On weekends, sometimes, he'd drive the two of us out to Long Island, to visit nurseries filled with budding plants, or to the picket-fenced homes of his many relatives. But no matter what we did during the day, on those weekend nights he'd allow me to watch television or read long after he collapsed into his twin bed beside my mother's empty one. He never asked me to close my book or turn off the lights; he left me alone, as if he understood the importance of solitary pleasure.

This kindness seemed unique in my life, a mark of some approbation never otherwise expressed. What he didn't know was that in my rebellion, I took advantage of his trust: I became a sneak, creeping into the streets of our quiet neighborhood, hot to commit the greatest sin of my life so far. With the help of a friendly, slightly odd usher named Sheldon, I regularly invaded the sole movie theater in our area that actually screened "foreign" films.

There I encountered the sensuous, black and white world wrought by geniuses like Bergman and Fellini. I discovered places and people that I would never otherwise have seen: one, a slightly mad, wide-eyed carnival performer with spiky hair, touring Italy with a brutal carnie strongman who didn't realize that he loved her until too late. In another wonderful film, a girl possibly even younger than myself, but merciless in the unfolding of her beauty, escaped on a stolen sailboat with her boyfriend, navigating the outer islands of the Baltic seacoast, exploring the variations of passion and ocean currents, both at once.

My father, bless him, slept. What would he have done if he had known where I was? A chubby fifteen, impatient to become one of my own heroines, I had never even touched a boy's hand, and was still so unsure of who I was that nothing was possible except an hour or two of fantasy.

And how did I repay him for those stolen moments of freedom? By embarrassing him.

Having been coached by my elder cousins, I sat beside him in a crowded subway car and looking up at him, asked in the loudest voice I could muster, "Daddy, what's a whore?"

He turned green with shock. No such words were ever used around our house. But I was only fifteen, my face as puffy as a kernel of popcorn, my eyes two blanks. Grateful for the noisy train he cleared his throat and offered some foggy euphemism.

"Thank you, daddy," I responded, as we rolled into our station. As, later, I whispered, "thank you, daddy," hurrying to my room after a night with Fellini or Bergman.

How sad it is, now, to come to understand that the only things for which I ever thanked my father were those about which I never told him. But which were symbols, nonetheless, of an otherwise indefinable love.

KARLA ANDERSDATTER

A Poet in the Third World

Dear Senators,
As a citizen of
the United States
of America
I ask that
my government
NO LONGER SUPPORT
the contras
in any way...
not by subversion
of private funds from Texas
to buy weapons or planes

not by suppression of
information or by military
presence in neighboring
countries

not by Ollie North or Fawn...
our military forces
misuse taxpower.
Americans do not want
to waste their lives, their
work energy, their minds
or hearts, and especially
their sons and daughters
on the tragedy
of military involvement
in the politics of
Central America.
For years it has been
known
that our government

> *of the people*
> *by the people*
> *for the people*

has been sending money
to the forces that *allowed*
these violations, ALLOWED
or looked the other way from

    TORTURE
      and
    RAPE...

ALLOWED

these violations
of human rights.
For shame
For shame

to pay for
TORTURE
to pay for
RAPE

When you pay for,
when you VOTE TO PAY FOR
this — YOU
become the torturer.
You
 become the rapist.

    for shame
    for shame

AVOTCJA

Cosmic Soul Mates
for Alicia Pierce, Eleo Pomare, Sylvia del Villard,
Pearl Primus, Gregory Hines & Katherine Dunham
whose truths are clothed in Dance

Time
Is a Dancer
Moving
Shamelessly
Through the Cosmos
The wise
Hear the call
In their bones
&
Become willing partners
Trying
Always to follow the lead
Of
The inexplicable forces
Which propel
The mystical beauty
Of its truth on its journey
Time
Is a Dancer
Moving
Proudly moving
Flowing
Eternally cognizant
That the alternative is
A guaranteed voyage
Into
The annals of obscurity
A nowhere land
Where
Even time forgets to dance

Blue To The Bone
Tribute to Reginald Lockett, 11/5/47-5/15/08

Reggie may have been born in a College town, but
Oakland moved herself inside his Soul & it was on
Country slick, tongue in cheek magnificent
A City sophisticate who never scraped the mud off his boots
He was an intellectual Trickster
Directed by the never silent voices of Ancestral Memory
Dined daily on mega doses of pride
Sprinkled with pain, sautéed in knowledge
Became fruit off the tree of "we're gonna make it"
Reginald Lockett was a straight shooting,
No nonsense, wise cracking, flirty kinda guy
A City/Country man who bled that slow, raw, regal
Keep on pushin' power of the Gut-Bucket Blues
You could hear it in every Poem he ever wrote
All Reggie had to do was smile & you felt it
Had a twinkle in his eyes that drew you into
Those makes you wanna "show out" & "act a fool" kinda Blues
While on the other side of town
The "high faluting" Literati wearing pity like perfume
Wallowed around in those comfortably fashionable Cafes
Discussing the lives of "poor misunderstood Artistes"
Who'd been dripping abstract angst so long
Their bleeding hearts overflowed all over the place
'Til even the dead knew they were in need of a transfusion or two
Reggie was simply an old school "Race Man"
All his life he worked too hard to whine
Loved him some Esther Philips, Bobby Blue Bland & B.B. King
Reggie'd smirk
And I could taste the Poetic irony in the words they sang
Loved the Music of Words, the rhythms
Of us & himself too much to piss away time
So he worked like a madman at his Craft
Worked with a fanaticism bigger than the Middle Passage
The name of his game was
"Ain't gonna let nobody turn me around" & he did it all for us
In the stench of this whirlpool of Wannabe's
Where a loud mouth &
Demeaning language is all you need to get to a Mic
Reggie was the real deal
No sequins, no frills, no tears, no rants
Just a one hundred percent "Citified" Country guy
Ten steps out of the Juke Joint
And always a few seconds ahead of the Lynch Mob
An intellectual Trickster from beginning to end
Reggie was Oaktown's Soul Man, Blue to the bone
A 12 Bar, dark brown, bitter sweet masterpiece
Our chocolate treasure
Who forced us to always look beyond "The Ceiling"
And keep on climbing
Reginald Lockett was a Blues Poem

DEVEREAUX BAKER

Reunion

My name is Laema. I came from the East
during the war. If you close your hands
over the tops of mine you can hear
nights unwrap themselves, bending over

from the waist down with their burden
of broken wood, or reaching deep
into frozen earth, fingers going numb
with their own memories.

Wrap this memory like a shawl of dreams
around your shoulders. My husband carried
our youngest son, ten days and nights
during the bombing

from our home to the camps,
moving like a chant through fields
of frozen birds, crying when he broke
their wings beneath his feet.

Pain was the swelling around the dark fruit
we were forced to eat for bread. It was the wafer
that melted against our tongues, causing us to carry
the dark seeds into our throats, rattling beneath our ribs

until they blossomed deep inside our bodies
and caused us to dream a pathway
for reunions with death time and again.
These are the flowers of reunion that bloom

when I try to forget. Carry this picture then
in your locket and wear it on a silver chain
next to your heart forever, as I wear it,
softly swinging on a thread of memory,

swinging between my breasts like a prayer,
repeating the same words over and over,
my name is Laema. I came from the East
during the war.

MARSHA LEE BERKMAN

Words That Transformed the World

In our fast-paced high-tech post-modern world, the abbreviated texts, twitters and similar correspondence that pass for communication between human beings have all but obliterated the recognition that words can give voice to the most profound longing of the human soul. In *Here I Am: Contemporary Jewish Stories Around The World*, the PEN Oakland Josephine Miles Literary Award-winning book co-edited by Elaine Marcus Starkman and myself, stories such as "The Ugly Jewess," "Miriam," and "A Room on the Roof" articulate the pain of the human heart and the power of words to pierce the armor that divides people.

I think of the words that have changed history by correcting the inequities that were once taken for granted. The *Magna Carta* limited the power of kings; Mary Wollstonecraft's *A Vindication of the Rights of Woman* pointed out the tragedy of not allowing women to pursue an education; *Uncle Tom's Cabin* by Harriet Beecher Stowe awakened a nation to the inhumane effects of slavery. And one could name many more words that have transformed the human spirit. Such diverse works as *The Republic*, by Plato; *The Rights of Man*, by Thomas Paine; Anne Frank's *The Diary of A Young Girl*, and even Rachel Carson's *Silent Spring*, which first made us aware of our abuse of the Earth and the non-human population who share our planet, have all directed our thoughts toward correcting the wrongs of society.

The continued violence of our age staggers the imagination. What better way than words to point out the brutality and corruption of our time and the slaughter of those people who are most vulnerable. We need words that heal and words that create peace, words to break down the differences that separate human beings and words to overthrow tyrants. In the Jewish tradition, words themselves are holy. To be cut off from language is to exist in the darkness of a nether world. Proverbs tells us, "The words a man speaks are as deep as water; a stream that flows from wisdom." The Nobel prize-winning writer, Isaac Bashevis Singer, once said, "We Jews, the people of the book, still believe in the power of the word."
Words evoke the divinity of God and have the power to create reality, to beat back chaos and to confront evil. The First Five Books of Moses—Genesis, Exodus, Leviticus, Numbers, and Deuteronomy—impose timeless commandments and moral order through words that contain life or death, blessings or curses, according to the choices we make—choices that enhance life or destroy it.

We have no greater example of the power of words than the Hebrew prophets who lived over 2000 years ago. Their words impressed themselves upon the human heart and addressed not only the injustices of an ancient age, but speak to us across the chasm of the centuries. The prophets continually strove to bring people back to the moral parameters of a just world. Isaiah reminded us that ritual is empty if not accompanied by true charity to others:
"This is the fast I desire: To unlock the fetters of wickedness… To let the oppressed go free; to break off every yoke. It is to share your bread with the hungry, And to take the wretched poor into your house; When you see the naked, to offer clothing"

And another prophet's words, the words of Micah, still inspire us to strive for the time,
"When nations shall beat their swords into plowshares/ And spears into pruning hooks," when "Every man shall sit under his grapevine or fig tree/ With no one to disturb him."

The prophets' ability to fight the transgressions they witnessed through the eloquence and power of words has always made me aware of the capacity of words to transfigure our perceptions and behavior. A few years ago I visited a restored 17th century home and marveled at the great Bible near the family hearth that was open to these words of Malachi:
"Have we not all one Father? Did not one God create us? Why then do we break faith with one another?"
Why indeed?

As writers, we need to realize our enormous potential to effect change, to alter the world for good, word by word, and to overcome bullets by using our own weapons to shatter the complacency to the injustices against humanity that afflict us today.

CHRISTOPHER BERNARD

Is There a Nazi in Your Future?

The strange click on the telephone line
is an insect caught in a circuit box.

The odd look you get at the office
is a spasm of envy, paranoia, or gas.

The shadow following too close behind you
is a beggar's. He whispers the end of your name.

The cops who, suddenly, are everywhere
have hardly slept. They drive and stare.

The problem at the bank was a common mistake,
the insurance company confused your accounts,

the credit agency will erase that debt
you never had and so never paid.

The helicopter hangs suspended from the sky
above the city, like a spider:
it watches and waits, its whirr a dream.

The knock on the door in the middle of the night
is a nightmare, a cliché. See? No one's there.

CARLA BLANK

A New New Deal for the Arts

In response to President Obama's call for all Americans to contribute to our nation's future, many suggestions gain inspiration from New Deal programs instituted by President Franklin Roosevelt to revive the nation from the financial devastation caused by the Great Depression of the 1930s.

As an artist, I suggest President Obama and Congress include projects that employ creative ideas and energies of artists, as did two famous New Deal programs, the Public Works of Art Project, instituted in 1933 and it successor, the Works Progress Administration (WPA), formed in 1935, when more than 8.5 million jobless Americans worked on arts related projects that paid the equivalent of today's minimum hourly wage.

The 21st century version of New Deal arts programs could feature creative partnerships between artists and scientists, engineers, businesses, educators, skilled labor, city planners, and community leaders throughout our nation's cities and rural communities. Besides reducing unemployment, the partnerships could add valuable creative thinking to projects that invest in infrastructure, revitalize education, and develop new and greener technologies. Based on 1930s programs and more recent models, three examples of programs that could be instituted are:

Innovative Technologies Projects: Like Xerox PARC, founded in 1970 as a computer research center in today's Silicon Valley by Xerox Corporation, which became the birthplace of many innovations that were developed into basic tools and components of computer science technology, this program could team artists with scientists and engineers to design innovations that help reduce energy consumption, increase use of recycled materials, convert empty malls and industrial parks for new uses, restore environments destroyed by natural disasters, and conduct experiments to invent materials and technologies for functions not yet imagined.

Federal Writers Project: By updating documentary research projects, such as the gathering of oral histories and the encyclopedic American Guide Series that preserved much of the nation's geographic, cultural and political heritage up through the years they were completed, writers, journalists and photographers could build on these great resources, retrieving memories and images from our present 50 states and territories that could be lost without an organized effort. This updated documentation could be stored in the Library of Congress or National Archives, digitized for retrieval by anyone online.

Community Art Projects: In addition to funding regional, state and local festivals and other events, this program could offer professionally directed classes and workshops in theater, dance, music, photography and visual arts, where people of all ages could gain access to training and appreciation of arts which are routinely omitted from public school curriculums and community services whenever budgets have to be cut. Programs offered since 1971 under National Endowment for the Arts' Expansion Arts and Community Cultural Programs have documented how increased understanding and respect for all arts, through greater accessibility, also increases the quality of life in a community, besides increasing local revenues as visitors partake of these activities.

The 1930s WPA programs financed projects other than those I have mentioned, including public art projects which continue to provide a source of wonder, such as San Francisco's Coit Tower murals that still draw tourists from all over the world. Moreover WPA projects provided enough income to make it possible for many artists to continue careers, making them today's canonized icons, such as Richard Wright, Orson Wells, Aaron Copland, Dorothea Lange and Jackson Pollack. Artists have collaborated with architects, educators and businesses for centuries. When such collaborations are successful, they are called a renaissance.

ABBY LYNN BOGOMOLNY

the bus station

I am a teacher, and each time my wound up, bouncy, cell phone-identified students stare up at me in thinly disguised boredom at my lesson or outright pity for my clothing, I feel compassion because they're just one bus stop away from flinging themselves into drama...so I wonder where the bus they take will go or how they will fare...

My classroom feels like a bus station:
to the west is the freeway—in line of sight to the distant city
that casts off commuters and refugees.
one student arrives with a deformed child in his chest
another will be late,
missing a shoe, an ear, a father.
he will try to listen,
but has already taken too many orders
from his manager at the drug store.
another student will fold last week's pink slip
in her wallet, next to the photo of her teenaged daughter.
she will sit in her bus station classroom,
next to a skinny, tattooed boy out of high school,
feeling free for the first time to think and have opinions,
no longer a crinkled woman folding
sweaters all day at Macy's.

At this bus station,
they keep cutting the schedule
and issue tickets to uncertainty.
long lines form for limited seats,
at a time when the roadways are littered
with throwaways and distractions:
my classroom bears the burden.

natural law

they will build over me,
pour their foundations over my lungs
and pollute my places of cleansing...
because they can.

this is not new
one day i will tilt and buckle,
changing altitude, winds, temperature,
taking them with me.
great military forces will be of no use
as i settle in my bed of the universe.

in their movies, brave scientists escape
to a distant moon.
in reality, no one escapes
the home of natural law.

they who have so much—want more,
but i do not care. still mother
of their bones forever,
i will turn over in my bed,
and bear a different shape:
watch my changing face carefully.

MAREK BREIGER

Who We Are

The Mexican music plays, the accordion and guitars and horns, and the plaintive male singer is joined by the soft voices of women on the chorus.

Tortillas are being ground and pounded.

I am on Mission Boulevard, across from Moreau High School, where I've taught English for more than ten years. I am at La Casa Latina, drinking coffee, reading and writing.

On the street, a family walks past, the mother wearing a shawl, followed by her four children. The oldest, a girl, pushes a baby carriage: the soulful dark eyes of Mexico define her face.

Inside, in broken English, a man asks his wife,

"Pine Yapple? or Dijet Pepsi?"

He speaks in the accent so easy to parody but that only fools mock, for he speaks the broken English that novelist Wright Morris once described as "the language of the soul, broken words, spoken to the heart."

Construction workers come in for an early lunch of beer and tortillas, easily mixing Spanish and American slang.

Everything is orderly. Everyone is polite in the Latin tradition, and I am not treated as a stranger—and perhaps I am not. For I am viewing an American and Mexican scene and more.

I am viewing immigrant America, the America of my Russian Jewish grandparents found on the West side of Chicago and the Lower East Side of New York and in Boyle Heights in Los Angeles.

It is the America of old country emotion and new country language and hope.

A taped sign, dark ink on white paper states, "*Velodores*, Candles, 12x 15," and I think of the Yarzheit, the memorial candle lit for my sister Miriam, for Mimi, every January 26.

What a price we pay when we give up the emotional language of the immigrants—our parents, grandparents, and great-grandparents.

Across the street, at the high school, for more than ten years, I've tried to teach the work of authors—writers such as Hemingway and Steinbeck, Elie Wiesel and Chief Seattle, Lorraine Hansberry and Martin Luther King—who used words to protest against our collective loss of memory and sense of justice.

For we Americans are a nation of immigrants and minority groups. We are not merely "whites" but Italian and Armenian and Irish and Spanish and German and Portuguese and Polish and all of the rest. We are not simply "people of color," but West African Ashanti and Filipino and Japanese and Chinese and Korean and Vietnamese and Cambodian and Ohlone Indian and all of the rest.

We have yet to learn a simple lesson—putting down or prejudging others because of race or religion is not an act of celebration or pride or an effective act of retribution; it is an act that works to divide and to make real progress impossible.

The accordion plays, the words are sung, the man behind the counter joins in and seems to remember a different time.

And outside it is still morning and there is no school and cars move past a scene of Hayward, Northern California and of the world.

CECIL BROWN

MC Cyrano

ACT ONE
SCENE FOUR

(FILLMORE AUDITORIUM–ON STAGE—MC FLUNKY)
(MC Flunky enters the center of the stage to great applause.)
(After bowing low, he begins rapping in the party style of MC Hammer.)
MC FLUNKY (RAPPING AND MAKING GESTURES A LA MOS DEF)
Hippty-hippity hop–
Busy Bee Can We Party? Can we party? Can we party? Put yo' hands in the air an' Wave 'em like you don't care!
A VOICE
(from the middle of the pit) :)
MC Funky! Did I not forbid you to show your face here for month?
(General stupor. Every one turns round. Murmurs.)
(The people stand up in the boxes to look.)
Luckily, the music is so loud that only a few people can hear this embarrassing interruption.
EMCEE CYRANO!
Do you dare defy me?
Fat fool, didn't I tell you to Leave the stage this instant!
(The voice utters the lines in the same exaggerated stagy manner as MC Flunky.)
(People look everywhere for the owner of the voice, which is somewhere hidden in the auditorium.)
(NEAR THE STAGE)
(Emcee Cyrano jumps up on the stage and makes his way to the bank of audio equipment that controls the sound system.)
(There are millions of connectors. Reaching into the tangled web of plugs and wires, Emcee Cyrano rips them out of their sockets.)
(Suddenly, the whole damn auditorium is so quiet that you could hear a rat piss on cotton.)
EMCEE CYRANO
(He turns Back to MC Flunky))
I said, Get off the stage!
MC FLUNKY
But—but...
EMCEE CYRANO
(turning to the audience))
I'm going to repeat it. Get off the stage!
EMCEE CYRANO
(to the audience)
I'm going to do what everybody wish they could do. When you see a no-rapping motherhumper on stage—and he can't rap, you wanna shut the motherhumper down, right! (Turning to MC Flunky)
Get off the stage!
MC FLUNKY
Where're my dawgs? Where's my pound?
EMCEE CYRANO
Your pound is here, you fat fool!
Off, off, you offal. Lug your guts away,
You miserable faker.

FIGHTIN' WORDS

(MC Funky is rooted to the stage.)
EMCEE CYRANO (CONT'D) Very well, then—stay!
(Emcee Cyrano runs across the stage over to the rap group—)
(The Three Mack–A–teers. He stands at attention in front of them.)
(Emcee Cyrano glances over at-the Mack–A–teers dressed in their blue musketeer's tunics with white crosses, with swords hanging from shoulder belts.)
(One of them steps up to Emcee Cyrano, right up to his long nose.)

MACK–A–TEER

Get Back! You long nose   Mother!
(Emcee Cyrano grabs the Mack–A–teer's sword.)

EMCEE CYRANO

No, you get Back, you short nose Mother!

MC FLUNKY ((TO THE MC) :)

Come to my help, my hip-hop family! My dawgs!
(Emcee Cyrano fences with the Mack–A–teer, all the while yelling to MC Flunky.)

EMCEE CYRANO

Fat man, I'm warning you !
(When Emcee Cyrano whips the sword out of the Mack–A–teer's hand, MC Flunky's eyes pop out in fear.)

CYRANO

I'm gong to clap three times!
(At the third clap, eclipse yourself!)

THE CROWD (AMUSED)

Oh, no!
(Emcee Cyrano claps his hand.)

EMCEE CYRANO

One !
(MC FLUNKY (In a state of shock)

A VOICE IN THE CROWD

Don't let him bluff you!

EMCEE CYRANO

Two!

MC FLUNKY

I-I-I...

EMCEE CYRANO

Three !
(MC Flunky disappears as through a trapdoor. A single thread of smoke remains.)
(The audience is like...what the f...k just happened!)
(Tempest of laughs, whistling cries, etc.)

THE CROWD:

Coward ...come back!

JANINE CANAN

We Are the Women

We are the women
who have been defeated
for thousands and thousands of years.

Not in any man's country
have we succeeded
in surviving as bold free women.

Yet we have our ways of continuing
underground like the rivers
and molten bowels of the earth.

We will never die, humanity will always
toddle behind us, and when the time arrives
like monumental geysers we will revive.

To Ayann Hirsi Ali & Hillary Clinton

Blessed

All complaints aside,
I cannot believe how blessed
I have been in this life.

First, I was given a human body.
You might say, doesn't that mean
an awful lot of suffering,

but I say, Would you really
rather be a cow or
a lizard?

Then I was born in the richest country
on earth where I would want
for nothing materially

and receive the best education
available—and wisely
I appreciated it.

As a result, I became one of the first
free women in the world
in thousands of years.

Freely I wandered, observed,
studied and pondered,
enjoying the greatest thinkers and artists.

Sure, I was insulted, mugged, raped,
beaten and glared at homicidally,
but it was worth it!

I sang my poems, wove my stories,
elaborated my essays as I sought out
the supreme spiritual masters

who taught me to open my mind and heart,
meditate and pray. I am still learning,
becoming ever more childlike and candid.

Yes, I have suffered, I cannot count the ways.
But even I cannot imagine the good Fortune
that granted me this blessed life.

NEELI CHERKOVSKI

At The Caffé Trieste

now I sit in the cafe drinking espresso
thinking it's got to be okay
me being contentious and ambitious and
vain, me being myself, an old man
but young when you consider that
somewhere in what is now Indonesia
we came of age, so some tell us,
when we chewed leaves and dug up roots
and hunted with stone

it has to be fine sitting here
while the earth burns and the population
spills into the sea which will soon boil over anyway

I worry about Mozart
and Bach, all those long hours
composing music for an ungrateful mob

that's how it is as I awaken in a fever
every night fearful of losing it
and falling down in a brick
courtyard with no help in sight

I worry about the Louvre Museum
and all that art so vulnerable
to a sudden nuclear strike
or a major eruption on the sun

what's going to happen to my little caffé
with its gossip and poetry?
the hissing espresso machine
echoes outside, I sip the fine dark scrim
and follow with cold water

it's all I've got now, this Golden Age,
as an old friend described it
listening to Italian arias
on the caffé's juke box and waiting for
a solution to arise

I close my eyes and take one final sip
tasting the soil on a faraway estate
and the interplay of sunlight
and cloud forest

the caffé has been here
since 1956, you'll find it
when you want it, maybe,
and maybe not, in a proper
season, in this new age
of splendor on a crowded
planet, all I ask
is that you smile
and lean back
to taste the tenor of the sky

JUDITH CODY

Truth. All of it at Once.

Its marble face stared
straight out at the
ever-changing multitudes,
an aura of impenetrable
magnificence clung to its
massive contours—
(bronze plaque beneath
the colossus reads, "Eternal
Perfection Right Here.")

Too big, no place for it anywhere
else, but everyone said that they
wanted all of it anyway.

After decades of cutting
chipping, blasting pieces off
Truth turned out to be more
fragile than it looked—
when it toppled over crashing
into brittle bits, each was
quickly seized. (Someone grumbled,
"Not so perfect after all.")

Going Home
battlements razed

When enough time had elapsed
so that some of the soul
could be deposited back
into the coffer of the body
the body then cleansed, coiffeured
contained in an unsullied
soldier suit, the old familiar
smile affixed to the sad face
the medals pinned upon the
anguished breast, only then
were the fathers
returned to their homes.

Did You Shoot Anyone, Daddy?

"I think so, yeah, I think I did.
This guy was truly quiet
not shooting at my
buddies we had to crawl
infantry-style on elbows
my gun safe inside my arms—
like I held you when you were little
before I went to the war—
I got a good look at him
when I bellied by him
maybe two inches away
from his arm where his gun
lay quiet near his hand I touched
it warm just like me his head
thrown back like maybe he
wanted to say something to me
with his mouth pulled open
could have been half a smile
could have been pain
he was maybe the same age
like me he had dark whiskers
poking from his chin
just like me he had dark
eyes looking like me at me
when Daddy went to pee
I saw him this morning
in the mirror over our sink."

GILLIAN CONOLEY

occupied

remaster, I got big sign I amble off
face lit as skin of someone bathing.
young frayed hoods smell saltier.
police refuse the stairs, one gropes a breast
under a sports bra. historical pic! crowd
shoots all then closes behind, laptop.
you sexy thang. anticrow anticrow
anticrows and swoops
the street, imperfectable, police seem
to have insatiable sexual
appetites, skyscraper bends over itself, as if to bow
or readjust, then lighthouses
a tangerine rolling out of a tent
is a real tangerine and people are
intemperate, out of air current   hot breath and other waves
of Being, wherein each calls for the other,
gives a sign. how to lift
the limit between the body and the world—
birds cry!   lovers die!
hermit can't eat the plastic

the sports bra snaps back

of great design
vet of bones all his brothers dead inside him stops to pose
with the lean of a milkman, smiles his truths of 1945.
the policeman's hand is gone
imaginal, archetypal
the best messages are mutual and free from all ambition, like a wishbone.
hermit licks the wrapper.
Steve Jobs we're sorry you died
images feel good taken into the human palm.
how to back into our new instruments
how light November rain

LUCHA CORPI

Berkeley Blues
1970   A Beatriz Pesquera y Roberta Orona

Entre mis ojos y la luna había
365 noches de insomnio
Una pequeña grieta en el estómago
El dolor de saberlo a él ajeno
El haz luminoso de una estrella
Una banda de mapaches desvelados
saqueando las arcas del basurero
Y mi vecino
que empapado de mezcalina
a medianoche corría por la calle
sin más defensa en contra de la luna llena
que un par de calcetines rotos
y la camisa de fuerza.

Entre mis oídos y la luna
ascendía la rasposa melancolía de Lady Day
Una nota repleta de espanto
Y el maullido del gato en celo
que ofrecía sus responsos de recién nacido
por la fé nuestra que agonizaba
entre los arrozales de la Indochina
en las aulas de San Francisco y Berkeley
y en las barriadas de Atlanta y Chicago
Los Angeles y Dallas.

Entre mis labios y la luna
se colaba el calor húmedo de otro otoño
Una brizna de azul de medianoche
que la memoria iba transformando ya
en polvo de oro
El chasquido de un petardo de gas
Y el dolor mudo del hambre
entre pecho y espalda
Y todos aquellos versos
escritos con la saqueada ortografía del silencio
en las últimas trincheras del instinto.

Entre aquella noche de octubre y la luna
no existía
ni Marx ni Lenín
ni la lucha armada
ni la revolución interrumpida
que nos dejara polvo y cansancio
exilio y desengaño
No éramos latinos ni chicanos
ni estudiantes en una institución
que apenas si nos toleraba.

Éramos gotas dormidas en el cubo del tiempo,
nombres acurrucados en los intersticios
de un sueño
Y entrábamos al poema
como se entra a un cetario
con los ojos líquidos de la memoria
a buscar entre fósiles de días nonatos
la geoetnología del planeta
la ecología cultural de la raza,
a beber un poco de intimidad y muerte
del remanso quieto de la nostalgia.

Berkeley Blues

1970   To Beatriz Pesquera and Roberta Orona

Between my eyes and the moon there were
365 nights of insomnia
A little crack in my stomach
The pain of knowing he belonged to someone else
The ray of light from a star
A band of wakeful raccoons
raiding the garbage man's treasure chests
And my delirious neighbor
running at midnight along the street
drenched in mescaline
with no more defense against the full moon
than a pair of torn socks
and a straitjacket.

Between my ears and the moon
the hoarse melancholy of Lady Day
One terror-filled note
And the yowl of a cat in heat
a newborn's requiem squall
for our faith as it lay agonizing
among the rice paddies in Indochina
in the classrooms in San Francisco and Berkeley
and in the 'hoods of Atlanta and Chicago
Los Angeles and Dallas.

Between my lips and the moon
the moist warmth of another autumn
A strand of midnight blue
already being transformed by memory
into gold dust
The putrid smell of a gas canister
and the mute pain of hunger
between breast and back
And all those poems
written in the looted orthography of silence
in the last trenches of instinct.

Between that October night and the moon
there was no
Marx, no Lenin
no armed conflict
no interrupted revolution
to leave us with dust and exhaustion
exile and disillusion
We weren't Latinos or Chicanos
or students in an institution
that barely tolerated us.

We were drops of liquid asleep in the cube
of time,
names nestled in the crannies
of a dream
And we entered the poem
as one enters the ocean where whales are
breeding,
our eyes streaming with memory,
to look among the fossils of unborn days
for the geoethnology of the planet
the cultural ecology of the race,
to sip intimacy and death
from the quiet pool of nostalgia.

*English translation by
Catherine Rodríguez-Nieto*

JOHN CURL

O Columbia

O Columbia
this is the temple
these endless waves of trees this wolfbirch dawn
these rivers of light bursting through crevices of cloud
this sweet fogdamp wombsky this starry flight of geese
this is the temple
this forestdrenched sunset this symphony of clover
these antelope mesas rainrumbling these snowloving islands
this threethousandmile bouquet of grainflowers returning to seedwarmth
this moondamp redwood knowledge
this thrushmelody shimmering through this golden spine
this marriage of root and earth this revealing of oceangreen valleysecrets
these clustered mountaintops singing to the dawn
this holy gift of rabbit leaf and wind
this joyous drifting continent
this is the temple

But the moneychangers have seized the temple
this cancer salesman this tv news disguise
this shattered glass betrayal this genocide of falcons
this prison corporation factory torture
this wageslave firing squad this starvation graft insurance noose
this money infection this poisoned barbedwire bank
this groaning captivity this gangster orgy this chairmen of the board conspiracy
this wagecut attorneysdelusional heartattack this stockholder deathship speedup
these neutron War Secretary embalmings
this incorporated lobotomy these brokenhearted bleedingroots
this crucifixion of robins this burning lake this storm of nails
the moneychangers have seized the temple

O these selfevident truths
O these alienated rights
O this consciousness streaming
O this vast comingtogether O this great castingout
O this refusal to obey orders O this national strike
O this army rebellion O this wilderness insurrection
O these marching saints O this deep plowing
O this whip of cords O this drivingout of the moneychangers
O this dissolving of the corporations
O this cleansing of the temple
O this tearingoff of uniforms O this bomb dismantling
O this fence downtearing O this prison unlocking
O this mind unblinding O this hurtlover healing
O this return to foreststars O this rebirth of our crystalhearts
O this sunburst of workerlove
O this seagull marriage O this rebuilding of the temple
O this collective jewel O this thought of love among us

O this emerald thunder O this tongue on your perfect lips
O this raven's shout O this festival of our ancestors
O this ceremony of dawnfamily
O this communal money
O this collective land
O these socialized machines
O this economic democracy
O this joyful workers' power
O this rainbow cooperation
O this circle of love around us
O these laughing children O these joined genitals shining
O this infinite sharing O this living prophesy
O this dance of liberation O these hugs among the cultures
O this love among the races
O this harmony of light
O this kiss blown from the sun to the moon
O this ocean of hearts

O COLUMBIA

STEVE DALACHINSKY

the snake reborn

(the work of keith haring 1978-1982)

the dog bit (its own aesthetic
chain / of language
individual shapes that make up a (w)hole
    as in buffet
the hanging nudes upside down
birthing big black holes (in stomach
delivering baby chatter
leashed unstrung monochromatic whose-it-whats
zapped by saucers – blown jobbed / handfked
& gave it to polka dotted dog thru the wall
with the spectators screaming give us more oh host
of the alien boner o(i)nk
"& Steve said" said the viewer behind my limbs
  not knowing
i was steve also >
        beheading the head of the giver of head
          its holy hoops of energy
      done with the judgment of resident aliens
          climbing the bastion of stick dick
      zapped by the light from the undark
          & therefore removing the dark from the circle
            in the speckled chest of treasure(r)s

    the time piece got crucified
      & the snake ate itself & all else to form a new crawling family
        naked jumbo-jackos leapfrogging over eachudders
          stuck up smooth as…asses
tech/tonic plated involvement here seen as even video frags detect
    the cut up presidents popes & art/scenes flattened on the sc(a)reen
      clubbing clubbing clubbing oneself to death with song
      painted into corners of know-me auto-journal didact
    then A.I.D.S. the vigilante ante's up &'s taken on board
the body as conveyer belt & another subway ride down to the chalk-line

**   the magic magic stick & the holy holy hoop**

flash freaks & god walled up / kickerflicked little spores beat down
    3 I.V.s & you'll own the penalty little man
  burning flattened pulse ground harder & harder into grounds
        inside the prison grounds
    monkey light held by its tail
radiating from yer under/currents currently behind glass

you hang there crucifix – eating the mermaid angel alive
your children lost in a bubble – big fish diving around yer corpse
you hang there – diving like the last breath gone
you hang there across the street – you hang there – beat down
    the public stuck up your little alien ass
    you hang there as the big snake cuts itself in too
feeds on itself & you & once again as always shits US out
    & all's reborn as you hang there
    & Steve where ever he is whoever he is
    owns all the penalties NOW
      as you hang there little soul hang there.

J.P. DANCING BEAR

Independence Day

1.
This breath, this hover
above the earth
the wind catching my clothes—
the small whispers of air in my ears
and my shadow the shape of a bird—
exhale and my body becomes lighter
the vision of a crane lifting into summer air.

In this moment of quiet
it is hard to remember
our violences
or a history of so many people
coming to new lives;

how all the ancestors
gave their tears
and still the rivers
were not enough.

I hold my breath too often
—it's true.

My tongue too.

Because everyone has a fight on their lips
everyone has a line at their feet.

2.

Most of the hot afternoon
was the sweaty glasses of iced tea
and muttering of this being the hottest

summer in memory.
If someone brings up global warming
it'll be another fight.

So I watch the ghosts of heat waves
shimmy off the asphalt
and pray for a breeze,

the bitterness upon my tongue
is sweat from my fingers
straining to hold on.

3.

There is the smell of gunpowder in the air—kids impatient for nightfall light their firecrackers and for a moment the veterans on our block flinch for cover. The fantasy of violence starts early: cowboys, indians, cops, robbers, yanks, jonny reb, back to our revolution. The day we threw off the corrupt political system and began a new one. But history books are not filled with the stories of entire systems, only one man or one color of an army's uniform, or a flag. Symbols to substitute our learning from the past.

A cloud of smoke in the air that calls back to a history unfamiliar. We love our myths, though. And we love those earlier men like they were gods or a son of a god. And here again belief bloodies the face of fact.

4.

my naked breath, my slight hover above—

removed from the grit of sand or soil.

LUCILLE LANG DAY

The People Versus Oscar Cole

A fat court reporter kneels before the judge
robed in black. An American flag
hangs on the wall behind them.
The defendant wears a velvet blazer,
white slacks and no socks.
A woman on the jury wonders
if he can't afford them.

In the chambers the other jurors
say it's just the style. Back
to business. They consider
the evidence. Did this man hold
in his palm a rock of cocaine, worth
about five dollars? Did he throw it
on the ground when the cops came?

The District Attorney has asked
for truth on behalf of the People.
The Public Defender says Mr. Cole
was waylaid by a dealer.
He was also ambushed by the police.
Mr. Cole is poor. This is his first felony.
But the judge has warned that sympathy

must not taint the verdict.
The jurors debate as the clock
ticks away. They eat lunch at a different
restaurant every day, watched
by the bailiff. The People spend
enough to send Mr. Cole to Harvard.
Instead he's sent up the river.

KATHLEEN DE AZEVEDO

Before the Ship Sailed

The early morning sun brightened the street of row houses, but in the shadows, a family of gypsies lay curled under one blanket against a wall. Rafaela wept even harder. Where was their home? Just yesterday her father had been washing his hands during Sabbath prayer. After their street was invaded by priests working for the Inquisition and her family scattered, she ran down to the Tagus River and jumped in. As she drifted clinging to a slab of wood, she realized: *I could end up anywhere in the world. This is no longer the Portugal I know.*

Rafaela was far from home now. She looked up and saw a candle burning in a balcony window. Too tired to fear the worst, she pushed open the door below and it gave easily. She worked her way up the stairs, touching the damp walls with her fingers. Her heavy wet dress practically tore off her shoulders. The room at the top was so dim, she thought at first it had been abandoned, but as her eyes got used to the semi-dark, she made out a man half-hidden by a damask curtain. He was writing on the wall. The man turned and approached her, coming into the light pouring through the balcony window. He stroked his Jewish cassock, running his fingers along the front trim. An old Jew. An old white-haired Jew, skin as pale and grey as street water.

"I was waiting for you," he said.

On a table, he had a plate with a chunk of bread and an orange. He saw her eye the food and ushered her forward.

"Eat it," he said and returned to his wall. "I will write you into my story."

She snatched the bread and stuffed large pieces into her mouth. The man continued writing as she grabbed the orange and bit deeply until the juice became mud in her hands and trickled down her wrists.

She moved up to the wall where the man was working. She could not read the words, but they seemed to fly. She imagined small intimate letters to be secretive prayers and plans, and big scrawls to be the story of ships sailing to new lands and what they found there. But it was unusual to see a man writing on walls unless he were a madman scratching his own skin with a quill pen. Or he'd be in the town square for yet another auto-da-fé. Or he wouldn't be here at all. He wrote with his eyes close to the wall as if blind. His lips moved slightly, as if reading. His cassock seemed a bit too large, his thin neck elegant or scrawny, depending how he moved his chin.

Rafaela finally felt bold enough to ask, "Why are you writing on the wall? And how can you tell what you have written, if you can barely see it?"

"I am writing all what will happen."

"Are you a prophet?"

The man did not answer but continued writing.

Rafaela went over to the balcony and looked onto the street, careful not to be seen. The mist rolled in from the sea like a heavy wool coat. A group of old rabbis talked, gesturing close to their mouths as if scooping out words. A man in ragged britches, pulled a cart of potatoes covered in rags, the wheels smacking on the cobblestone. A Moorish boy mocking his friend as they both ran up the street, called out, "Come on, what do you know of Allah anyway? Is He good to everyone? Tell me that, amigo."

Rafaela had heard ships were going to Brazil, far from the Inquisition. She had drifted for so long, it was like she was halfway there, and she could leave–completely. Rafaela looked back at the wall, wondering if the old man were writing about what would happen to her. He just stays here and writes, she thought. Won't he be caught, even if he cleverly hides his words behind a damask curtain? The old man wrote with one hand, and stroked his beard with the other. There was no clumsiness in his gestures; they were both Jews, no need to explain. He smiled a bit. She hoped he saw her future a good one. She heard an argument just outside his window, between a woman and a man with a donkey cart about whether the next *auto-da-fé* would happen today or tomorrow. Who is a better judge of human nature, God or the Devil? They argued. Prophets are only clever when the future is inevitable. Otherwise they are fools. Rafaela was about to call the old man to the balcony, "Come and listen!" but the woman called the man a mule; and the argument became so pointless it was hard to tell why the words had become so heated, except to say a mule was involved.

WENDY DONIGER

You Can't Make an Omelette

Writing about the ancient history of Hinduism has now become highly politicized, and the fight raging around the issue of Hindu pluralism in India has plagued me in the United States. The problem arises with Hindutva ("Hindu-ness"), a territorial, racial, and fundamentalist form of Hinduism that has inspired violence against Muslims, violence against Christians, and the pervasive infection of fundamentalism, particularly on the Internet. My encounter with the Hindutvavadis (as the adherents of Hindutva are called) first began in 2002, when a retired Indian business man living in Princeton started harassing me, and my students, on the internet. Then in London on November 12, 2003, in the middle of a lecture that I gave at the University of London, chaired by the historian William Dalrymple, a man threw an egg at me. (He missed.) A message that a member of the two-hundred strong audience posted the next day on a mailing-list website referred to a passage I had cited from Valmiki's *Ramayana* in which Sita, the wife of Rama, accuses her brother-in-law Lakshmana of wanting her for himself. The web message stated:

"I was struck by the sexual thrust of her paper on one of our most sacred epics. Who lusted/laid whom, it was not only Ravan who desired Sita but her brother-in-law Lakshman also. Then many other pairings, some I had never heard of, from our other shastras were thrown in to weave a titillating sexual tapestry. What would these clever, "learned" western people be doing for a living if they did not have our shastras and traditions to nitpick and distort?"

The parts of his own tradition that the website writer objected to are embraced by many other Hindus and are, in any case, historically part of the record. To the accusation that I cited a part of the Hindu textual tradition that one Hindu "had never heard of," my reply was: "Yes! And it's my intention to go on doing just that."

In an article entitled "India: The War Over History" (NYRB 52: 6, April 7, 2005), William Dalrymple reviewed a number of recent books about Indian history whose authors have been attacked—through words, threats, occasionally blows—by reactionary forces in India. He listed some of the most egregious examples of the rewriting of school history books in India and general misrepresentations of the history of Hinduism, a list to which, alas, many new examples have been added, or resurrected, since he wrote, in 2005. And he mentioned the egg affair, concluding:

"During the questions that followed the lecture, Doniger faced a barrage of heated insults from a group who had come with the egg-thrower, and who maintained that as a non-Hindu she was unqualified to comment on their religion. Other SOAS lectures on India have since been broken up in similar circumstances."

Dalrymple alludes to the fact that the man who threw the egg at me also threw eggs at two other (Indian) scholars who had spoken in the same series of lectures in which I spoke. It was therefore not really an attack on me, personally, at all.

But the incident that I have come to think of as "the egg and I" was not the end of the controversy over my representation of Hinduism. I took the episode as a gauntlet that I could not resist picking up, and it inspired me to write *The Hindus: An Alternative History*, which was published in 2009. Several critics used the word "courageous," the full significance of which I was then too naïve to appreciate. The book was one of the five finalists in non-fiction for the National Book Critics Circle Award.

In India, The Hindus (published by Penguin Books, Delhi) hit the top of the best-seller list in non-fiction for a while and then remained further down on the list for a while longer; it is still selling very well. But at the same time, the book came under attack by the Hindutvavadis. Hindu bloggers accused me of hating Hinduism and of sexualizing and/or psychoanalyzing Hindus. They flooded Amazon.com with their lurid opinions of the book. They wrote me obscene and, occasionally, threatening emails. Hindus protested outside the U S Embassy in Delhi, calling for the book to be banned world-wide. And there were counter-protests;

Salman Rushdie came to my defense.

    In 2010, six elderly gentlemen brought a criminal suit against Penguin, India, and me, demanding that the book be withdrawn from publication and all extant issues dropped. They argued that the book had offended them, thus violating an Indian law that makes it a criminal offense to offend a Hindu. In February, 2014, Penguin, India, decided not to go on defending the suit, and agreed to withdraw the book from publication and to pulp all remaining copies. In fact, not a single book was destroyed; Penguin had only a few copies in stock in house, and all the copies in the bookstores were quickly bought up. Outside of India, sales of the book soared astronomically; it was #11 on Amazon for a while, and then settled down to #17, and so forth. Many PDF's were downloaded from several Indian websites established for that purpose. Other Indian publishers volunteered to publish the book there. More important, there was an astonishing volume of international protest against Penguin's actions and against the blasphemy law; several branches of PEN sent in petitions, as did a number of academic institutions and many, many individuals. There was terrific media coverage. The storm is still raging as I write this, on February 18, 2014, and I am hopeful that much good will come of it all. Quite an omelette! The fight goes on.

SHARON DOUBIAGO

Maybe The Revolution

I love your poem insisting good will return,
we have to have faith. But now is
bad. At the Foreign Film Festival Awards
the filmmaker of The Road to Guantanamo
broke down on stage, mid-acceptance speech, and sobbed.
And didn't quit sobbing. Maybe
this is the revolution, that we all break down,
start crying and not stop.

The next day three men at Guantanamo Bay
were found hanged and a poet friend took the opportunity
to inform me of my lifelong misuse of hung for hanged.
I didn't want to believe this
especially for my published poems. But the headlines
confirmed the King's English:
3 Terror Suspects Found Hanged

I like what you say, they're just idiots, not evil. Just
going for the bucks (the proper English). But these days
the opposite keeps insisting: this is a well-planned,
long-planned coup. What do we do
about those just going for the bucks?

My daughter called me to her laptop
to show me Guantanamo after our first Afghanistan war.
Hundreds of young men hogtied face down,
so shocking I still marvel that any of us are still standing.
Maybe this is the revolution that we all break down
and not get up.

My grandfather was the hangman of Globe, Arizona.
Disinherited by his Confederate father
for marrying my grandmother whose grandfather was Union
his training to be a doctor cut short, but which got him, starving,
the only job he could find, he hanged his fellow man
for bucks, ruining himself and assuring
the ongoing family ruin, especially our bucks, our English.
Maybe the revolution is finding the names
of everyone he hanged (tell me again, O King of my tongue, I
hang a man, I hanged a man, I hung a bunch. Tell me
the good your proper is.

Maybe the war would end if we all start wailing
like the women at the funerals of their children we've bombed.
like the women who haven't taken off their black clothes in years
because every time the mourning is completed, another love is killed.

Maybe the revolution is to tear at our clothes, to screech
and wail, fall on our backs, everyone gone mad
like the Afghani man this week
with his car in our streets, the blood
running in the streets, maybe
that's the revolution, tears
like labor that can't be stopped

crying and crying, the whole world
not getting up. Imagine that sound, everyone sobbing, that

correct language, tears running
maybe that's the revolution
the tears running   the tears running in
the tears running in the streets

CAMILLE T. DUNGY

Daisy Cutter

Pause here at the flower stand—mums
and gladiolas, purple carnations

dark as my heart. We are engaged
in a war, and I want to drag home

any distraction I can carry. Tonight
children will wake to bouquets of fire

that will take their breath away. Still,
I think of my life. The way you hold me,

sometimes, you could choke me.
There is no way to protect myself,

except by some brilliant defense. I want
the black iris with their sabered blooms.

I want the flame throwers: the peonies,
the sunflowers. I will cut down the beautiful ones

and let their nectared sweetness bleed
into the careless air. This is not the world

I'd hoped it could be. It is horrible,
the way we carry on. Last night, you catalogued

our arsenal. You taught me devastation
is a goal we announce in a celebration

of shrapnel. Our bombs shower
in anticipation of their marks. You said this

is to assure damage will be widely distributed.
What gruesome genius invents our brutal hearts?

When you touch me I am a stalk of green panic
and desire. Wait here while I decide which

of these sprigs of blossoming heartbreak I can afford
to bring into my home. Tonight dreams will erupt

in chaotic buds of flame. This is the world we have
arranged. It is horrible, this way we carry on.

MARGARITA ENGLE

The Observer
Fredrika Bremer in Cuba, 1851

Freeing her mind with words,
the traveler in a suffering land
described it as a paradise of nature

and then she described
slavery

and even though she could not
change the hot, sunny, tropical island,
she soon discovered that her written words
had changed her own cold, northern homeland
where sugar in tea now tasted
like the sweat of shackled cane cutters

and readers were moved
to go out and gather
wild honey.

MARIA ESPINOSA

Dying Unfinished

In Penn Station Eleanor glanced at the windows which sold tickets to places like Chicago, Baltimore, and Raleigh. How tempting to buy a ticket at one of these windows, obtain a small tube of toothpaste and other toiletries from one of the drugstores here in this underground station, and disappear.

"Where is she?" Aaron, her husband, would ask when he came home. "Where is she?" the children would ask. They were birds with hungry beaks who pecked away at her soul and body.

She would disappear. She might surface in New Orleans or Tucson or perhaps Vancouver as a waitress or librarian, a slender middle-aged woman with graying hair and without a past. But as always, she went to the Long Island Railroad section and boarded her train. They rolled past miles of Queens suburbs, identical houses with television antennas. She scribbled the beginning of a poem in a small green notebook.

Am I me? Are you really you?
Or do we only see shadows
We mistake for the other?

She paused. This was only a fragment. The root of what she wanted to say eluded her, in the way that the sky is obscured by clouds. Those clouds covered her thoughts, her memories, and only a few clear bits of blue sky remained.

What if she did follow her longings? Eleanor imagined Heinrich, her lover, and her together in a cozy Village loft. She began to sob.

"Lady, are you all right?" asked the conductor.

She nodded, put her pen and notebook back in her purse, and held out her ticket to be punched. Held out her neck to be beheaded.

Ah, shades of Madame Bovary. She and Heinrich were hopelessly romantic. Let her thoughts stream out into the atmosphere. To formulate them in words was dangerous. So let them dissolve into mist.

oooooo

Rosa once asked her mother, "What is love?"

Eleanor thought of Heinrich, of Aaron, of anonymous hands wandering over her body. Hands became billowing clouds. Both question and answer faded as she noticed with particular clarity the green shade of the watercolor on the wall.

oooooo

"Mother, you write so well," she said. "Why didn't you continue?"

"Every writer has one book in them. Their life story," said Eleanor. She dug at a clump of dandelion weeds. "But . . ." She rubbed a sore reddish spot on her palm.

"But what?" asked Rosa impatiently. "What else were you going to say?"

Clouds swirled through Eleanor. She swayed dizzily for an instant as she squatted. The trowel trembled in her fingers. "Father used to urge me to write stories. He thought I had a gift. But I have nothing to say."

Rosa bristled. "You had plenty to say when you were younger. I'm sure you do now. You wrote so well."

Inside Eleanor, structures rumbled as if through the impact of a minor earthquake.

"I suppose a true artist is driven to create." Her voice sounded brisk. The structures were settling back in place. "Aaron is driven. An artist seems to have a mysterious gene, an extra amount of vitality. I don't have it, but your father does. I enjoy music, and I enjoy my garden. My art lies simply in living life."

Rosa, in white shorts and a dark sleeveless top, deeply tanned, was sitting down on the grass beside her mother, who wore a large straw hat and a faded blue gardening dress. She sniffed a felled dandelion and said, "I don't believe you."

"It's true," protested Eleanor. Inside her, though, was a huge dark mass of fear, kept at bay until Rosa's words stirred it up. If she wrote the true stuff of her life, if she wrote about Heinrich and her hidden thoughts, all the structures would come tumbling down.

ADELLE FOLEY

60 Years Later / After the Camps

They were our neighbors
Torn from our community
  How could this happen

How could this happen
Nurseries and barber shops
  Sold at bargain rates

Sold at bargain rates
"Please, take the horse and chickens"
  And the fields left fallow

And the fields left fallow
Crying for children's laughter
  Young lovers' meeting

Young lovers meeting
Near barbed wire, guard towers
  Boredom and hot dust

Boredom and hot dust
Faded memories. At last
  Soft voices speaking

Soft voices speaking
To those who did not witness
  Utter disbelief

Utter disbelief
It will not happen this time
  They are our neighbors

JACK FOLEY

H.D. Moe (1937-2013):
Fluxional, Vehicular and Transitive

In early July, 2013, the poetry community learned that poet H.D. Moe was living at Salem Lutheran Extended Care Faculty in Oakland. Moe had been seriously ill with liver cancer for some time. He was now in hospice care. Alameda Poet Laureate Mary Rudge suggested that H.D. Moe should be given a medal for his many achievements in the art of poetry. I enthusiastically agreed, and together we planned an event at which David could be given the award. We fund-raised in the community for the event and received far more than was necessary to pay for the medal—which, as it turned out, was donated by Natica and Richard Angilly. Among the people donating money were three poets laureate: Robert Hass, Mary Rudge, and Al Young. The money we raised ($560) was given to H.D. Moe, who exclaimed that it was the most money he had ever received for a poetry reading!

Hearing about the project, people began to send me comments and poems about H.D. Moe. I collected them and placed them in a little pamphlet that I gave out at the medal ceremony and emailed to people who couldn't attend. More comments and poems arrived after David died. I found myself the possessor of pages of sometimes amusing, sometimes grief-stricken, always respectful praise by people who had been touched by David's poetry or whom he had helped in their careers. I remember running into him on the street in 1985. "Hey, Jack," he said, "I mentioned your work in *Poetry Flash*." Those were the days when David seemed—to use an old-fashioned word—preppy. Later, he abandoned that affectation and began to look like what he always was: a deep, starry-eyed bohemian, a poet who made the rounds of the various series that appeared and disappeared throughout the area. He had a quiet laugh and a button, perhaps procured from Stanley McNail: "HIGH ON POETRY." Everyone knew him; everyone liked him. If there was a single word people used to describe him, it was the word sweet.

Norm Moser, a close friend of H.D. Moe's, said, "Moe eats, drinks and defecates just like the rest of us. After that the resemblance ends." Another friend, Julia Vinograd, said, admiringly, "H.D. Moe, oh, he's a character!" He was, indeed. What are we to do with a passage like this?

BLUFF TOWING A DESERT   PHILHARMONIC
Titurel urna
yama yaffling
qualalah gimel chokmah ketber tiphareth
viracil lombox marshal macluen fried radar
 hitchhiking by lavastone endearments
 gypsy filmstar parallelism to our endless out
  lineup churchmouse

The answer of course is: read it. Or, failing that, listen to it, read it aloud. The passage is exactly what it says it is—literally phil-harmonic, full of the love of music. There are references in David's work to (among other people) Lester Young and Anita O'Day, and they evoke what has been said of Moe more than once: that he is a jazz poet. But perhaps, even more than that, he is "a character," an original—more like nothing else in the world than like a "jazz poet." The jazz is there, but it seems to be there as a kind of background, an enthusiasm still present but no longer able to account for everything. When I got to know him, he seemed to be more genuinely—as he puts it—"PHILHARMONIC," Classical even. The poem I have quoted ends with the marvelous line, "buggy flight into the sweet unknown," and "flight into the sweet unknown" is exactly what H.D. Moe is all about. And he is "buggy" in all the senses of that word. The poems "bug" Moe's critics, but they "bug" his admirers too—stay with us, remind us of an extraordinary openness, a "place" in which an intentionally misspelled "marshal macluen" can hobnob with the likes of "qualalah gimel chokmah kether tiphareth / viracil lombox" and "fried radar." That openness might be called the fundamental condition of Moe's poetry, and it is certainly responsible for much of the poetry's enormously attractive flash and glitter, its terrific noises:

  you tuck in my bones
    mutating goons
      android balloons
dust clowning photons
 strumming man with a woman's thumb

In the rush of the verse one hears sound happening over and over again: the off-rhyme of "bones," "goons," "photons," the true rhyme of "goons," "balloons," the echoing of "strum" in the word "thumb."

It is, I believe, in this condition of openness—a state in which Any Word May Happen At Any Time—that Moe's poetry occurs, yet individual poems and passages, even individual words, create specific emphases. There is comedy, of course (at one point the poet cries out, "it's only the uugggaabougah") but there is much else besides. This is from a love poem:

pebbles in the
sun's mouth
 raven on the
  waves
   roots kicked
  up by
   crutches
  of
  Ireland
   she
    is
     the
      wonderful
       dark -

And this is an ecstatic response to a poetry reading:

what is the communal name now
    for us evolvers
beyond the boundaries
     of our own known glowing?
  who is the googol of I
    soundlessly remote in the oceany rows?
        my mind an empty boxcar
     clicking along a new country side of thoughts
       abe lincoln the earth
         O immortal cologne
        & lavender waterfall
           imbued in this room

> I hear so many translations
> my individuality
> is sometimes happily lost
> O bright nomenclatures
> O quiet wisdom
> Like the black beetle I touched
> who refused to climb upon my thumb,
> alone digging

There has always been a place in American letters for the "experimental," the "new," and, beyond this, for what might be called the "transcendental," the headlong thrust into the universe. Here is Ralph Waldo Emerson:

> *The quality of the imagination is to flow, and not to freeze. The poet did not stop at the color or the form, but read their meaning; neither may he rest in this meaning... [The mystic] nails a symbol to one sense, which was a true sense for a moment, but soon becomes old and false. [For the poet] all symbols are fluxional; all language is vehicular and transitive....* ("The Poet," *Essays, 1844*)

Moe's language is definitely fluxional, vehicular, and transitive. So many American "classics" are the products of people who seem both isolated and profound— "eccentrics." (Emerson, Dickinson, Melville, Ives.) H.D. Moe speaks of such people as "evolvers" and ends his poem with a particularly apt description of both his and their activity: alone digging. He told me he used to encourage editors to rearrange his verse— "Surprise me," he would say— and "surprise" is certainly a characteristic of this poetry. But there is also a child-like quality which sometimes produces passages like this:

> WHAT'S WRONG WITH THE NUTTEHUMPYO
> GRAND CANYON EARS
> nuttiehumpyu
> nuttee   nuttehumpyo
> nuttiehumpyee
> nuttium
> nute humpyu

But if H.D. Moe is a child, he is a child who has been amazingly metamorphosed into a sort of encyclopedia as absolutely everything finds new and extraordinary uses in his work. His poetry is an enormously refreshing production of a mind which interests itself in everything that is. "Passage to more than India," wrote Walt Whitman, "are they not all the seas of God?"

Now that Moe is gone, who can we find to remind us that poetry—poetry, not "light verse"—is the mind finding ways to lighten up, to illuminate, to be brilliant, to have more fun than a barrel of nuttehumpyos?

"The Name is Popularly Interpreted to Mean 'Wanderer'"

I've been thrown out of Hollywood night spots for being too rowdy
        Wanda
have picked cotton from the roadside in Fresno
        Wanda
was once pulled over by the CHP for spilling apple juice on the roads of King City
        Wanda
Allen Ginsberg hugged me in Oakland
        Wanda
I've seen L.A. riot twice
        Wanda
I've been blissed out at Mt. Shasta, stoned at Wolfgang's, and nauseated in Palm Springs
        Wanda
My heart lives in Lancaster and my grief dwells in the Russian River
        Wanda
I am a Black Californian, but I am forever married to a New York Jew.
        Wanda
I was born here. I intend to die here.
        Wanda
At home.

*

"in cold grey morning
comes the forlorn honk of workbound traffic
i wake to the video news report

the world is going off

rising, I struggle free of the quilt
& wet dreams of my lover dispel
leave me moist and wanting

in the bathroom
i rinse away illusions, brush my teeth and
unbraid my hair
there're the children to wake
breakfast to conjure
the job
the day laid out before me
the cold corpse of an endless grind

so this is it, i say to the enigma in the mirror
this is your lot/assignment/relegation
this is your city

i find my way to the picture window
my eyes capture the purple reach of hollywood's hills
the gold eye of sun mounting the east

the gray anguished arms of avenue

i will never leave here"

people speak
of the violence and dignity
of your presence
but what
of the beauty
of your language?

CB FOLLETT

Words to the Mother Whose Son Killed My Son

He's just as dead,
killed by your son, or someone else;
muddy where they dragged him
through the jungle, bruised
when they tossed him over the compound wall
while blood was still doing its work,
rushing to protect, cushion, heal
a boy already dead
ready to stiffen and cool.
It could as easily been your son, chilling
in moist soil, awaiting the carrion beetles:
left behind by my son
as he high-fived his buddies.
The truth is, I would have killed
your son that day to save mine.
We who once sat grateful for no news;
we did not choose this for our sons.
I have no need of your country,
where my son trespassed under orders
from shoulders with bars and oak leaves.
Your country endlessly trying to edge free
from invaders; each more technocratic,
with improved death,
with the sear of napalm
that kills people as well as land.
We were no match for your sons
defending their crops, their villages.
They knew each hill and sightline,
each beetle and snake;
were willing to lie among them, dig
into them to quiet and wait.
My son, used to sidewalks
and one apple tree in spring,
was good on his feet, quick of eye,
but not acclimated to yellow light
flicking through thick forests,
where vines move in heat waves
languid as the enemy.
His eyes blurred from straining to see
what was leaf
and what was not.
I mourn for my son,
for his quick laugh,
his perfect spiral pass,
delicate touch with fly and reel,
and his big size twelve feet.
My son is lost forever,
and in ways perhaps more powerful
and corroding, you have also
lost yours.

The Jackdaws Come at Noon

Swoop over our heads threatening
our skin, our skulls, as they used
to sweep over the corpses of our fathers
and brothers; who could not get away;
who were seized from our houses,
dragged into the streets, lined up
in front of our windows and shot.
Fathers,
who worked the fields, or repaired
the water pumps; our young sons
and brothers grown an inch
too tall, barely a darkening
on their chins; their faces
innocent but their eyes old,
so old – and now
we are a village of women. The corpses
are bones under the dirt and the crows
flap black and uncivil to protect
their own young.
When I was a child,
my grandfather would put a piece of tape
on the nail of his right pointer, another
on the nail of his left, and recite some little
silliness about crows: 'Fly away jack. Fly away
jill. Come back jack, Come back jill"
The farmers shot
the crows in the field. They had no corn
to share and no clothes to spare for
Straw Toms to prop up in the rapeseed
and they didn't scare the crows, not for long.
And now we are
our own farmers, tiny plots of vegetables
in houses we can't maintain against rain
and the jacks build their nests in our
stunted trees or our chimneys, and treat us
as the poor relations.
Some men have come
back from the fighting, and there are now
small boys playing jacks, hopping over rocks.
A threadbare woman has started a school
in the old barn and some of the children
go when they can, when they are not sick,
or too hungry to sleep.

JOAN GELFAND

Good Morning America, Where Are You?

Now that the buck has stopped
The jig is up
The well done run
Dry your eyes. You're done.
The party's over the game is played
The bad boys took off
With the cache.

Now that the buck has stopped
Where are you?
What's your place?
What's really on your mind?

Now that the buck has stopped
Did you make the right choices,
Sacrifice the best of times?
Can you remember your kid's last season?
Who won, who lost, who's behind?

Good morning America.
The drug of distraction's worn off
The cocaine high of overvalued
Done gone good-bye.

And this downturn, this turn down,
This big big disappointment, bummer slump
Might just be Nature's way of cooling us off
Cooling us down - all that dough
Rising and rising making us feel
Super, natural but you know she's the boss
Nature had to cool off!
Man! She was feeling the heat.

You have lost and I feel for you
All that hard work and
Faith in The Street.

There's a knock knock joke
In here somewhere
Something along the lines of
"How many Investment Managers
Does it take to screw…"

Or was that greed I heard knocking
Your knees back there?

HERBERT GOLD

Cri de Coeur – Cri de Spleen

A kindly friend decided that I should meet (be fixed up with) a recently-divorced woman who was about to publish her first book. Our encounter was not productive in the match making area. The lady (let's call her Electra) asked me to "have a look" at her manuscript and possibly comment for the publisher. Because of some rash sense of obligation, I agreed to read it. It turned out that I was not taken with the person or the book. Politely, I excused myself for not blurbing. The meeting had not been productive in either the man-plus-woman or the aspirant-writer area, which seemed to cover all the fields under cultivation.

Electra turned out to be a popular success. Our friendship continued not to flourish, perhaps because I wasn't admiring of her person or her work. San Francisco having a small but social literary community, she responded to invitations by saying, "If you invite Herb Gold, I'm not coming."

I've managed to survive despite a few missed dinners. But I happened to be in a restaurant having lunch with Judy, my second daughter, when the lady sat across the way with one of her friends. She said loudly, causing a few people to raise their heads, "There's Herb Gold with another of his young chicks."

On the way out, I led my daughter past her table and introduced her. Electra had the good grace to blush, for which I hereby give her credit.

A few years later, I was sharing a sushi platter with my youngest daughter in a booth next to the booth in which the same relentless colleague sat with a friend. I went to the men's room (lots of green tea). When I returned, my daughter whispered, "Why does that person hate you? She thinks I am your underage girlfriend." I now take away the previous credit. Unfortunately, although I also frequent restaurants with my third daughter, the irate lady—lets continue to call her Electra—has been deprived of a trifecta in the inappropriate-sex accusation sweepstakes.

Over the years, other squalls. One of my books received an exceptionally bad review (not an unfamiliar phenomenon, alas), and someone I barely knew commented casually, in passing, by the way, "Electra showed me your review." I didn't need to ask which one.

At another regretted occasion, a large New Year's Eve celebration, I failed to recognize Electra after one of her drastic facelifts. I introduced myself to her. Big mistake. But there was a crowd into which I could disappear, slinking.

And then there came the public demonstration at which we both spoke, Perched on a narrow platform above a gathering in front of the main San Francisco library, Electra passed in front of me, teetering in high heels. Fearing she might trip, I reached out to steady her. "Help! Help!" she cried. "Herb Gold is harassing me!"

We were not destined to be close friends.

RAFAEL JESÚS GONZÁLEZ
Al fin de la Cuenta Larga

(solsticio invernal 2012)

El baile eterno y vasto de las galaxias,
de las estrellas y los planetas,
los soles, las lunas, los cometas
marca la suma de la Cuenta Larga—
cinco milenios, un siglo, veintiséis años solares
desde que dicen los mayas empezó este mundo.
Los temerosos temen que se destruya la Tierra;
los optimistas esperan salvación de las estrellas.
Son ya ruinas los templos y los observatorios,
desaparecidos los reinos, cenizas los libros,
los antiguos escritos apenas
descifrados por extranjeros.
No son buenos los agüeros—
la Tierra está gravemente herida;
han desaparecido miles de plantas y animales;
el sagrado maíz mismo está contaminado
con el veneno de alacranes.

En vigilia y en rito esta noche
saquemos las plumas y los cristales,
encendamos el fuego,
ofrendemos del copal el humo perfumado.
Hay que celebrar la vida, tener por sagrados
la Tierra, el Sol, el Universo.
Despertemos y con el corazón abierto
empecemos la cuenta de nuevo.

At the End of the Long Count

(Winter Solstice 2012)

The eternal and vast dance of the galaxies,
of the stars and the planets,
the suns, the moons, the comets
mark the sum of the Long Count—
five millenniums, a century, twenty-six solar years
since the Mayas say this world began.
The fearful fear the Earth will be destroyed;
the optimists expect salvation from the stars.
The temples and observatories are now ruins,
disappeared are the kingdoms, ashes the books,
the ancient writing barely
deciphered by strangers.
The auguries are not good—
the Earth is gravely wounded;
thousands of plants and animals have disappeared;
the sacred corn itself is contaminated
with the venom of scorpions.

In vigil and in ritual this night
let us take out the feathers and the crystals,
let us light the fire,
offer of the incense perfumed smoke.
We must celebrate life, hold as sacred
the Earth, the Sun, the Universe.
Let us awake and with an open heart
begin the count anew.

RAY GONZALEZ

A Judge Orders the Opening of Federico Garcia Lorca's Grave

Leave the dead alone.
Federico is not with the other 18 bodies that were dumped there.

Do not rewrite the myth.
Federico is not there because his poem about

the moon lifted him away long ago.
No poet leaves bones as clues to where they must go.

Do not open the earth.
Federico emerged long ago and hid among the black trees

to get away from the death song, the others slowly moving
to the sound of his footsteps, their bodies stripped of possessions,

though the murderers left a folded piece of paper in Federico's pants.
Do not unfold it and read what they did not read because Federico

took the words off the bloody page and ran.
He is gone and will not greet the shovels because your law is not

for tracing the saint. It is for entombing the written word,
but you will discover that poetry is not buried down there.

They Call the Mountain Carlos

They call the mountain Carlos because
it is brown, though its purple slopes
at dusk suggest other names.
Those who name it have to brand
the earth with something they know—

a name, a face, even the heat that says
"I know Carlos and he is the mountain.
I am going to cover his eyes in light."
They call its peak Carlos because
it is the sharpest feature on the face
that stares south, watching people
cross the border, pausing to catch
their breath and meet the cliffs of
Carlos because he is there.

When they ascend the canyons inside
the face, Carlos shifts and the climbers
discover what he has done.
The moving earth changes everything
and they are forced to stop playing
the game of naming a mountain
that keeps touching the sun.

NATHALIE HANDAL

On the Way to Jerez de la Frontera

Maybe you are missing
a part of you,
or you are out of questions,
or you are nowhere in sight
and everyone's looking for you.

Maybe noise
is where pleasure lives,
where a version
of death hides.

Maybe we know nothing
of what surrounds us,
and the sherry we drink—
fino, amontillado, oloroso—
fills us with what we can't desire
for too long.

We need to invent something
about ourselves:
the country we are from,
this striking white color,
this empty shadow,
and the paper burning
inside of it, inside of it
the distance
moving
ash in the back of our eyes.

PETER J. HARRIS

American Man

So many of them ... on the avenue of speechlessness ... Please come Great Voice" —Larry Neal

militant falsetto
subtle as background radiation   indivisible as dark matter
disciplined as a second-string infielder poised to turn two in an exhibition game
umpired by prison inmates   leaping to avoid concussion of one-note meanings barreling out of American history

whose child am I?
genuflecting to the reverb of Curtis Mayfield's mantras in 3-minute anthems?
even spreading bubble gum to repave the avenue of speechlessness
whispering the Great Voice so gentle a Christian aunt feels my love

I still get asked

how can you be an American man?
just nudging my volume past protocol frightens the uninitiated
how can you be a Black man?
just frowning in concentration intimidates Topps card collectors
            Peter, you ain't Black. You vegetarian!
is how Jessica put pestle into mortar after class one day
virtuoso grand daughter of the voice for integrity
converting agony of foremothers chained within clauses of declarations
flinging alchemy & medicine from tectonics of puberty
            vexing barometers of who can I be
throwing out inevitability at first base by a mile with her brash jubilation
wise-cracking adolescent   resolution in her exuberance   discerning *comadre* of my masculine independence

GERALD HASLAM

The Great Biblical Colloquy

Wylie Hillis sauntered into the Tejon Club Bar that day sportin' one of them pointy, old-time hats like George Washington used to wear. Us boys couldn't help bustin' out laughin'. Now what?

"You guys'll quit laughin' whenever them damn liberals start up with them death panel deals and your asses are on the line!" he snapped, wavin' this little pamphlet at us. He was always bringin' junk like that into the Club where us guys enjoyed our after-work beers. And he was always preachin' since the Democrats was back in office. "Now that they're a-takin' over, we'll all be bossed by coloreds and gay deals, too."

Big Dunc grunted, "You damn rights," without looking up from his mug of beer.

"Wait a minute," I said. "Last week you told us that A-rabs were takin' over and we'd all have to wear those towels on our heads…speakin' of which, where'd you get that silly hat?"

"Yeah, where'd you get that goofy hat, anyway?" asked Bob Don Bundy that's a graduate of Bakersfield Junior College so he's a smart sucker. "And where in the world do you get your so-called information? What's the authority behind those fliers and pamphlets you're always quoting?"

"Them's true facts in there," Hillis asserted. "Yer liberals're in cahoots with them A-rabs and gay deals, too."

"You damn rights," grunted Big Dunc. "It's right in the damn Bible."

"What about that hat?" I added. "Is that in the Bible?" Wylie looked ready for Halloween to me with that pointy, old-time thing on his head. "You goin' out trick-or-treatin' tonight, posin' as ol' John Paul Jones?"

Wylie scowled. "You'll think trick-er-treatin' whenever us patriots take over. Me and the Missus bought us hats at the Tea Party rally out at the fairgrounds last weekend. We bought us one of them snake flags, too: 'Don't step on me'. We're a-takin' our country back!"

"From whom?" Bundy asked, adding. "And it's 'tread' not 'step'."

"Oh it is, Mr. Fancy Pants. We're a-takin' our country back from the dang liberals like you, that's who. I got me a gun! We're gonna stir us up a militia!"

"Yeah," I grinned, "I seen your old bolt-action .22 and I even seen you shoot it. The safest place to be is in front of your target. I can just imagine you and Duncan with his single-shot .410 out there takin' on the Russians or the A-rabs or who-the-hell-ever it is. I'll bet the enemy's shakin' in their boots right now."

"I'uz the best shot in my outfit back in the army," asserted Duncan.

"Yeah," I replied, "that's why you spent two years handin' out underpants to recruits, you were such a deadly sniper they kept you protectin' boxer-shorts from the Russians."

"Eat shit."

Wylie ignored us and repeated, "We're a-takin' our country back!"

Earl that owned the joint he grinned and rolled that toothpick around his mouth, then said, "You ever think to try votin'?"

"Votin'!" exclaimed Wylie. "Oh hell no. You do that and they get you fer jury duty and shit like that."

"What're retired old farts like you doing that's more important than jury duty?" Bob Don asked.

"Just mind your own bee's-wax, perfesser," snapped the patriot.

"And how come you're such an upstanding citizen when you told us how you busted your ass to get a deferment so's you didn't have go in the service like the rest of us did, and you told us the other day you want to kick out all those gays that volunteer and put their lives on the line?" I demanded. "What qualifies you to criticize?"

"The Bible! The Bible, that's what! It says them gay deals're a abomination."

"A what?"

"A damn abomination is what!"

That's when Duncan, still slouched over a beer with half his ass-crack smiling from the back of his jeans, reentered the conversation. "Me and the War Department we're fixin' to join that Tea Party deal, too. She read this deal all about it. And besides, we might could run off that colored president that he's not even a real American. Besides, he likes them A-rabs." Dunc's eyes narrowed and his voice lowered when he added, "I think he might even be one."

I just shook my head.

"Well, there's a noble cause for you," smiled Bob Don.

"God, guns, and guts…and white guys…made America great!" added Big Dunc, his favorite slogan.

"You damn rights," agreed Wylie.

"In that tricorner hat, you look more like Martha Washington than George to me," said Bob Don.

Wylie stood, his face red. "Cain't talk no serious politics to dumb peckerheads like y'all," and he stormed out of the club.

"He'll be back whenever he gets thirsty," said Earl, chewin' on his toothpick.

"You boys oughta believe on the Bible like me and the War Department do," said Dunc.

Bob Don smiled. "When was it you read the Bible, Duncan?" We all knew he'd never finished a book in his life.

The big guy just grunted. "The War Department she told me all about it, see."

"Well, I took a 'Bible as Literature' course at Bakersfield Junior College," Bob Don continued, "two semesters—Old Testament then New Testament—and I'll bring my copy in, read you a couple little excerpts. We can have a little colloquy."

"A what?" demanded Wylie.

"A colloquy," said Bob Don. "A discussion."

"Don't be talkin' that damned Spanish to me, perfessor fancy pants!"

"You don't have to bring nothin' in for me," said Dunc. "Me and the War Department're right on top of that deal."

"I'll bet you are," I said.

The very next afternoon while we were gathered for suds after work, Bob Don brought this dog-eared old Bible with lots of bright pink post-its sticking up from pages. I asked him what was up, so he read us some passages that he said he was going to spring on Dunc and Wylie when they got there. Me and Earl, neither of us very familiar with the Bible, probably looked shocked.

When the patriots finally showed up, Wylie wasn't wearing his John Paul Jones hat, but Dunc had one on, and his had three tea bags dangling, one from each corner. "You are one silly lookin' specimen, Duncan," said Earl, rolling his toothpick around his mouth and shaking his head.

"I'll wear whatever I goddamn want, see," snapped Dunc, adding with his usual eloquence, "Eat shit."

Wylie ignored that dispute. He'd come in carrying a handful of fliers he said were from his church, and on the front page it said in big letters, "Homosexuality! ABOMINATION! Leviticus 18:22." He cast is eyes at each of us, then demanded, "How d'ya like them apples, boys?" He thrust a flier directly at Bob Don Bundy, who waved him off, saying, "Keep it."

Wylie didn't let go. He said to Bob Don, "See what that deal says? Well stick that in yer damn pipe and smoke it, perfessor! It's still an abdomination!"

"You damn rights," added Big Dunc.

"Let's see," responded Bob Don, grinning, "you two like to blaspheme and cuss all the time. Let's see what Leviticus says about that. Ahhh, here it is, 24:10-16." Bundy turned toward me and Earl and said, "Well, I guess we've got to stone these two blasphemers to death." He shrugged, "Hate to do it, boys, but it's in the Bible."

Big Dunc blinked.

"What?" I said. For a second, I thought he was serious.

Earl he caught right on. "I've got some old bricks out back from that fireplace we took out. Will they do?"

"They'll do," said Bob Don.

"What the hell're you guys talkin' about... ," sputtered Wylie. "Talk sense!"

"Oh yeah, you two also had haircuts last week, didn't you?" Bob Don added, "Leviticus says that's a no-no, too."

"Get the bricks," Earl winked at me.

Duncan slid off his bar stool, teabags swinging. "You boogers're crazy, see," he said.

"And you, Duncan, were telling us about eating clams over at Pismo on the weekend. They're shellfish as far as I know, and Leviticus says eating shellfish is an abomination, too. I think we get to burn you alive for that one if we want."

"You'll play hell," threatened the big guy, suddenly looking worried.

"Where you gettin' all that crap?" demanded Wylie.

"Well...," Bob Don grinned, "well, I'll be. It's in the Bible." He raised the book over his head for a second. "But there's some good news, too," Bob Don continued. "Leviticus says we can have slaves from neighboring nations, so I'm gonna get myself a Mexican and a Canadian to help me stone you two peckerheads and burn your carcasses."

Duncan was easing toward the door as Earl asked, "Can I get me a young gal?"

"I don't see why not."

"Boy howdy," he replied, his toothpick quivering. "You want one, too, Jerry Bill?" he asked me.

"No, I'm good."

The door slammed and Duncan was gone, teabags and all.

Wylie, was uncharacteristically mute for a spell, finally he slid off his stool and said, "I don't believe in none of it."

Bob Don said, "You don't believe gays are an 'abdomination'?"

"Hell yeah, I still believe that part, but none of that other crap."

"Show him your Bible," I urged Bob Don, who extended the open book toward Wylie.

That old Arkie, Wylie, he pulled his hands back as though a serpent had been offered him. "No sir," he said, "I'm not touchin' that deal. I'm not lookin' at it! The real Bible don't say none of that shit."

"I'm afraid it does," responded Bundy. "But the thing is, Wylie, times change. Times really do change."

JUAN FELIPE HERRERA

Photograph with Tony, Francisco & Jorge Outside Brava Theatre, San Francisco, 9/15/12

We are embracing—after thirty-two years poets on the road about justice

Tony's hair is long-gray mine is short-gray we are bowing down

monks outside the hut &

Jorge drops into the back half-shadow smile

In '81 out of El Salvador he was mourning his familia short-time gone

Francisco is laughing with full belly heart with beads & crimson shirt

for a moment stand together

all the trails come to one   no words

we bow again

we laugh again

The More You (Hotel Realization Poem #1. 9/22/13, Washington D.C.)

The more I
Travel the more
I realize I am an artist the
More I live
The more I realize
I am no in particular no
One special –

Think of what Judy Baca
Said – about imagining and seeing
A little further
Than where we
Are now
A little beyond –

I am discovering that that is
How art – poetry
We – our
Inner life
Finds new
Skies how
We
Really truly breathe unfettered
By the tight obligatory
Frames we cast
For ourselves

(it does not matter—nevertheless)

The question is
What are you
Going to do w/all
This life? For some odd
Reason
It is yours. You
Can live it not all
Of it but
You can live it
For a little
While and
If you do
You really
Will not need
To live all
Of it

JACK HIRSCHMAN

The *Da-Sein* Arcane

"Gesang ist Dasein" —Rainer Maria Rilke

At the very beginning
of the memory of my
discovery of poetry,
you were here as Da

(so easy to say: *There*
fused with the Russian
for *Yes,* you were where
I first read Da-sein)

before Heidegger would
deconstruct it years later,
and now from this old
hindsight of 60 years,

I put my finger on it:
you didn't so much make
me a poet as reveal what
poetry really is, and how

its resonance streams
all the way down into
the profounds of the
foundation of inwardness.

So even after I turned
the body of the dancer
inside-out with Artaud,
and entered the scream

of silence attending the
funeral of the West with
Celan, even forgetting you
as I ran headlong down

Mayakovsky's street,
drum-pumped aortas
beating out the raps of
facts of the class act

of that flaming tract of tracts
engined by those engineers
of soul into the Revolution,
you found me after all,

in the Soviet Memorial Park
in East Berlin, insisting
(by way of Russian space and
the global sorrow that would

have evoked your voyage to
Russia with Lou Salome at the
outset of the 20th century)
on death-in-life for yourself,

and it did and it does for me
as well...the glorious D,
the greater purport, as Walt
called it so accurately. O David,

my own, who's deepened my
way through. At the end of
whose never-ending life,
prophetic of all that had

already occurred in the last
century, and would to this
very day, O *Duino*
Elegies, that found me

with its total cry. And now
that the world is dying of
the hedony of consumerism
and the call to be poet is

above all inward, (for that's
what's given in a book and,
more essentially, originally,
in a poem in a book)

—O may Song break the glass
of ether that sustains the things
of the world and "Who if I cried..."
be from the mouth of a body of

souls for years gathering griefs,
sufferings and rage to a cry that
might occupy all of *Dasein* so
that we each of us actually hear

each other from the sun's soul
and our deaths embrace as
one heart, O ray of the son of
Love's resplendent Glory.

MITCH HOROWITZ

Black Moses: The Radical Metaphysics of Marcus Garvey

The late nineteenth and early twentieth centuries saw a Renaissance of alternative spirituality in America. Many Americans were fascinated with positive-thinking metaphysics, or the occult cosmology popularized by Madame H.P. Blavatsky and her Theosophical Society.

When we remember this era today, it is rarely understood that these mystical trends were often joined to a passion for social reform. The most stirring, and little known, marriage of spiritual and political radicalism can be seen in the career of black-nationalist pioneer Marcus Garvey.

Garvey, who sojourned from Jamaica to America in 1916, envisioned the creation of a pan-African superpower that would take its place among the empires of the world. For a time, he came closer than many would have imagined possible, attracting tens of thousands of cheering followers to rallies and parades in America, England, and the Caribbean, and assembling the first and largest international black political organization in history.

In a pillar of Garvey's program often missed by those who scrutinized him, the political leader believed that positive thinking, or New Thought, metaphysics could build the dreams of disenfranchised men and women around the world. Garvey's movement represented the boldest – and least understood – effort in history to combine mind-power metaphysics with the quest for political gain.

Born in northern Jamaica in 1887, Garvey traveled through Central America in his early twenties. He was appalled to witness the second-class status occupied by black laborers completing the Panama Canal. "Where was the black man's country?" Garvey wondered. The young journalist looked for answers in Booker T. Washington's *Up From Slavery*. Washington's philosophy of self-sufficiency hit Garvey with the force of a religious conversion. Garvey merged this influence with his own search into New Thought spirituality.

"Always think yourself a perfect being," Garvey told followers, "and be satisfied with yourself."

Garvey's philosophy of faith-in-self and perpetual self-improvement formed his deepest appeal – and it took a leaf directly from the American metaphysical tradition. The newspapers and pamphlets of Garvey's Universal Negro Improvement Association (UNIA) abounded with tell-tale phrases of New Thought, such as the call for a "universal business consciousness" which appeared in his *Negro World* newspaper. Garvey's Negro Factories Corporation advertised shares of stock by declaring, "Enthusiasm Is One of the Big Keys to Success." And a front-page headline in Garvey's Blackman newspaper announced: "Let us Give off Success and It Will Come," adding the indispensable New Thought maxim:

"As Man Thinks So Is He."

One of the only books that Garvey publicly recommended to followers was Elbert Hubbard's *Scrapbook*, a collection of life lessons by Hubbard, a social-reform journalist and motivational hero within New Thought circles. Garvey's favorite poet was Ella Wheeler Wilcox, the poet laureate of mind-power, whose lines he used to conclude a 1915 UNIA rally:

Live for something, — Have a purpose
And that purpose keep in view
Drifting like an helmless vessel
Thou cans't ne'er to self be true.

Garvey made little direct reference to the source of his ideas. A degree of secrecy and confidentiality characterized almost all of Garvey's affairs, including those of the mind. Yet in a speech he delivered in January 1928 in Kingston, Jamaica, Garvey articulated his New

Thought ideas more clearly than any other time in his career. "Get you[rself], as the white man has done, a scientific understanding of God and religion," he told his listeners, continuing:

> What marks the great deal of difference between the Negro and the White man is that the Negro does not understand God and His religion. God places you here in the world on your responsibility as men and women to take out of the world and to make out of the world what you want in keeping with the laws of the spirit. God has laid down two codes that man cannot afford to disobey: The code of Nature and the code of the Spirit. The code of Nature when you violate it makes you angry, makes you unhappy, makes you miserable, makes you sick, makes you die prematurely…Every sickness and every disease, I repeat, is a direct violation of the code of God in Nature.

Making a definite spiritual use of the term "science," Garvey told the audience that whites "live by science. You do everything by emotion. That makes the vast difference between the two races…Get a scientific knowledge of religion, of God, of what you are; and you will create a better world for yourselves. Negroes, the world is to your making."

Contemporary readers of Garvey's words could easily miss, or simply wonder at, the political leader's references to religion and science – but the signposts abounded in Garvey's day. The New Thought movement rested on the premise that religion was, above all, a lawful phenomenon guaranteed to produce certain results. Garvey's spiritual "science" also had roots – occult roots – in his Caribbean boyhood. In the West Indies, the term science was a slang word for magical practices.

Garvey's speeches and articles bear the telltale signs of a political metaphysics, couched in language to which every American, black or white, could instantly relate.

DOUG MEGAPOET HOWERTON

Fighters Fight the Wars

This lifestyle is sheer mockery
Just a perverted scheme
An ageless illusion... a major intrusion
A warmonger's tour de force

This underhanded suspenseful scenario
Is divisive habitual and degrading
Leading to holocaust slavery atomic warfare
This mayhem is the irresponsibility of plotting
Fighters fight wars... Lickers lick sores
The alleged crazies behind lock doors
This detailed fiasco but today

Fighters fight wars...Lickers lick sores
The alleged crazies behind lock doors
This detailed fiasco is but today

Seen through eyes that are realizing
Conditioned leaders lead a contented populous
Utilizing simulative text from ancient symbols
Implementing control with drugs propaganda and
Militaristic force so quasi governments can rule

The political process is corrupt beguiling
All manner of people sacrifice their life for war
Bombs fall on moonless nights killing racial foes
Wars and rumors of wars Persist

Fighters fight wars...Lickers lick sores
The alleged crazies are behind locked doors
This detailed fiasco is but today
Seen through eyes that are realizing

KITTY KELLEY

Unauthorized, But Not Untrue

Shortly after my book *Oprah: A Biography* was published last April, one of Oprah Winfrey's open-minded fans wrote to her website saying she wanted to read the book. Oprah's message-board moderator hurled a thunderbolt in response: "This book is an unauthorized biography." The word unauthorized clanged on the screen like a burglar alarm. Suddenly I heard the rumble of thousands of Oprah book buyers charging out of Barnes & Noble—empty-handed.

Days before this exchange, I had felt the chill of media disdain when my publisher began booking my promotion tour. Larry King barred the door to his CNN talk show because, he said, he didn't want to offend Oprah. Barbara Walters did the same thing, proclaiming on *The View* that the only reason people wrote unauthorized biographies was to dig "dirt." There was no room for me at Charlie Rose's roundtable and no comfy seat next to David Letterman. The late-night comic had recently reconciled with Oprah after a 16-year rift and did not want to risk another. On my 10-city tour I made few, if any, appearances on ABC-owned-and-operated stations because most of the stations that broadcast The *Oprah Winfrey Show* are owned by ABC or its affiliates. No one wanted to displease the diva of daytime television. Although they had not read the book prior to publication, they assumed, given the author and the subject, that my unauthorized biography would be a blistering takedown of a beloved icon. The reviews ranged from rocks (*The New York Times*) to raves (*The Los Angeles Times*). My publisher, Crown Books, aimed for sales from the fan base fondly known as "Opraholics" and "Winfreaks," but once Herself publicly denounced the book as "a so-called biography," the fan base dwindled, and to date the book has yet to sell 300,000 copies (a disappointing figure for an author paid to sell millions). It's true that traditional publishing is getting slammed by the Internet and can no longer guarantee commercial success to writers, even those who, as I did, hit number one on *The New York Times* best-seller list and on Amazon.com. Sadly, the demand for books has decreased in the last 10 years, which may or may not explain why the United States has fallen from number one to number 12 among developed nations in the percentage of college graduates.

Priced at $30, my book was too expensive to flourish in a sour economy, especially in the target audience of Oprah fans, who, demographics show, are low and middle-income women with little disposable income. But there was more at play than economics. Even among Oprah fans there is a bit of Oprah fatigue, following 25 years of her appearing on the air five days a week. Some people feel they know all there is to know about their idol, and whatever else there may be to learn they will read in the weekly tabloids at the grocery store. Others want the myth and do not want to be disillusioned by an unauthorized biography.

In today's celebrity culture, that word unauthorized carries immense freight. It signals an independent appraisal that will reveal more than floss, and some people cannot accept their idols with flaws. Instead, they need the illusions they see on the screen or the fantasies they read. To show anything less makes them feel shortchanged, even conned.

Journalists are just as susceptible to the power of celebrity as the adoring housewives who watch *Oprah*. Lara Logan, CBS News chief foreign correspondent and a contributor to *60 Minutes*, appeared a few months ago with Howard Kurtz on CNN's *Reliable Sources*. She castigated Michael Hastings for his *Rolling Stone* article that led to the firing of General Stanley McChrystal.

When Kurtz asked her if there is an "unspoken agreement that you're not going to embarrass [the troops] by reporting insults and banter," Logan said, "Yes, absolutely. There is an element of trust."

Hastings said that reporters like Logan do not report negative stories about their subjects in order to assure continued access. No reporter would admit to tilting a story toward favorable coverage to keep entrée, but they do, and that is one of the dirty little secrets of journalism today. The kickback I got from many of the media mandarins who refused to talk with me, and who had themselves been subjects of unauthorized biographies, reflects the fear and loathing of the genre.

Still, I believe that the best way to tell a life story is from the outside looking in, and so I choose to write with my nose pressed against the window rather than kneel inside for spoon-feedings. Most of the great biographies are written about people who are dead, and thus the biographies are unauthorized. Championing the independent or unauthorized biography might sound like a high-minded defense for a low-level pursuit, but I do not relish living in a world where information is authorized, sanitized, and homogenized. I read banned books, I applaud whistleblowers, and I reject any suppression by church or state. To me, the unauthorized biography, which requires a combination of scholarly research and investigative reporting, is best directed at those figures, still alive and able to defend themselves, who exercise power over our lives. So I only pursue the kings (and queens) of the jungle.

Whether authorized or unauthorized, a good biography is nuanced and complex, because that is the way most people are. Being imperfect, most of us are messy and mixed-up in our private lives, inconsistent in our intentions, misled in our motives, and contradictory in our actions. Powerful public figures seem to have even more exaggerated faults and frailties, probably because their legions of publicists have spent years bleaching out the stains. The most authentic parts of a life are often quirky and filled with secrets that might startle the admissions committees of colleges and country clubs. What if they knew about Grandpa's bootlegging, Grandma's gambling, Dad's tax evasions, or Mom's affection for spirits? So there is a natural tendency to erase what is real, painful, or unflattering; sadly, those deletions deprive a life story of its depth and dimension.

As Shakespeare wrote, "men are molded out of faults, and for the most, become much more the better for being a little bad."

The Family: The Real Story of the Bush Dynasty was published in 2004 in the midst of a contentious presidential campaign, and I was lambasted by the Republican National Committee ("an assassin of honorable statesmen"), the White House communications director ("untrue garbage"), the White House press secretary ("garbage and sleaze"), and the White House deputy press secretary ("fiction and garbage"). House Majority Leader Tom DeLay wrote to my publisher, saying that I was in the "advanced stage of a pathological career," and that Doubleday, the house of Rudyard Kipling, Booker T. Washington, and Anne Frank, was in "moral collapse" because they had published my "scandalous and mendacious enterprise." Days later, DeLay was publicly rebuked by the House Ethics Committee three times for unethical conduct. Within a year he was indicted in a criminal investigation in Texas and charged with a felony that forced his resignation from the House of Representatives. After six years of litigation, his trial began on November 1, 2010. He was last seen on television in 2010 wearing sequins and "dancing with the stars."

Promoting the unauthorized biography of the Bush family dynasty was daunting, because of the "how-dare-you" attitude of the media, which could not accept the portrait of the elder Bush as a man who did not live up to the orchestrated public image they had bestowed upon him. A prime example of the mythology surfaced after M. Charles Bakst reviewed the book for *The Providence Journal*. A political columnist in Rhode Island, Bakst had interviewed George H.W. Bush in 1991 about his war experience and took issue with my reporting on the discrepancies between Bush's 1944 recollections in his personal letters of being shot down over the Pacific during World War II and what he later claimed in a 1988 book he had written with Doug Wead.

In 1944, Bush bailed out of his plane and maintained that he never knew exactly what happened to his two-man crew, who were never found. In 1988 he changed his story and said that he saw his gunman killed by machine-gun fire and his radioman parachute out before he was fired on. If one accepts his contemporaneous accounts in 1944, plus official Navy documents, then the 1988 account is a fabrication. Bolstered by documents showing that there were no machine guns and no dog fights involving machine guns, the inescapable conclusion is that George Bush plumped up his war record for political gain.

Running for president in 1988, Bush called his book *George Bush: Man of Integrity*. Bakst wrote that he had never heard of the book or the two different versions Bush had told about his war experience. Bakst sent a copy of his review to the former president, who responded with a handwritten note:

"As for Kitty Kelly [sic]—she is a liar and a smear artist. I had not heard of the Wead book. I never talked to Wead about jumping out of my plane. Nor did I write a book with Doug Wead ever. This is but one instance of the Kelly smear. But my family has no chance in a court so Kitty & others are free to lie and smear. Enough! All best, George Bush."

I was reeling and so was my publisher, who faxed Bakst a copy of the book jacket from Man of Integrity, which showed that George H. W. Bush had indeed collaborated with Wead. Even Bakst was taken aback. When he contacted the former president again, Bush responded through Jean Becker. She said he "felt guilty" about not remembering that he had written the book, but he stood by his contention that Kitty Kelley was "a liar and a smear artist." Bush did not provide specifics to substantiate his accusations. Nor did he cite one error, one mistake, or one misrepresentation in my book. Apparently, he wasn't bothered by the facts—just the fact-finder. The former president, now retired in Texas, spends a few days a month at the George Bush Presidential Library in College Station, where he autographs leather bomber jackets like the one he wore as a Navy pilot in World War II. He sells them for $985.

Presidential wrath has its niggling little consequences. After almost 30 years as a contributing editor for *Washingtonian* magazine, I was suddenly removed from the masthead. The editor said he disapproved of my Bush book because of its intimate revelations and its timing, but then he might have been doing the bidding of the magazine's owner, Philip Merrill, who was a presidential appointee of both Bushes and a close personal friend of Vice President Dick Cheney. In any event, Bush was delighted with the news. He told *Time*'s Hugh Sidey:

"Kitty Kelley. Did you see where somebody handed her her hat the other night? The *Washingtonian*. I loved that."

Relieved of my masthead status, I crept back into my writer's cave, determined to keep a low profile and stay out of trouble. But then Fox News commentator Bernard Goldberg published a book titled *100 People Who Are Screwing Up America* and I found myself listed as culprit number 80. Granted, this was not nearly as illustrious as being on Nixon's enemies list, but when the Associated Press called for a reaction, I said I was proud to be included in any group with President Jimmy Carter, Nobel laureate Paul Krugman, and actor/activist Harry Belafonte.

VANDANA KHANNA

Echo

I cannot make it lovely,
this story of my father: his body
raw under the lights like a skinned

almond, surrounded by sandalwood,
pickled carrots, and the hush
of rice settling in a bag.

I can't help it, I need metaphors:
his body curls like the curve of a cheek,
a knife lies beside him, done with its work.

This story in metaphors. Not simply:
You lie on the floor. You've been cut
by two men you don't know. They wanted

money and you were too slow, didn't understand.
But rather: bruises braid his skin, the bitter black
of leaves, eyes red as the swollen sting

of chili powder. *Why do I write in the past?*
He smells only sweat, sickened blood seeping,
nothing familiar—not black and red pepper pinched

into the air, not the jasmine of his mother's
kitchen. Nothing—until his breath is like a tea
bag twisted, pressed into the cup of the room.

But it's not an Indian grocery, it is a shabby
downtown hotel, the kind that lock their doors
at ten, have security guards to stop the prostitutes

from coming in, from warming themselves
in the lobby. The kind where hallways echo
of accents. The phone is off the hook.

Not, *why do I write about the past?* but, *what story
must I tell?* You lie there dreaming, but I'm
not sure, dreaming of your childhood in Lahore:

the city escaping the finite lines of a map, erased
by riots, civil war. You remember the hot nights,
chattering birds—how the world was never silent then.

You tell me over and over but I can't write it:
the same story, but I know we are leaving
things out. Embellishing. What they must

have said, the words, harsh like Bengali, you never
tell, the first cut and then the next, how you fell
like a sack of mangoes into a heavy tumble.

You have left the spaces empty for me to add
in colors, the smells, to translate to English.
To translate into the present, into beautiful.

PAUL KRASSNER

Remembering Kesey

One afternoon in 1971, Ken Kesey and I were smoking hashish in a tunnel inside a cliff which had been burrowed during World War II so that military spotters with binoculars could look toward the Pacific Ocean's horizon for oncoming enemy ships. All we spotted was a meek little mouse right there in the tunnel. We blew smoke at the mouse until it could no longer tolerate our behavior. The mouse stood on its hind paws and roared at us, "Squeeeeeek!" This display of mouse assertiveness startled us and we almost fell off the cliff. The headline would've read: Dope Crazed Pranksters in Suicide Pact.

I once asked Kesey, "Do you see the legalization of grass as any sort of panacea?" "The legalization of grass," he replied, "would do absolutely nothing for our standard of living, or our military supremacy, or even our problem of high school dropouts. It could do nothing for this country except mellow it, and that's not a panacea, that's downright subversive." Kesey had been disinvited from a Nightline panel on drugs because he was pro-marijuana. He made a distinction between pot, mushrooms, LSD, psilocybin—"the organic, kinder, gentler, hippie drugs"— and cocaine, crack, ice— "drugs that make you greedy and produce criminals." He called drugs "my church" and confessed that he had taken psychoactives "with lots more reverence and respect than I ever walked into church with."

In 1978, Kesey said to me, "Hey, why don't you come to Egypt with us? The Dead are gonna play the Pyramids."

I did not play hard to get. The Grateful Dead were scheduled to play on three successive nights at an open-air theater in front of the Pyramids, with the Sphinx looking on. Drummer Bill Kreutzmann had fallen off a horse and broken his arm. He would still be playing with the band, using one drumstick. Or, as an Arabian fortune cookie might point out, "In the land of the limbless, a one-armed drummer is king." Basketball star and faithful Deadhead Bill Walton's buttocks had been used as a pincushion by the Portland Trailblazers so that he could continue to perform on court even though the bones of his foot were being shattered with pain he couldn't feel. Having been injected with painkilling drugs to hide the greed rather than heal the injury, he now had to walk around with crutches and one foot in a cast under his extra-long galabea. Maybe Kreutzmann and Walton could team up and enter the half-upside-down sack-race event.

An air of incredible excitement permeated the first night. Never had the Dead been so inspired. Backstage, Jerry Garcia was passing along final instructions to the band:

"Remember, play in tune."

The music began with Egyptian oudist Hamza el-Din, backed up by a group tapping out ancient rhythms on their fourteen-inch-diameter tars, soon joined by Mickey Hart, a butterfly with drumsticks, then Garcia ambled on with a gentle guitar riff, then the rest of the band, and as the Dead meshed with the percussion ensemble, basking in total respect of each other, Bob Weir suddenly segued into Buddy Holly's *Not Fade Away*.

"Did you see that?" Kesey said. "The Sphinx's jaw just dropped!"

Every morning my roommate, George Walker, climbed to the top of the pyramid. He was in training. It would be his honor to plant a Grateful Dead skull-and-lightning-bolt flag on top of the Great Pyramid. This was our Iwo Jima.

In preparation for the final concert, I was sitting in the tub-like sarcophagus at the center of gravity in the Great Pyramid, after ingesting LSD that Kesey had smuggled into Egypt in a plastic Visine bottle. I had heard that the sound of the universe was D-flat, so that's what I chanted. It was only as I breathed in deeply before each extended Om that I was forced to ponder the mystery of those who urinate there.

I told Kesey that I had a strong feeling that I was involved in some kind of lesson. It was as though the secret of the Dead would finally be revealed to me, if only I paid proper attention. There was a full eclipse of the moon, and Egyptian kids were running through the streets shaking tin cans filled with rocks in order to bring it back.

"It's okay," Kesey assured them. "The Grateful Dead will bring back the moon." And, sure enough, a rousing rendition of *Ramble On Rose* would accomplish that feat. The moon returned just as the marijuana cookie that Bill Graham gave me started blending in with the other drugs. Graham used to wear two wristwatches, one for the Fillmore in San Francisco and the other for Fillmore East in New York. Now he wore one wristwatch with two faces.

There was a slight problem with an amplifier, but the sound engineer said that it was "getting there."

"Getting there ain't good enough," Garcia replied. "It's gotta fuckin' be there."

This was a totally outrageous event. The line between incongruity and appropriateness had disappeared along with the moon. The music was so powerful that the only way to go was ecstasy. That night, when the Dead played *Fire on the Mountain*, I danced my ass off with all the others on that outdoor stage as if I had no choice.

"You know," Bill Graham confessed backstage, "this is the first time I ever danced in public."

"Me too," I said.

And Kesey chimed in: "That was your lesson."

MICHAEL LALLY
Fighting Words

Poetry saved my life.
There is no life without poetry.
What life isn't a poem?
Open my brain, poems fly out.

How do I get the poems back?
That's not a poem, that's my life.
"My Life" was my most famous poem.
What life isn't a poem?

Poetry literally saved my life.
It made me feel not so alone.
It's not so easy now to write a poem
since the operation on my brain.

But I'd do it again, and again,
because in the end, what isn't a poem?

NHUAN XUAN LE (THANH-THANH)

Just Cause

You asked me to tell about my native land,
And you made as if you did all understand;
But, I was aware you gave to it no priority,
Except to amuse yourself with your curiosity.

Would it be too demanding if I asked back
Your opinion on the war that became a crack
As the longest and most controversial conflict
To bedevil and cause people to contradict?

Do not mention the fifty-eight-thousand lost,
One-hundred-and-eighty-billion dollars cost,
And the way it happened in that painful past,
Its social and mental syndrome thence to last.

Just tell me what you feel, think, and react
When they claimed lack of Just Cause a fact
While National Security and Interests' scope
Is asserted to include anywhere on the globe!

Why not to let Europe for the Nazis to take,
And Asia for the Mikado militarists to invade,
And West Germany for the Soviets to fool,
And South Korea for the Red Chinese to rule?

Of course, the States had to pay some prices
To win and gain the biggest and best slices!
Thus, they had recourse to "No Just Cause!"
Only because they came to a defamed pause!

Wait and see! I bet, it will be taking actions
To intervene for and against certain factions.
The Middle East, Africa... the cons and pros:
No more "Far! Strange! Misjudging the foes!"

Now, you have got it: It is remedying things!
Iron fists? Velvet gloves? Just tactical swings!
The Free World must win to redeem its pride
And justify that the Just Cause is on our side!

RABBI MICHAEL LERNER

Loving Words To Heal and Transform the World

"Have you heard that Rabbi Lerner has just been killed?" asked the anonymous phone caller to *Tikkun Magazine* at our Oakland office. "I just heard it on the radio!" My coworkers were quite upset 'till I called in a few hours later. But having gone through false bomb threats and endless hate calls, plus a steady string of death threats to me personally, no one was totally shocked. *Tikkun Magazine* has consistently editorialized that the Israeli Occupation of the West Bank and blockade of Gaza is both self-destructive for Israel, a violation of Jewish ethics, and immoral toward Palestinians. These fighting words had consequences: bomb threats, withdrawal of financial support, and frequent death threats. These reached a crescendo in 2011 and 2012 when my own home in Berkeley was physically attacked on 4 different occasions by right wing Zionists who plastered its outside with posters proclaiming that I (rabbi of Beyt Tikkun synagogue in Berkeley) am a "self-hating Jew, a Nazi, and a danger to the State of Israel."

Danger to Israel? In my *Jewish Renewal,* HarperCollins 1995, and in *Embracing Israel/Palestine,* North Atlantic, 2012, I insist that those of us who believe in non-violence and peace must be both pro-Israel and pro-Palestine, that both sides have a legitimate story, and both sides have acted in provocative, and at times violent and immoral ways. Each side wants us to believe that they are the "righteous victims" and the other side is "the evil Other." My message: The well being of each side is intrinsically connected to and dependent on the well-being of the other. In fact, that's *Tikkun's* larger message: The well-being of all of us in the U.S. is intrinsically dependent upon the well-being of everyone on the planet and the well-being of the planet itself—so it's time to stop all the nationalist chauvinism and recognize and celebrate our mutual inter-dependence.

Tikkun is rather unique: both a magazine and a movement for non-violence, peace, social justice, environmental sanity and human rights. To make it clear that *Tikkun* was not just for Jews, we've called our movement NSP—The Network of Spiritual Progressives.

Many of who formed *Tikkun* had been 1960s social change activists. We experienced the Left's implicit religio-phobia. And its willingness to believe that working class people (whose economic interests were better served by the Left) must be fundamentally irrational when attracted to the Right, motivated to do so because they were racist, sexist, homophobic or xenophobic. Yet we discovered in our own massive empirical studies that while some section of the Right fit that description, a lot of middle income people were seeking a framework of meaning and spiritual purpose for their lives that transcended the materialism and selfishness of American society, and didn't hear that spiritual need being addressed by a Left whose main promise was to eliminate discrimination and then give people "equal opportunity" to compete in the war of all against all that is global capitalism.

So from our start in 1986 we've been advocating for a "politics of meaning" or spiritual progressive vision. We call it A New Bottom Line. We want every economic and social and political institution or policy, every corporation, government policy, the educational system, the legal system, and even our personal behavior to be judged rational, efficient or productive not only to the extent that they maximize money or power (the Old Bottom Line) but ALSO to the extent that they maximize our capacities to be loving and caring for each other, generous and kind, ethically and ecologically responsible, and capable both of seeing every other being as a manifestation of the sacred and responding to the natural world with awe, wonder and radical amazement at the grandeur and mystery of the universe. A "spiritual progressive" is anyone who supports this New Bottom Line—you don't have to be religious or believe in God—in fact, many of our members are secular humanists who agree with our goal: "The Caring Society—Caring for Each Other and Caring for the Earth..."

We translate this immediately into two campaigns:

1. The Global Marshall Plan to eliminate domestic and global poverty, homelessness, inadequate education and inadequate health care

2. ESRA—the Environmental & Social Responsibility Amendment to the US Constitution to ban all monies except public funding from elections, require media to give free and equal time to all major candidates, and require large corporations to prove—once every five years to a jury of ordinary citizens—a satisfactory history of environmental and social responsibility

Unrealistic? Yes. Feminism, civil rights, all were originally dismissed as "unrealistic." Our advice: DON'T BE "REALISTIC" because it's always the sycophants of the established economic, political, cultural and academic powerhouses who get to define what Americans are taught is realistic. Building planetary generosity and caring for each other and for the earth is actually the only way we will survive in the 21st century. Join us and the NSP—and together we can still (even at this late date) heal and transform our world; which is what the Hebrew word "tikkun" really means.

Join us.

LEZA LOWITZ

Stop the Bullet

Lincoln resisted going to war,
against the "better angels of our nature."
And when the civil war was over,
even the photos were discarded,
their glass plates sold to gardeners
for conservatory walls.
As the sun burned the images away,
hundreds of red roses
absorbed the light to grow.

Over a century and a half later,
an 82-year-old surfer rides the waves,
recalls being strafed by machine-gun fire
on Pearl Harbor
as the planes flew low,
the red circle on the fuselage
etched in memory.

So many bodies, not enough caskets,
they had to put two men in each—
young American men along
with the Japanese pilots
who killed them.
Is there a better metaphor for war?

When the soldier arrives,
bleeding in the doorway,
can you recognize him as yourself
and let him in?
Once you let him in,
you'll meet many more like him.

Let him turn himself inside out
like a kimono—
black on the outside,
pattern on the inside—
the heart's hidden wounds exposed.
Let his sorrow intensify with each breath.
Let him live.

Turned inside out,
he will show you two kinds of hearts:
one that moves
and one that is frozen.

Do not temper outrage.
Do not try to craft perfection.
Only do what you have to do
to forgive.

The greater the battle,
the deeper the peace.

Released from the pull of separation,
go forth with the intention
to save your own life.

If you want to see peace in the world,
kill the anger within your own heart first.

If you're still suffering,
if you must live in the night sky,
seek still to uplift others.
Do not live alone!

Remember—
even the stars
keep company
with the moon.

KIRK LUMPKIN

Occupy Poem

Where have you been my brothers and sisters
    just caught up in the day to day of making a living,
    lost in TV shows
    where the advertisers bought
    time in your mind,
    or out somewhere in cyberspace
    trying to live some life
    that marketing departments
    made up for you,
    or too drunk, too stoned, too medicated
    to care
    or at least
    to do anything about it?

I understand,
    I've been there myself.

And we've all been occupied
    by corporate America
    and the military-industrial complex
    just like our government has.

But it's time to come back to ourselves:
Occupy your own life
    fully and deeply,
Occupy your own body,
    your own mind, your heart,
Occupy the present moment,
Occupy the place that you live,
    your neighborhood
    your community,
    your farm,
    your watershed,
    your bioregion,
    your continent,
    your planet,
    and damn it
    your government
Occupying not
    like invaders, colonizers, developers, or corporate profiteers,
    but like native citizens,
    like native plants
    reclaiming,
    re-inhabiting
    their own,
    reaching down roots
      that connect us
      to our billions of brothers and sisters
      around the world,
    to Mother Earth,

    to the life energy flowing through all living things.
We can become
        a home grown grassroots rainbow volunteer army of love
        occupying the soul of America.

Two Poems for My Father
Don Lumpkin 1922-2011

I. Your spirit opened
    up so wide
    it could not be held
    inside of you

Your soul it grew
    to be so sweet
    that it was time
    to be harvested

II. Looking back
    after cleaning out
    my parents' apartment:

Golden dust motes dancing
Inside an empty room

ALISON LUTERMAN

Day's News: Oakland

Five cops got shot last week. A few miles up the street.

(Blue and white mums in a white plastic bucket.)

We were watching TV, behind barred doors.

*(Half-mast flag leaning precariously.
News crews jostling for a shot of anyone.)*

The SWAT team crouched between parked cars:
popoppoppoppop and rattatatat.
as if there were a war on,
which there was.

(Today cops cruise the neighborhood, tight-jawed.)

Five cops got shot.
Three died on the spot.
One lay comatose at the hospital
while they harvested his heart
his liver and his eyes.

(The fifth survived.)

And today the drifters drift.
Garbage blows against people's legs.
They'll tighten up
patrols, they say.   Investigate.   Shit,

I could show you the teenage girl
dragging her kid
by one pipe-cleaner-skinny arm,
right past the spot,
yellow danger-tape and orange cones
the blood not even properly cleaned up.

Well someone's got to sweep
this broken glass.
Someone's got to tell that kid
to watch out or his ass
will land in jail just like his old man.
Someone has to plant stiff flowers
in dingy plastic buckets,
someone's got to lower the flags.

MARY MACKEY

Walking Upside Down on the Other Side of the World

Quando falamos nesta cidade perdida
when we speak in this lost city
our words bubble out of our mouths
like the *orações*/prayers of drowned children
through air so hot and green   it holds us
in suspension like bottled glass

here *perto deste grande rio*/near this great river
on the edge of this great forest of stumps
anaconda clouds glide over us like sinuous birds
and the throats of lovers fill with mud and black water

here you can get anyone killed for $50
by the *jagunços* in cowboy boots and aviator glasses
who sit in the bars nursing cold beers

here iron ore is sucked out of
the earth like blood   and a section
of bamboo filled with
gold dust will buy a you a quick death

in this Anopheles democracy of sudden disasters
mosquitoes spread malaria equally to everyone
garimpeiros, caboclos, assassins,
colonels who ride in air conditioned cars
babies who sleep in hammocks

here the dead speak the words
the living are afraid to utter
and each kiss   given in fear
is as swift as the tongue of a bat
probing a flower

MIKE MADISON

Polite Fighting Words

President Reagan was to address the nation on television. The cameras had started rolling, but he had not yet been given the signal to begin reciting his lines, and in that brief interval, he winked at the camera. It was a friendly, jovial, wink intended for his people: the Cadillac-driving, golf-playing, stock-and-bond owners of whom he was the champion. Surely he was not winking at the rest of us: the unemployed, the disabled, the working poor, single mothers, immigrants, and people of color.

The message of Reagan's wink to his followers was that he was well on his way to carrying out his programs of eviscerating the labor unions, cutting taxes for the rich, and dismantling government regulations so that the corporations and banks could go about their business without any scruples forced upon them. Now, thirty years later, these programs have succeeded more than he might have anticipated. The politicians, depending on the banks and corporations for gifts of cash, have enacted only the weakest possible regulations. And the regulators, hoping for a future lucrative job with those whom they regulate, shirk their duties. Big businesses plunder the nation and the planet unimpeded, and when times are good, profits are enormous, and when times are bad, the unpaid bills are passed along to the taxpayers.

It is difficult to fight when your enemies are powerful, wealthy, unscrupulous, and diabolically clever, and when they own the institutions that are meant to regulate them. But the criminal big banks—Bank of America, J.P. Morgan Chase, Wells Fargo, Citibank—have a weak point. We can refuse to play their games. We can transfer our checking accounts, our savings accounts, our mortgages, our auto loans, and our credit cards to small local banks, or to credit unions.

If one customer walks into a branch of a big bank and closes his accounts, no one notices. If ten customers do it, the branch manager raises an eyebrow. If one hundred customers close their accounts, the manager is severely worried. And if three hundred customers close their accounts, the branch is out of business and is shut down. Collectively, we can do this, all across the country—shut down branches until the criminal banks are put out of business.

Fighting words needn't be harsh; they can be polite. Try these: 'I'd like to close my accounts, please.'

TONY R. RODRIGUEZ

Preface to the excerpt from
The Meaning of "Western Defense"

To the impatient, unlearned or pedantic reader, the following essay published in the spring of 1954 by iconic American writer Norman Mailer may come across as outdated or irrelevant. Such a reader's first instinct might be to pass it over. This fickle instinct, however, serves only to perpetuate the flawed concept that older essays from decades past are fruitless and inconsequential. Such a reader will be unable to connect the universal and ageless dots of human struggle strategically mapped out by Mailer. We can even call these dots "fightin' words."

In this essay, Mailer raises a clenched fist and waves it agonizingly at the political disillusionment of a country accepting the ways of strict conformity and one-sided nationalism. *The Meaning of "Western Defense"* is an intellectual philosophy published in a time when America was facing severe quandaries with foreign policy; much like the perplexing troubles America faces in 2014.

Today our nation's enemies may function differently or similarly in many ways; but it's the hunger of Mailer's contemplative ideologies that a reader should study under a literary microscope. The historical records of our nation's conflicts during the spring of 1954 are in place. The facts and opinions presented in this very essay possess the universal fightin' words that surpass time. This very essay reminds readers of the complex threads of human struggle that unite us all throughout past centuries, and right up to today's time. In the spring of 1954, when this essay was first published in *Dissent* magazine, literary aficionados and political chieftains both big and small examined and debated Mailer's positions on American policies with the Soviet Union and beyond.

This is an essay of importance—then and now. It's an archival reminder of a universal fight taken on by a wordsmith who threw his gloves off and charged dutifully. On a side note, if one recalls, there was even a prominent mention about this very essay in the 1994 Robert Redford film *Quiz Show* (near the 120 minute mark of the film), starring Ralph Fiennes and John Turturro. That's the effect of this essay. It's not potent merely because it was mentioned in a popular film, but because Mailer exposes greater truths to a wide audience of inquisitive and diverse readers. And now, dear reader, you are a part of that "fighting" audience, gloves off and all.

NORMAN MAILER

The Meaning of "Western Defense"
-an excerpt

For the liberal, the problem of defending the West is perhaps even more critical a question than for the socialist, since it is the liberal who eschews Utopias and therefore finds himself without an exit. On the one side he is becoming increasingly depressed, if indeed not terrified, by the movement in America toward conformism, hysteria, and McCarthyism; as an alternative he can only see the heavy danger of "Soviet Imperialism." Before such a prospect he feels impelled in the words of Dwight MacDonald to "prefer an imperfectly living, open society to a perfectly dead, closed society."

I would argue that the mistake is precisely in so establishing the choice, and that the implement of this choice—Western Defense—has the ultimate and most abominable meaning of Western annihilation.

I must add that in support of this I will present no documentation nor any research. Such a project would be not only beyond my capacities, but I see small purpose unless it were done on an heroic scale. I offer this argument therefore in all modesty. I am neither wholly convinced of it, nor confident of my political insight. Still, it is a thesis I have held for several years, and I have found it, for myself at least, a not unfruitful hypothesis by which to understand events.

The nominal reason advanced for Western Defense is that it is the bulwark of civilization against the predatory and aggressive aims of the Soviet Union. If one inquires why the Soviet Union is "predatory," the answer is almost always the descriptive and circular response that it is in the nature of totalitarian regimes to be aggressive and imperialistic. Which of course answers nothing at all.

One finds it perfect that our third-rate imitation of Stalinist distortion of history, our government by public relations, should have coined the phrase, "Soviet Imperialism." It is a wonder the next page was never borrowed from Stalin's book which would give the USSR the credit for inventing imperialism. Whatever the Soviet's crimes and horrors and total perversions of socialism, and we know the list unbearably long, they can hardly be accused of imperialism. The guilt for imperialism belongs to the West, that chalice of civilization, and not all the public relations from here to the millennium can word it away. Imperialism, since one is forced to go back to the ABC's of these things, is still the employment of excess surplus value to create new markets, dominate backward countries, superintend partial and specialized development of their industry, and establish spheres of influence. For a modern example, Venezuela comes to mind.

What must be emphasized is that imperialism is exclusively the problem of finding investments for the collective idle profit of monopoly capitalism, and it has been the difficulty of finding such markets and backward countries which has dominated the history of Western civilization through World War I, through panics and depressions, through the loss of the world market and World War II until the only solution left since the Second War has been the war economy which marries full production to a necessarily crippled market—the Soviet Union having absorbed too many of the backward countries of the world.

This is the crisis of Monopoly Capitalism. Arthritic through most of its members, suffering from high-blood pressure in America, it can continue to function only so long as it manufactures armaments whose "ultimate consumer"— (I regret I cannot find the source for this quotation)—"is the enemy soldier." The liberal will advance the argument that "Keynesian economics" and the "welfare state" will dispose of capitalism's contradictions, but since this has proved politically impossible until now in anything approaching its intended form, the burden of proof is still upon him. In fact, one can hardly visualize the cure of capitalism's chronic agonies through a nostrum which in effect asks private financial empires to accommodate themselves to the dissipation and eventual transformation of their power. As easy to ask the state to wither away! I feel it is not too extravagant to say that if the Soviet Union were Utopia, the United States would be forced to invent a Stalinist nightmare.

The economic problems of the USSR are congenitally different. Its chronic crisis has been the inability to increase production organically rather than the need to find a market for surplus profit. There is no need to recapitulate the history of its disasters, some due to Leninism, some due to capitalist encirclement, but the "great experiment" should have proved if it has proved nothing else that one cannot build socialism in an isolated bloc let alone an isolated country. When the country is backward as was Czarist Russia, everything is made worse, of course. Trotsky once said that socialism means more milk, not less milk, and the Soviet attempt to build a major economy was driven to put its emphasis upon less milk. One cannot create giant steel works and coal mines and railroads and other heavy industry at an accelerated pace without inflicting upon one's labor force a demand for longer hours of work at smaller real wages. Marx once mentioned the economic inefficiency of slavery as a productive system, and the USSR has given a further demonstration. The heart of its inability to increase the rate of its productivity vis-à-vis the United States and Western Europe has been the irremediable dilemma of being forced to demand more and more of its workers in return for less and less goods and creature comforts.

A man as well as an animal can be worked to death, and the horror which besets the Soviet bureaucrat is the recurring breakdown of economic arithmetic. To double steel production in a given sector—let us put it arbitrarily—he discovers that he must triple his labor force. Under such conditions, aggravated, repeated, and multiplied, the state of the Soviet Union can only remind one of that swelling of the joints which accompanies anemia. Far from being imperialistic, Soviet aggression bears much greater similarity to primitive capitalism. It is the need for plunder, economic plunder, which has forced its expansion since the war. With such plunder, equivalent to economic transfusions, there is the hope of breaking out of their economic trap. For plunder may be translated into consumer goods, and with more consumer goods, more efficient production can legitimately be expected of the Soviet worker. It is mainly this reason, I would argue, which has motivated the brutal and apparently irrational conduct of the Soviet bureaucracy in the Eastern satellites, rather than any theories or explanations which depend upon a mystique of totalitarianism.

devorah major

political poem

what makes a poem revolutionary
does it violently refuse the page
construct a chaos of grammar
that denies metaphor or defeats meter
is it armed and ready for prolonged struggle
is it loud and insistent assaulting your senses
full of gun powder and iron pellets
is it unavailable for canonization
despite an early death as martyr
or does it instead
find guerrilla survival
hidden
underground
exploding in unexpected places
appearing once again   just
when you thought it dead

CLIVE MATSON

Thank You

Thank you wall. Thank you air
for not ionizing.

It's 6:42pm in the Midwest.

Thank you Obama, Bush Jr., Clinton, Bush Sr., Reagan,
Carter, Ford, Nixon, Johnson, Kennedy, Eisenhower.
Thank you President Truman
for doing it only twice.

Thank you Peacemaker, Pershing, Cruise,
Nautilus, Polaris, Titan, MX.
Thank you 200,000 microchips times 20,000
microchips times 20,000 microchips.
Thank you 476 orders to "Fire!"
for being discovered as accidents.

Thank you Three Mile Island.
Thank you Chernobyl.
Thank you, Fukushima. Thank you,
big accident, for not happening.

It's 6:43pm in the Midwest.

Thank you Putin, Yeltsin, Gorbachev, Chernenko, Andropov,
Brezhnev, Kosygin, Khrushchev, Bulganin, Stalin.
Thank you Batwing, Scud, SSX-24, SS-20, IRBM, ICBM, MIRV.
Thank you older generation. Thank you my generation.
Thank you younger generation.

Thank you maniac. Thank you neurotic.
Thank you normal person for not ending it all.
Thank you two keys for not turning.
Thank you, earthquake, for not cracking
SIOP's Headquarters, Nebraska.

It's 6:44pm in the Midwest.

Thank you mind for keeping track.
Thank you mind for usually keeping the process hidden.
Thank you billions and billions and billions
of dollars spent on the last six minutes.
Thank you last six minutes for not happening.

Thank you regional conflicts for not going nuclear.
Thank you Korea, Viet Nam, Cambodia, Nicaragua,
Afghanistan, South Africa, Iran, Iraq, Cosovo.
Thank you, Saddam Hussein, for moving slowly.

Thank you, spontaneous combustion.
Thank you air. Thank you walls for not vaporizing.

It's 6:45pm in the Midwest.

Thank you U.S.A., U.S.S.R., China, England, India, France, Sweden, Pakistan, North Korea, maybe Israel, Argentina, South Africa.

Thank you. Thank you.

MICHAEL McCLURE

Solstice Thumbprint
for Robert Duncan

PATHWAYS OF THE SENSES
IN CALM TURBULENCE.
CHAOS. TASTE OF BLACK SUGAR.
Flowering branches ready
to burst
in the trunk. RAIN BECOMING
BUNDLES
of flowers. Storms
beginning in the heart.

Growing to full brightness as
BRIGHTNESS
GROWS
out of the dark. Singing with sense
new senses everywhere

WHIRLING AND STREAMING
in shapes and directions
endlessly unknown
over
and over
always the NEW BORN
GLEAMING
archetype

of never-repeating pathways
interflowing
chaos and mountains of
turbulence
with yellow sun
upon it.
Yellow sun
BRIGHT.
BRIGHT
beginning in the HEART—

CHAOS black sugar
of flowers.
Streams of rain bundles
flow becoming branches,
flowering branches ready
to burst
in the trunk

COLLEEN J. MCELROY

The Tongue

the most powerful
             muscle in the body
is the tongue
          it takes all
available   space
          always seeks another
nook
     or cranny
               a fault line
that needs filling

a panther has a purple tongue
a bull dog's tongue is black
hissing in shadows across the road
a black cat humps its back

Einstein's inimitable tongue

pull a tooth and the tongue
aches to fill the space

two penny five penny
gopher guts
go around the corner
to lick 'em all up

French kisses
       fill music scores
1000 tongue warbling ballads
       of loves lost and found

the tongue whips
         the rest of the body
in brutal swipes

today there are enough weapons
to equal 400,000 Nagasakis
so little spoken with the blunt
tongue of war

what's the point: how many
times can we kill each other

KIM McMILLON

Pele and Yemaja, The Goddesses

I was born from the ocean
I am made of sand, rocks, and seashells
blue and white waves caressed me into being
my skin is as black as coral
that in Hawaiian is called
ēkaha kū moana
I lay on the beach, and talk to the ocean
Yemaja, Ocean Goddess
Did you swim with the mermaids today?
I brought flowers for you
Because today I go to the ocean to be reborn

Excitement Junkie

I am an excitement junkie
I need to feel like
I'm taking a risk
I'm a stimulus addict
I need to feed on
be on
Where's my top
I'm sick of being in a cradle
with too many sides
I need to be out
There's too much earth
under my feet
not letting my flights of fancy
take me higher
and higher
always spinning
always topping myself off
again and again
Yes!
I feel the pleasure
the excitement
that one quick fix
Just let me have my
own personal needle

Cosmopolitans and Passion

If passion were a person
it would dress in red
and drink cosmopolitans
and gossip with strangers
but when doors close
passion takes off that red dress
and is bold and naked
and does not drink,
does not smoke
and does not give a damn
passion comes clean, and open
passion is a Goddess
that knows no equals.

A Hat Full of Butterflies

I would be happy
with a hat full of butterflies
reminding me
that I am always free
I have wings
they are just invisible
to everyone, but me
I travel at night
stars light my way
I go to the planet of dreams
It is always light on my planet
except when I go to sleep
my planet knows I need my rest
and so cuts off the lights
until I awake
when it greets me with the
kiss of day

ADAM DAVID MILLER

My Nisei Friends are Dying, a Colloquy

They are dying from diseases of the heart

We did not want to kill them. Just get them
off the West Coast, where they couldn't
do no harm, ya know. Yeh.
Some of the old ones might die?
Some, a few. They're tough, and Japanese
anyhow.

>   No, they didn't tell us nothing, they just
>   came and said, "let's go." We didn't
>   know where, and they wouldn't let
>   us ask.
>   No, they didn't show no warrant.
>   Nothing.
>   They didn't let us take clothes or things
>   we might need.
>   "Don't go out of our sight," they barked,
>   when I started to go get my overnight stuff.
>   Our wives wanted to know where they were
>   taking us, and why. "Down to the station
>   for questioning," was as much as they could get.

*The Issei, slipping away
without a trace.*

TAKE ONLY WHAT YOU CAN CARRY
Reads the notices

>   How would you like to be born in Tanforan
>   stable, and you were not a horse?
>
>   How would you like a tag around your neck
>   and a number, and a soldier with a gun
>   guarding you, and you (were) only five?
>
>   How would you like to come of age behind
>   barbed wire in your own country, charged with being
>   yourself, a charge you could not deny,
>   a guard with a machine gun and itchy fingers
>   overlooking your evening stroll?

The Nisei were dying even then.

>   How would you like to see your parents cry
>   both outside and in?

We knew we could help and we wanted to
The government gave you some money: bitter money

>   How can we explain these things to the children?

The issei are all dead.

E. ETHELBERT MILLER
Wounded by Words

Maybe there are too many fightin' words in the air these days. I know there is a battle between narratives. All I have to listen to are people who want to "reclaim" America. This would never have been a problem if the color of our nation had not been changing over the years. Words like multiculturalism and diversity were disturbing for people attempting to maintain the status quo. When power shifts in a society, fightin' words will always be released. Change is often reduced to a slogan or just a word. Take the word "occupy" which forced itself on us last year. But why can't we fight for love, nonviolence or peace? Might this be a contradiction? Are these words fightin'words? I think they are. These words push back against what is wrong in the world. They are not passive terms. Love is always in a battle against hatred. Nonviolence must conquer the ideas that lead to conflicts and wars.

As writers we must be selective and careful of the words we select for our poems and stories. Those of us, who are visionary, will be challenged to give birth to a new narrative. Is a common language the new language? Democracy today is a fightin' word. How do we bring people together under its banner? How do we master the tightrope without the net below?

How do we learn to embrace the same metaphor? When will we look into another's eyes and no longer see—the other? How many fightin' words will no longer slip from our tongues when brotherhood and sisterhood become a reality? When will the healing begin? Too many of us have already been wounded by words.

YASMIN MOGUL

It was the Feast of Purima

It was the feast of Purima. Processions filed past my bedroom window. I peered out at them, my heart beating at the thought of joining them, dancing in their midst, fleeing with them to the nearby beach, sitting on sand, watching the moon, watching…a silver gold disc, expanding, igniting the waves of the ocean, pulling them in closer over the populated shores, scattering the people; black crows over silver white sand. Purima—the feast of the high tide, of the full moon, a feast of feeling.

"It's not like Christmas, Merrick. We don't have to worry about buying presents, go crazy shopping. It's a feast, a real feast with nature."

"Sure." Merrick was dressed in jeans. A blue plaid shirt, unbuttoned. "Sure, Umri. My forefathers celebrated the same kind of feasts. So, I suppose I too should prostrate myself on the sand before the moon."

"Stop teasing me. I'm much too happy today. Happy, happy." My arms coiled, caressing his neck. "Happy that you are here in Bombay, in India. I want to take you all over the city. To all the places I've loved and talked about. Want you to meet all my people."

"Take it easy, honey. I'm really not in the mood to go flying all around. Ain't you ever going to get your head screwed on tight, Miss Chicken Little?"

"Stop teasing, Merrick."

"O.K. I won't argue with you today. I know you want to gallivant, gad-about. You hear the bongos outside and your feet start moving to the rhythm. And, yes, I'd rather spend the evening at home. Read a book. God, what I'd give to spend a day reading at home. Someday, Umri, someday you will want to stay home and read."

"I've stayed home enough for a lifetime. Damn it, Merrick. I've only just come out of the prison you kept me in in Cambridge. I don't ever want to see another book, and certainly not Naipaul's books, which you seem to read all the time."

"You don't know nothing about Naipaul, Umri. Why don't you read him?"

"I don't have to read that over-inflated pompous pariah who lives in London and thinks he knows my India."

"Perhaps he knows more of your Indian than you ever will."

"If he does, then I have nothing to love about India. Naipaul has never loved anything. Let me show you. My home is out there. Let's see it together. Let's see it, instead of reading about it in books."

"You can see in books," Merrick said, shaking his head. "But I won't argue with you. Not today." His arms coiled around me like twisted Banyan tree roots hugging the earth. "I love you, honey. I've come to your India, but our home is back in Massachusetts. We must return together. Don't leave me again, honey. I've come to take you back with me."

Merrick unbuttoned his shirt. I watched him and clasped my hands around his chest.

"Tell me you loved me last night."

"I loved you last night." His hands pulling me into bed. His hands engulfing me; wings of dragonflies settling over still waters, delicately folding over fragile abdomens.

Outside, the sound of bongos, louder. Their beat lapping against my ears, each lap pulsating with shuffled footsteps. Women dancing in the streets. Silver anklets on silver streets. The moon, too, silver and distant, rising, settling on the oil chandeliers carried over the heads of the men who led the processions.

We joined the processions. Merrick uncomfortable in the crowds, holding on to me. I, leading him, feeling the jubilation of the crowds, as I always did with the crowds, even those of the Boston Hay Market.

"Now, don't go crazy." Merrick's warnings at regular intervals. "It's mad out there, Umri. It's a stampede." His voice drowning in bongos.

We joined them, let them lead us to the Juhu Beach. There, the men formed a circle.

The women gathered inside the circle. They stretched, moved to the music; narrow hibiscus stems creeping out of the petals. They stood a moment, silently listening to the chants from the men around them. Their feet moved slowly to the chants, barely rising above the sand, until the chants became shouts. Then they jerked. They released strands of copper cymbals from the folds of saris. They pulled the strings with jerky motions. The sound of the cymbals silenced the drums.

I watched Merrick. I pointed out that I thought he wasn't really seeing. The people blending into the moonlight, into the sand.

"Unity," I said.

"Tumult," he said.

The smell of burning wood. Merrick pulled me. There was no place to move.

"Fire," he said. "Move, Umri, move."

No place to move. Flames visible above the shadows around us. Merrick pulled me away from the flames. I pulled him back.

"That's Ravan, the villain in the epic Ramayana. Remember, I told you about him. He's the one who kidnapped Sita, the heroine. Look, they are burning Ravan. We must watch Ravan burn."

Merrick protested. The flames rose over the crowds. They ignited the face of the sixty-foot effigy.

"We must see Ravan burn," I pleaded. He pulled against me. "There's no way to get there," he said. "It's crazy out here."

A hush fell over the crowds.

JEFFERSON MORLEY

Unspeakable: My JFK Lawsuit

In December 2003, I sued the Central Intelligence Agency for certain records related to the assassination of President John F. Kennedy in 1963. Was I another one of those crazed JFK conspiracy theorists whose incoherent ravings reveal a flight from reality into the paranoid style of American politics? Not really. I sought the records to understand the causes of President Kennedy's death on November 22, 1963. Like a lot of people, I don't think we have a convincing explanation of why the 35th president was violently removed from power. I've heard a lot of implausible theories about JFK's assassination, and the notion that one man alone was responsible is one of them.

When I filed my lawsuit at the E. Barrett Prettyman Courthouse in Washington on December 17, 2003, I wasn't looking to answer the eternal and very daunting question of who killed JFK. Rather, I was looking to clarify a simpler query: Which CIA employees knew the most about the events that led to JFK being shot and killed in front of a friendly crowd in Dallas on November 22, 1963?

I had a solid lead. A number of Cuban-American men in Miami who had worked with the CIA told me about an impressive undercover officer named George Joannides. He served in south Florida in 1963 and had a unique perspective on events before and after JFK was killed. My Freedom of Information Act (FOIA) lawsuit to obtain his files from 1963 attracted support from a wide range of JFK authors, including Norman Mailer, Anthony Summers, and Vincent Bugliosi, who endorsed the effort in open letters published in the *New York Review of Books* in 2003 and 2005.

Now, after almost a decade of wrangling in federal court, the CIA has succeeded in defying common sense and the scholarly consensus by keeping the Joannides' files out of public view. The agency has largely prevailed in obscuring information crucial to understanding the intelligence failure of November 22. The federal judiciary has abdicated its responsibility to pass independent judgment on the government's extreme claims of secrecy.

The Obama White House approves. Despite President Obama's pledge of "a new era in open government," the Justice Department has embraced the extreme secrecy claims of the CIA around ancient JFK assassination records. A chance to clarify the circumstances of JFK's death has been lost. Secrecy clouds the truth. And it is U.S. government officials—not the much-maligned JFK conspiracy theorists—who are distorting the historical record.

But Morley v. CIA was still pending in early 2014 and it has succeeded in shedding some new light on a dark chapter in American history. It has identified one of the agency's sorest spots in the JFK story: the role of certain CIA counterintelligence officers in the events that lead to the gunfire in Dallas. While there is no proof of a CIA plot, the lawsuit has added to the evidence of CIA negligence around President Kennedy. To be specific, the records that have emerged since Oliver Stone's "JFK" indicate that the actions of certain career officers involved in anti-Castro counterintelligence activities—including George Joannides—contributed to the breakdown of presidential security in Dallas. At a minimum, these men and women failed to report in an accurate and timely way about what they knew of Oswald.

To put it another way: If the Warren Commission and the American people had been told in 1963 what we know now about Lee Harvey Oswald, at least two top CIA officials would have lost their jobs: counterintelligence chief James Angleton and deputy director Dick Helms. Both were central to the intelligence failure that culminated in JFK's death on November 22, 1963.

This is the new documentary record of the JFK story that people need to know today. An office under Angleton's aegis, the Special Investigations Group, monitored Oswald closely for four years before JFK's assassination, according to newly-declassified records. Helms, a canny power broker with a well-deserved reputation as "The Man Who Kept the Secrets," also failed President Kennedy on November 22, 1963. The record now shows that Helms presided over two different intelligence collection operations in late 1963 that picked up on Oswald as he made his way from New Orleans to Mexico City to Dallas. One of them, codenamed AMSPELL was run by Joannides, a decorated undercover CIA officer who died in 1990.

The lawsuit did not crack the case but it has illuminated Joannides' central role in the CIA's post-assassination cover-up. A well-dressed lawyer from New York, Joannides was a trusted ten-year veteran of the clandestine service in 1963. At the behest of deputy director Helms, he served as chief of the "psychological warfare" branch of the Agency's Miami station. His specialty was deceptive operations that could not be traced to the U.S. government. On November 22, 1963, his assets helped shape early media coverage of JFK's assassination.

I've told the story in *Salon, Talking Points Memo,* and theatlantic.com. Scott Shane of *The New York Times* has confirmed its accuracy. In 1963, Joannides used CIA funds to subsidize an anti-Castro student organization fighting to overthrow Castro. The group received $50,000 a month from the CIA according to a memo I found in the JFK Library. In August 1963, members of the group's New Orleans chapter debated and denounced Oswald on a local radio station in August 1963. They even issued a press release calling for a congressional investigation of his pro-Castro activism. Three months later, when JFK was killed, Joannides's agents immediately called reporters with the news that Kennedy had been killed by a supporter of Castro. This propaganda blitz—made possible by CIA funding—generated front page stories in the *Miami Herald, Miami News, New Orleans Times,* substantial coverage in the *New York Times,* a short item in the *Washington Post,* and headlines in many other newspapers around the country. As chief of psychological warfare operations in Miami, Joannides could take credit for getting out the story that JFK had been killed by a communist. Yet a half century later, the CIA still disavows any knowledge of Joannides' actions.

I sued the agency because his story deserves official explanation, not a conspiratorial speculation. Certainly Joannides' assignment to Miami in 1963 delivered him into the murky heart of the JFK assassination story. His psychological warfare responsibilities required he generate propaganda and disinformation so as to hasten the overthrow of Fidel Castro's revolutionary government in Cuba. After JFK was killed, he did that. As a counterintelligence officer, Joannides was also responsible for making sure that certain CIA operations had not been penetrated by Castro's security service. After JFK was killed, he learned that his Cuban allies had tangled with the pro-Castro Oswald in the summer of 1963, but he never breathed a word of his actions to investigators. His behavior was curious, to say the least.

When people following the lawsuit ask me, "Was George Joannides part of a JFK conspiracy?" I reply 'That's a question for a prosecutor, not a journalist.' Put aside the question, "Is there proof of a criminal conspiracy?" Consider JFK's assassination in a different way: as a matter of civil litigation. In a civil case about JFK's assassination, we would not ask, "Who killed JFK?" We would ask "Who was responsible for the wrongful death of the president?"

In the civil law perspective, I think Dick Helms and Jim Angleton were guilty of negligence in the case of the murdered president. Their action served to relax normal security measures around Oswald in late 1963, contributing to the breakdown of presidential security in Dallas. The proof, I believe, can be found in the files of George Joannides, the counterintelligence officer with responsibilities for reporting on Oswald.

If nothing else, Morley v. CIA has confirmed that key details of the intelligence failure of November 22, 1963 are beyond the reach of the law and the eyes of the American people. The CIA asserts that it cannot share certain counterintelligence activities related to Lee Harvey Oswald and his pro-Castro activities in the summer and fall of 1963 without endangering American lives today. It is a preposterous claim yet legally valid. Unless the Congress acts or the Justice Department changes its position, CIA officials will not have to talk about these events any time soon—and perhaps not ever. In terms of U.S. secrecy law, no Americans are permitted to talk publicly about the classified details of the JFK story I sought when I went to court in 2003. Almost a decade later, the curious case of George Joannides remains officially unspeakable.

JILL NELSON

Old Dog, Old Tricks

Fifteen years ago, before most of us had even heard the name Barack Obama or dared to imagine him, I asked my father, then in his early eighties, how he would summarize his life as a Black man in America. A native of Washington, D.C., my father was one of four children born to parents who were the children of slaves who worked the plantations and horse farms of Virginia. Neither of his parents went past third grade. They were hardworking, decent people who were never able to gain purchase in the middle class. They spent their lives scuffling upwards and falling back down, but succeeded in lifting their children on their shoulders and into the middle class.

I expected my father would need time to respond to my query. Instead, he asked me to sit down with him at the table and told me the following story.

"There were a bunch of mean, racist crackers and one night they decided to catch them a black man. They grabbed a man off the street and took him deep into the woods to a clearing, dug a hole deep enough for the man to stand up in, and buried him up to his neck. Then one of them went and got his dog, an enormous, vicious, drooling Boxer named Tag. The men formed a big circle around the Black man's head, and then let Tag go. Tag ran past the man and ripped a piece off his cheek. Then he ran by again and tore the man's lip with this teeth. Then he ran past again and damn near tore the man's eye from the socket. The black man was bleeding and moaning in pain, and the next time Tag ran over him he opened up his mouth and bit down on Tag's balls. And Tag twisted and struggled so hard to get away he pulled the man clean out of the ground, and the man jumped up and ran away. And the white folks shook their heads and said, 'That damn nigger didn't even give old Tag a chance.'"

To say I was startled by my father's story is an understatement. I knew that my father had been confronted with many race based obstacles in pursuit of an education, a profession, and entry into the middle class, but he'd made it, hadn't he? How could it be that the story of Tag the Dog, a story told to him by his father and to my grandfather by his father, and to my great grandfather by his father, a story handed from fathers to sons across generations, still summed up his quintessential American experience?

My father, born in 1916, turned ninety-eight in January 2014. Over the past decade he has delighted in witnessing, supporting, and voting for citizen, candidate, and President Obama. I asked him right after the 2012 re-election of President Barack Hussein Obama if he'd like to rescind or amend the Tag story. My father's old eyes, once brown and now a deep, almost navy blue, twinkled and he laughed heartily as he shook his head. The story of Tag the Dog continues to sum up an awful, seemingly intractable truth about being a Black man in America for my father and many, many others.

Karl Rove's arithmetical meltdown and insane accusation that Obama won because he "Suppressed the vote"; Donald Trump's rant that Obama's victory means it's time for "revolution"; Bill O'Reilly's lamenting the demise of "the white majority"; the GOP's insistence that re-election brings with it no mandate; the assertion that Obama won because he gave "gifts" to minorities, women, and young people; post-election calls for secession, or myriad other racist responses from decrepit cheerleaders of the dying white culture, remind us that Tag the Dog lives. Whether in the woods of memory with allegorical rednecks, in the workplace among co-workers who cling to white privilege as they deny its existence, or in the halls of Congress amongst deranged Tea Party members and avatars of the Old Confederacy, being a black man and top dog still isn't fair to old Tag.

GERALD NICOSIA

The Greeks Who Stole Kerouac

On July 24, 2009, Judge George Greer, known as "the toughest judge in Florida," ruled the unthinkable—at least unthinkable for the Sampas/Viking Penguin literary empire—that the will of Gabrielle Kerouac, giving the Sampas family the right to exploit Jack Kerouac's works, image, belongings, and even his gravesite, was a forgery. Greer couldn't have been more forceful in what he said about that crime.

"She [Gabrielle Kerouac] could only move her hand and scribble her name," Greer wrote in his landmark ruling. "She would have lacked the coordination to affix that signature. The [probate] court is required by law to use a clear and convincing standard in determining these matters. However, even if the criminal standard of beyond all reasonable doubt was the requirement, the result would certainly be the same. Clearly, Gabrielle Kerouac was physically unable to sign the document dated February 13, 1973 and, more importantly, that which appears on the Will dated that date is not her signature."

There were many of us who knew that something was wrong about that will—even if we weren't sure it was a case of forgery. I used to think that there was undue influence—perhaps the old lady was just "out of it" when the will was signed. But it was a well-known fact that Gabrielle Kerouac loved her grandson, Paul Blake, Jr. The Blakes and the Kerouacs lived together for long stretches of time—on Long Island; in Rocky Mount, North Carolina; in Orlando, among other places. Gabrielle taught her grandson Paul to sing French songs and she cooked French treats for him. Gabrielle was absolutely devastated by the early death of her daughter Ti Nin, Paul's mother, in 1964—after being devastated by the death of her first child Gerard 38 years earlier. It was inconceivable that she would then, in her right mind, write Ti Nin's child, the grandson she loved so much, completely out of her will.

Jack died in 1969, leaving everything to his mother in his will—which also said that if his mother wasn't around to inherit his estate, he wanted his nephew Paul Blake, Jr., to get it. Gabrielle, "Memere," outlived Jack by four years, and when she died the will leaving everything to Stella Sampas Kerouac was suddenly filed in the Pinellas County Courthouse—though the living Sampases now claim they "had nothing to do with it." How the Sampases managed to hide the theft for so long is a long story. It involves the fact that neither of Gabrielle's grandchildren, Jan Kerouac nor Paul Blake, Jr., was notified of her death, though the Sampases had the addresses of both.

In one of Jan's notebooks, now on deposit at the Bancroft Library in Berkeley, she scribbled at the top of a blank page: "The Greeks Who Stole Kerouac." She never lived to write the story.

The Sampases were banking on the fact that the victims they were robbing were two dysfunctional kids. Jan had grown up on the streets of the Lower East Side in the drug-ridden Sixties—with no dad, and a marginally effective mom. Her veins were filled with methedrine and LSD, and at 13 she was working the streets to pay for drugs and parasitical boyfriends. That this kid had any chance of discovering a forged will was virtually nil. As for Paul Blake, Jr., he came home from high school at sixteen to find his mother dead on the couch—having starved herself to death to punish herself, a good Catholic woman, for losing her husband to another woman. He rambled through Alaska and elsewhere, working as a carpenter and losing job after job, as well as two wives, because hitting the bottle was the only way to quiet his ghosts. Again: no chance this deeply troubled kid was going to start probing courts for an answer to his disinheritance.

Within weeks of Jack's death, the Sampases had scooped up his manuscripts and papers and spirited them to a small apartment above Nicky Sampas's bar in Lowell. A friend recalls Tony Sampas tapping on one of the cardboard boxes of Kerouac files, saying, "These things will be worth millions—not now, but some day."

After Jack's widow Stella died in 1990, her youngest brother John was elected by the Sampas brothers and sisters as their literary representative, and he took off selling Kerouac papers and belongings as quickly as he could. But apparently, rich collectors like Johnny Depp were a little uncertain about dropping 50,000 bucks for items they weren't sure Sampas had a right to sell. So Sampas began handing out copies of Gabrielle's will to his best customers. One such customer sent me a copy of the will a few weeks before Jan Kerouac and her lawyer Tom Brill arrived at my home in January 1994, planning to talk about her problems getting royalties from the Sampases.

Instead, Jan took one look at the will on my kitchen table and yelled, "This thing is a forgery!" Her grandmother's signature was way too strong to have been made by an old lady who'd been lifted on and off a bedside potty for seven years. You could see where the lines started and stopped, and the last name was misspelled "Keriouac."

The Sampases fought for fifteen years to keep that case from going to trial. When Jan died in 1996 and made me her literary executor to carry the case to trial, the Sampases made a deal with her heirs, John Lash and David Bowers, to dismiss the case—and when I refused to dismiss it, the Sampases and Jan's heirs fought together to get me thrown out, succeeding in 1999. But Judge Thomas Penick in Florida refused to let Lash dismiss Jan's entire lawsuit. He let Lash dismiss *Jan's part of the lawsuit*. Penick pointed out that there was another potential heir, if Gabrielle had died intestate: Jack's nephew. Paul Blake Jr.'s lawyers Bill and Alan Wagner finally won that forgery verdict from Judge Greer.

Postscript to "The Greeks Who Stole Kerouac"

The Sampas family, the brothers and sisters of Stella who had inherited the Kerouac Estate from her when she died in 1990, immediately took an appeal of Judge Greer's decision. Co-heir and Literary Executor for the family, John Sampas, told British journalist Stephen Maughan, "We do not believe the Will of Gabrielle Kerouac was forged and do believe the Judge based his ruling on fictitious accounts by a doctor who never met Gabrielle Kerouac." Sampas also lamented that a strong defense of the will had not been put on before Judge Greer. Why he and his family did not mount such a strong defense, he did not explain. "Our lawyers," Sampas claimed to Maughan, "would have demolished Alan Wagner and his corrupt father Bill Wagner."

While the appeals process continued, Paul Blake, Jr.'s lawyers were prevented from going after assets of the Kerouac Estate, and even from getting any sort of accounting of those assets. All that is now changed.

On August 10, 2011, the District Court of Appeal of Florida, Second District, ruled against the Sampas family and affirmed Judge Greer's ruling that Kerouac's mother's will was a forgery. The way the decision was written, it is a final decision and cannot be appealed further. That means it is now in the history books that the Kerouac Estate, arguably the most valuable literary estate in recent history, was stolen.

As things now stand, however, the Sampas brothers and sisters are still sheltering under the protection of a Florida "non-claim statute" that allows people to inherit stolen property, and keep it, so long as no one complains within two years. Since Jan did not see the forged will until 1994, the two-year waiting period after the filing of Stella's will (in 1990) had expired; and unless Paul Blake, Jr., can find a federal law to go around the Florida state law, the Sampases will get to keep all their literary loot.

A.L. NIELSON

Technology Transfer 41

Sweet crude

Target air

Significant Strike

                                We went in with a bunch of guys
                                Like Christmas lights

Acquired aircraft
At some point you become comfortable
At some point you become an unfriendly
Huge fireball

                Technology transfer

We ran a touchdown
And the enemy didn't show up

We're on that problem big time

We want to talk to that battery
At an interval we can predict

                              Continuous
                              Breaking developments

Intermittent
Leaders
Spoke holy places

The market continues its wild ride

Continuous coverage of carpet bombing will resume after this

                We get more punch per bomb

A struggle to the last child

                              Sell on the rumor
                              Buy on the news

IN A MACRO SENSE

                            I'm getting some information in my other ear

SO FAR IT'S A BLOWOUT

ELIZABETH NUNEZ

Boundaries

In this scene, Anna tries to persuade her boss, Tim Greene, to publish more literary fiction by black writers, rather than strictly commercial fiction. He disagrees.

For Tim Greene, chick lit and ghetto lit tell the real stories about African Americans. It wouldn't matter if Anna told him about the mirror and the lamp. It wouldn't matter if she said to him that she agrees that fiction should mirror life, but that the lives the books he wants to publish mirror only a tiny fraction of the lives African Americans really live, that he is perpetuating a pernicious stereotype by promoting these books. It wouldn't matter either to argue that books have the power to give us insights to the past, the present, the future, to give us something to reach for. That books can inspire us to be more than what we are. If she should say these things to him, he would respond that he is working for a company that does business for profit. His job is to keep his eye on the bottom line.

As if he has read her thoughts, Tim Greene says, "It not just about the money, Anna. It's about literacy."

She stares at him in disbelief.

"Young people like these books," he says. "At least these books get them reading."

She has heard the argument many times before—though it still shocks her that intelligent people, people in positions of leadership, with the responsibility of guiding the young, still promote such drivel. *At least these books get them reading.* It is an expression of despair, of the failure of schools to educate the young. Reading scores of black children in the inner-city are dismal and blame is cast on the powerful, seductive force of the visual media. Educators throw up their hands and surrender. The battle against the lure of cable TV and video games is one they cannot win. *At least these books get them reading.* But reading what? Young people, like young people throughout the ages, get pleasure from the stimulation of their imagination, and Anna is convinced that no other media stimulates the imagination more than reading. For the reader must transform black and white symbols into colorful pictures in his mind. He must bond with people he has not met in the flesh or seen on the screen. He becomes judge and jury in battles between good and evil. If all we can say is at least they are reading, we have failed to pass on to the next generation the pleasures that come from good books that challenge us to imagine lives we have not lived, to empathize with those we do not know.

Books, Anna believes, are our defense against those who would lead us like lambs to the slaughter house. Books teach us to think, to use our intelligence to sort out right from wrong, good from bad, the beautiful from the ugly, to make decisions based on what we know is right and good, not on what we have been told to do or think by powerful people concerned with their welfare instead of our own. Books can prevent wars, keep us from destroying ourselves and our planet. Why else do dictators and warmongers burn books in the public square? Why was a fatwa issued against a novelist, calling for his execution?

"And is it enough that these are the only types of books they read?" Anna asks.

"It's a good beginning," Tim Greene says. "These books open up the world of reading to them. They get to find out there's fun in reading, and who knows?" He smiles brightly at her. "They may get to like the books you read, Anna."

She does not think that reading poorly written, exclusively plot driven books will lead a young person to seek out more challenging books. She believes children have to be taught. She believes teachers must do the hard work of giving children the tools to decode words on the printed page, to appreciate the beauty of a well turned phrase, to ponder the validity of ideas they had not considered before. She believes a society is in danger when good books are neither written nor read.

Was it reading the kind of books he wants to publish that turned him on to Ellison?

Anna seriously doubts that. He and too many like him seem to lack faith in the possibility of remedying an inferior education, of resetting the clock for young men and women whose deficiencies in reading and writing have accumulated after years of neglect. Yet these are the vulnerable young minds most in need of inspiration and hope; these are the underprivileged youth whose notion of the good life will remain limited unless expanded by good books that could open the way for them to the beauties of the world.

Tim Greene is still holding Ralph Ellison's novel in his hand. With studied deliberativeness, he places it on the coffee table. Ridges form on the sides of his face. They contract and loosen, making tiny waves along his temples. "Tomorrow." He does not look at Anna. "If you could clear out your office by this afternoon, I'd appreciate it."

PETER ORNER

Plaza Revolución, Mexico City, 6 A.M.

A woman who sells television antennas in the zocalo walks slowly through the mostly empty plaza and thinks of her sister who lives in Coyacan now. Her sister who was beautiful before she had children. She never had children herself, but she was never beautiful to begin with. What does all this mean? She crosses the plaza in the lonely light and thinks the idea of having a sister is a strange thing. Her sister's name is Rosella, a name her sister always said she hated though it went so well with the beauty. Her sister lost her beauty and she lost a sister. Some days this is the only word there is: lost.

The light slants across the plaza, slightly pinkish now. The four-sided arch looms. It's really an unfinished building they call an arch. They started to build a new parliament here but then they realized the land was too marshy. Didn't they take off your shoes before they started to build it? Maybe politicians never take off their shoes. But aren't all buildings, people, unfinished? We build and we build and still we're incomplete? You want to think things on a morning like this. In silence like this. You want to remember. You want to find what's lost. I know where to find Rosella and still she's lost? It's a question for God who looms above this arch as indifferent to sisters as he is to parliaments as he is to so many other things. She carries her sister in a small hungry place in her stomach that food won't satisfy. When she was a girl Rosella once banged her on the nose with a teapot. She forgave her sister that afternoon. She forgives her again this morning. For the tea pot. For not being beautiful anymore. For being lost. Rosella. Rosella! From her eyes not her mouth in the now noisier morning.

CLAIRE ORTALDA

NO-Body

Totally, I can do the hip-jerking strut in 5-inch heeled boots. I can straddle the mic and let the blues of a thousand traditions rise up and out my voice in what some snarks term my cat yell and what my fans call soul holler. My songs are the stories of my dreams and the lyrics come from the street. I was the first to dye my hair in spots, like a leopard, to let it hang high and knotted like a circus pony, to dress in silks the color of birds. All this and the pounding bass of my drummer, the writhing cry of my sax player, the wail of my lead guitarist like the arc of a live power line. We always touched the soul, and that's why our gigs covered the globe and that's why I saw what I saw.

Riots in London, burning down, burning down, the streets thick with bobbies, people thronging the streets and squares of Greece, Egypt, Syria, Libya, Moscow, New York, Oakland. Occupy, occupy. Tear gas and batons and bean bags and rockets and live ammo and tanks and Al Qaeda and IEDs. The poison tsunami has hit our shores. The pelican starves blackly in the oil slick.

The world's been stolen. You've given us no choice. Our song "Infanticide" rose to the top of the charts in three days, "Walking 6 Miles to School in Bullshit" right behind. Why bother to give birth to this generation then steal our future? Kill the baby in the womb or leave it exposed on the hillside. Save time. Save tax dollars. Save all of that wasted commodity you call "love," because there's no such thing without hope. And no, you didn't have it tougher. We've got it tougher. Because we've got nothing. The world has united to say one thing to us. In the end was the word and the word is NO! No jobs, no place to live, no country to call our own, our vote an inky sham, our education an indoctrination into denial. We thrash and pace like zoo animals, caged. On the streets, your limo splashes us with the gutter water of our trashed dreams. No, no, and no. I scream it, back so arched, the tail of my hair touches the stage, sax like a missile tearing the sky, drumbeat like bullets, guitar the electric arc of the torturer.

And they were texting me on stage, some holding up the lights of their phones in the darkened arena and some fast-thumb messaging their stories to me.

And one text just said: THIS IS LAST NO CAN TAKE. RZR BLDE RDY.

And that's when I lay down on the stage, right on the edge where the front-rowers could touch me, and extended my wrist to the crowd.

And somebody cut me and I bled, just a little.

Hey, it's symbolic, man, and then I got up and sang, my bird-scarf wrapped around the wound, turning rusty-brown with the corpuscles of the disenfranchised.

And the NOs came, texted to me. They worked so hard, they played the game, they studied the book, they tried for fame. And no, no, no. No to the job, no to the college slot, no to the money, no to the apartment, no to the house. No medical care, no benefits, no respect, no interview, no scholarship, no audition. Nada, nix, nyet, no, baby. On the bench, off the team. And we can see the future and nothing's going to change, except we'll be old with the no instead of young with the no. The screen glitters with everything we're told we want and life brings us nothing. We're going to get old without stories, without accomplishment. We have no place, our dreams are dust and there'll be no babies born of this generation. Just like the best aphrodisiac is the brain, the cleanest infanticide is the cherry-flavored condom. It all ends here, yeah with that whimper we all read about when we thought literature was the answer if politics wasn't.

I read their texts over the mic and they echo back over the massed dark heads and the phones wave with light. And I lay down. Now, every show, I lie down for them. They cut me…my wrists, my legs, my stomach and I bleed for them because I love them, because I am them, because I scream for them up here, their NO-texts become song in my throat.

But soon, like the cutters out there with their lines of crusty scabs, their white furrowed scar tissue, that thin, almost golden, membrane that blankets the most recent wound, there are fewer and fewer sites on my body to cut. I bare more and more of my self to them, and their starving, vampire souls want more real estate of flesh.

Tonight, I sing of the dead God, the one sagging on the cross. Devout lips kiss this corpse, his flesh is eaten in the mass. He swings from the belts of nuns and monks. It is Easter but he has forgotten to rise, the stone refuses to roll open the mouth of the tomb. The world is dead, the land sere, the kingfisher lies ill in the castle, the sheep will not lamb, the crops wither and die.

I sing, nearly naked, to show there is nothing left of me to give. But still they text their NOs and the cries rise for the healing balm of my blood. I can not deny them, I who have always said Yes to them. I lie down and loose the bird scarf from my throat.

I never know the hand that holds the blade and I do not tonight, but this time the razor finds my throat and this time I do not rise to sing again. I can feel the pulse of my heart in my neck and in the rhythm of the expulsion of blood. My drummer times his beats to mine and the sax lowers to a warble. I can feel the flutter of the kingfisher's wings in my chest. Come back to life, fly over the land and make the crops to grow once again. Your people are starving with a new kind of hunger. Possessed of the souls of lions, their bodies are trapped in the lab rat's maze. Let them go, let them go, let them go.

Oh, I can taste money in my mouth, the metal of money-blood they have drained from us. My guitar is crying in looping, liquid reels, a mobius strip of wailing that goes on and on and on as the teenage heart of my public cries with it, cries with me, silenced, bloody, prone on the stage. Am I savior or example? The canary in the mine or the first lemming over the cliff? I don't know, I don't know, I don't know, as even the LED lights of their texting phones held high, their NOs swooshing in electronic illumination over their heads by the thousands, even that light dims. I can only hear now and it is the sound of a small river, and within my breast, just the tiniest stirring of wings. And then the river slows its flow and there is warmth in my breast and on my breast and I think I hear them singing. My fans are singing, they are singing all together. Their voices sway as if they have linked hands and they are singing in one voice. Oh, sing in one voice.

Sing the word yes. Take it back. Put your name on it. Claim it. It's yours.

SANDRA PARK

If You Live in a Small House

On the isolated, northernmost island of Ni'ihau, the war was fought on different terms. Nobody there listened to the radio or watched television. Honolulu people thought that everyone on Ni'ihau was a little crazy, inbred over many generations. If not crazy, they were surely thought of as backward, a bunch of locals, mostly Hawaiians, living under the land ownership and largesse of the Robinson family. After the attack on Pearl Harbor, one Japanese pilot did not make it back to his carrier, unable to locate that floating dot in the Pacific. He landed in a dry, scrubby field. A Hawaiian man took his boots and identification papers. Another Hawaiian went through the damaged plane and carried away the ammunition from the machine guns.

But a local resident named Yoshio Harada recognized the face of this pilot, the face of someone he had not met before, a sign that something important was going to happen. Shaking with excitement, he gave the pilot a shotgun, a small tribute to a nearly overwhelming vision: for the first time in his life, he had met someone who could have been him, speaking in Japanese and jabbing the air with his finger. Yoshio spoke only baby talk Japanese, but he nodded, looking at his mirror self with comprehension. Together they wrestled the machine guns off their mounts, only to discover there were no live shells.

The Hawaiians kept looking out for the Robinson sampan that carried weekly supplies from the island of Kaua'i, but the U.S. Army had forbidden the sampan from sailing. Desperate, the pilot burned down the house of the Hawaiian who would not return his papers. He confronted the man who had taken his ammunition with Yoshio's shotgun. Without his boots he looked like a scared boy. He fired three times into the big Hawaiian's stomach. The Hawaiian overpowered him and smashed his head against a stone wall. Yoshio leaned over the shotgun and pulled the trigger, falling next to the bloody head of the pilot. When the sampan finally returned, Robinson told his people that they had fought their own war. Benehakaka Kanahele, the man who took three shots in the stomach, survived and went back to his wife. Of all the stories that were told, the one about the downed pilot on Ni'ihau was almost forgotten, an orphaned occurrence that only grew murky and more ragged with time. There were no songs or stories about the short, fierce war that was waged on the island of Ni'ihau.

Whenever there was drinking and men of a certain age, war stories were told. The old stories were the best, how a young man almost dies of boredom, then almost dies advancing under fire, then dies and rises to heaven with a girl in his arms. With the onset of the Korean War so soon after the end of World War II, people's feelings about war, its moments of deprivation and glory, sunk into a tired muddle of changing alliances and embarrassing incidents. Returning soldiers said the Korean countryside was nothing but rubble and snow. The most pitiful stories were about mistaken identity, the problem of the wrong face and the right uniform.

Author's note: *Based on a historic incident, this passage reminds us that all wars are wars by proxy, directed from outside the field of combat and what happens on the ground is another story. On December 7, 1941, the day World War II in the Pacific began with the air attack on Pearl Harbor, a Japanese fighter pilot crash landed on tiny, remote Ni'ihau, the northernmost inhabited island of the Hawaiian archipelago, privately owned, population a few hundred, almost all native Hawaiian.*

MARGO PERIN

Entropy

The classroom glares like a radiation chamber
Rectangular funnels of light ricocheting off walls of concrete and steel
Between more concrete and steel
The stratosphere of San Francisco County Jail

I stand in front of the chalkboard
Littered with broken psalms, gang emblems
I'm there to teach writing, to turn the classroom into a lighthouse
Show how a pencil can be used as a laser beam
To illuminate the scars of those thrashing about in the waters

Incarceration is being caught in shark's teeth
Three rows pointing inward
One falls out, a lawyer fucks up
No time off for time served, no possibility of parole
Another tooth pulling each one of the men closer to the throat
Closer to being swallowed up
Our society's disappeared

I tell my students to think of their confinement
As a writing retreat, all expenses paid
While I go to jail armed with three dots and a jot
To dig into where I am not

We say light is life and dark is death
But when a seed rises above the ground
It starts to die, when a baby leaves the womb
It starts to die, when the leaves of a tree
Get too much light, they wrinkle and fall.

What if the shadow was really the light
And the light the shadow?

My students are hidden in the shadows because …
Tall, black, and short on green, wrote the one with the moniker Hallmark,
Because …
Moms didn't love me, wrote Shanice
Because …
My stepfather said choose me or him and she chose him, wrote Janice
I've been homeless since I was twelve
When I refused to do the laundry she burned my books, wrote Peter
    That way I learned the importance of education
My babysitter made me stick my pee-pee in my sister, wrote Tom

Because
Because
Because

How many crimes are committed
In the name of
I exist, I matter?

How many crimes
In the name of
I don't matter
And you're going to pay?

Let us set up a memorial
DEDICATED TO ALL THE
MEN AND WOMEN LIVING INSIDE
Let's announce in the obituaries
The names of those
Who serve on the battlefield
Of society's wastelands

The sores and wounds of outrageous fortune
Living in a sea amongst us
Seen and not seen
Sewn and not sewn
Inside the seams of prison walls

RICHARD PRINCE

Interview by Ishmael Reed

Ishmael Reed: I want to ask you about the race discussion that followed the verdict finding George Zimmerman, killer of Trayvon Martin, innocent.
Richard Prince: Yes.
IR: After the president made a speech.
RP: Yes.
IR: MSNBC had Toure moderate a panel of four White men, who don't get profiled, racially. I noticed that the major media have featured the comments of people today; Bill Keller of the *New York Times* was in there, George Will, and Joe Klein of *Time Magazine*.
RP: Joe Klein?
IR: Yes, Joe Klein of *Time Magazine*.
RP: Oh, Joe Klein, yes.
IR: He's been a Black dysfunction hustler since 1989. As a matter of fact I have a piece in a major Jewish Magazine called *Tablet*.
RP: Oh, you really get around then.
IR: I call him a *'Kaiser Juden'* meaning he has been trying to please the
anti-Semitic court of The One Percent. He agreed with the Zimmerman verdict.
RP: Yeah, so did Rem Rieder of *USA Today* and the *American Journal Review*.
IR: Bill O'Reilly also tried to hustle the verdict for ratings. It's all about Black dysfunction. Let me ask you something. Do you believe the Black correspondents, reporters, pundits—the ones that are remaining in the corporate media—are under what I call 'opinion control?'
RP: I don't think they are under "opinion control." The only "opinion control" I think is that they are in this society and they are following what everyone says, but I don't think anyone is telling them what to say.
IR: Jeff Zucker, head of CNN, is not telling Don Lemon what to say? O'Reilly, preaching to people about moral lapses—I find that ironic.
RP: I don't think that Jeff Zucker is telling Don Lemon what to say. I think Don Lemon unfortunately didn't put much thought into what he was going to say. He is too naïve.
IR: He agrees with Bill O'Reilly that Black values are the pits. He said that O'Reilly had a point.
RP: If he had thought about it, he was saying the same thing that Bill Cosby said years ago. He should have thought about the response that Bill Cosby had gotten and said to himself, "I don't want the response that Cosby got. What did Cosby do wrong?" He should have thought and analyzed that and come out with what he had to say in a different way.
IR: [At the time about which Prince speaks, Cosby was on a tough love tour; scolding Blacks about their values.]
RP: [I'm not sure that Cosby was scolding all Blacks about their values. His original comments in 2004 were about "the lower economic people" not parenting properly. See: http://mije.org/richardprince/still-talkin-about-bill-cosby]
IR: The media concentrated on the Black dysfunction parts in the president's speech. They like that part.
RP: Yeah, well I think that they talked about some other parts, too. The point that people talked about was that he talked about racial profiling in stores and all that other stuff that happens to Black men. Even though Obama got all the flack from saying that Trayvon Martin could have been his son, he went back to the same place and expanded on that point, saying that Trayvon "could have been me thirty five years ago." That was what was news to me.
IR: According to the CDC, sixty-two percent of Black on Black homicides are drug related.
RP: Oh really? I thought they were gang related.
IR: No. Sixty-two percent are drug related. I sent you my *Wall Street Journal* piece. I live right here in the ghetto.
RP: I saw the *Wall Street Journal* piece. That was the one about the neighborhood watches,

right? I thought that was interesting.

IR: The Black on Black homicide rate has doubled since 1984. Why doesn't the president connect that with the contras bringing drugs into the inner city?

RP: That's too complicated for one thing. The contras didn't directly bring the drugs into the inner city if I remember that story.

IR: But the state department knew about it.

RP: What's that?

IR: The state department and other agencies knew they were bringing drugs in.

RP: It wasn't as direct as that. They used "Freeway" Ricky Ross as a middle man.

IR: Kerry's report has Government agencies being aware of it; John Kerry's Sub-Committee on narcotics trafficking. He criticized agencies of the government for looking the other way. The Reagan administration's acquiescence to drug peddling by their allies coincides with an uptick of Black on Black homicides traceable to drug turf wars. [On March 16, 1986, the *San Francisco Examiner* published a report on the "1983 seizure of 430 pounds of cocaine from a Colombian freighter" in San Francisco which indicated that a "cocaine ring in the San Francisco Bay area helped finance Nicaragua's Contra rebels." Carlos Cabezas, convicted of conspiracy to traffic cocaine, said that the profits from his crimes "belonged to... the Contra revolution." He told the *Examiner*, "I just wanted to get the Communists out of my country." Julio Zavala, also convicted on trafficking charges, said "that he supplied $500,000 to two Costa Rican-based Contra groups and that the majority of it came from cocaine trafficking in the San Francisco Bay area, Miami and New Orleans." I.R.]

RP: I have to go back. That was twenty years ago by now. I think that this is interesting about the drugs. You say they were drug related. People make an argument that Whites do more drugs than Blacks do.

IR: Yeah, but the kids in the suburbs steal money from their parents to buy drugs. That's why you don't have the violence. Here in Oakland—and I'm sure this is true in other cities—these are turf wars with different gangs competing over the drug market. Other ethnic groups are involved, but they're never mentioned by the media.

RP: I think that what's interesting about that Fruitvale movie that you will see is that they had an Asian guy as the drug dealer.

IR: That's what happened on our block. The gang leader on our block was Vietnamese and he was murdered a couple of years ago. In the WSJ piece, I talk about how the police knew about this and didn't do anything about it. When I go to the meetings the people complain that the police are chummy with the drug dealers. The president can't talk about that. Okay, a couple more things. In the *Nation Magazine* a woman wrote an article that the media was reluctant to mention that there were five White women on the jury. They always referred to them as women.

RP: Yeah, but it did get out that there were five White women and one Hispanic.

IR: Mark Geragos, this attorney on CNN, said that the case was settled when they chose five White women. He got disputed by Jeffrey Toobin, and Michael Jackson hater Toobin said that they voted on the basis of the evidence.

RP: Well, I don't know what to say. The only two women who spoke on that jury were both saying that they both felt compelled to do what they did because of these instructions that were given by the judge about Stand Your Ground laws.

IR: Yeah, well I tell you what. The way I read that was that these patriarchal defense attorneys looked these women in the eye and said, "This can happen to you. A Black guy can come into your house." I have a piece out called "The Anne Card" like "The Race Card." That's been evoked throughout American history: that they use the safety of White women as a decoy to take people's land. Before Blacks it was Native Americans. Lincoln did not want to be embarrassed by the people of Minnesota executing three-hundred Sioux. It wouldn't look good to Europeans. The authorities in Minnesota used what I call 'The Anne Card,' to say that the Sioux were violating White women. Under this pressure Lincoln ordered the execution of 38 Sioux, the largest mass hanging in American history. (They hanged a 39th by mistake.) Joy Reid of MSNBC was the first to question whether these women could return to their right wing communities after having convicted Zimmerman of murder, Zimmerman being a folk hero among the right. When Zillah Eisenstein, a White feminist, started to comment on the White women on the jury Melissa Harris-Perry had her shut down. (In a piece she wrote about the trial she said that the jury chose race over gender.) MHP said that the women on the jury shouldn't be demonized and blamed for the verdict; even Michele Bernard got cut off by Chuck Todd when she tried to broach the subject. Do you think that MSNBC is trying to ease up on the White demographic? They don't want to embarrass them?

RP: I can't say. Like I said, I didn't notice that. What I recall is that it was weird that there were five White women on the jury and one person of color. Why weren't there any Black people? Somebody answered that question on Anderson Cooper's show.

IR: The demographics in Sanford, Florida?

RP: No. They said there were Black people who were waiting to be seated but by the time they were called to be questioned about being on the jury they had all of the people that they needed.

IR: The week that the president talked about dysfunction in the African American community, the *New York Times* had a piece whose headline was "Heroin in New England, More Abundant and Deadly." The addicts were White. Do you think that Black dysfunction is easier to sell products with than White dysfunction?

RP: I don't think that was the point of the speech he was making. I don't think the speech was about dysfunction. I think he was making a speech about why Black people are upset about this verdict. That was just one of the things he mentioned. That wasn't the point of his speech.

IR: Now let me move on to progressives and the media. We had thirty thousand prisoners on a hunger strike, California prisons are so bad. We got a progressive governor who defends a prison system that the federal court has said constitutes cruel and unusual punishment. The progressives are spending more time on 126 prisoners in Gitmo, than the 30,000 White, Black, Brown prisoners out here in California who went on a hunger strike. Why do you think they spend more time on Gitmo than they do on these American prisons?

RP: I think it was a campaign issue.

IR: I see.

RP: In 2008. They are upset because the campaign promise hasn't been kept. Obama wanted to close them down. He didn't make a promise about the California prisons.

IR: Do you think the Black and Brown prisoners need to join Al-Qaeda, get captured and sent to Gitmo in order to get sympathy for their cause?

RP: I don't know. What does Diane Feinstein say about all this?

IR: Oh, God, forget about her.

RP: Oh, really? I think that Guantanamo gets more sympathy because it is international and it's not just the United States. People all over the world talk about that while the California prison system is a local issue. Not local, local but an internal United States issue. The Supreme Court ruled about it, which was why they had to do something about it, and you have Attorney General Kamala Harris who is an ally of Obama, so I don't know why it isn't talked about. It's really something Eric Holder should talk about, too.

IR: Okay, now, let me move onto Tom Roberts and Rachel Maddow. Tom Roberts announces that he's gay and so is Rachel Maddow. I have a piece in the July/August, 2013, *Playboy Magazine* about it.

RP: You're in *Playboy Magazine*? You must have contacts with all of these newspapers.

IR: Well, I might get one article published for every five or six that I turn in.

RP: But still, that's a lot.

IR: I still need to learn a lot. I need a translator for Melissa Harris-Perry's show. There's a lot of academic jargon. I need subtitles.

RP: Oh, I see, so back to Tom Roberts and Rachel Maddow.

IR: Why doesn't anyone acknowledge racism in the LGBT community that Audre Lorde, Marlin Riggs and Barbara Smith have reported? [LGBT: Acronym for Lesbian, Gay, Bisexual and Transgender. Sometimes shown as GLBT. Ed.]

RP: There is a group called GLAAD (Gay & Lesbian Alliance Against Defamation) that has said they tried to address that. They pointed out that there had been a lot of Blacks in the

LGBT community who have been harassed and assaulted and all that. They say more attention should be given to that. They promised they would elevate the issue of racism within the LGBT movement.

IR: Okay, now, my piece in *Playboy*; I learned from the professor of Queer Studies, the battles against the gay oppression was fought by Black and Puerto Rican transvestites. One was in 1966 at a cafe in San Francisco where they fought the vice squad. Then Stonewall, they played the most important part in that, yet Tom Roberts and Rachel Maddow never mention that.

RP: Well, I didn't know that that was the case.

IR: Do you think that Tavis Smiley was right that the president focuses more on the LGBT issues than on Black issues?

RP: No, I don't think that's correct. I don't know how much attention he pays to these issues. What the White house is saying is that the LGBT issues are out front and everyone knows about them. The White House's position is that "You may not see me addressing Black issues, but I am." There are a lot of behind the scene ways. The Black issues are on the Q.T. Their position is that you might not see all that the president is doing for Black people, because he is doing it behind the scenes. Executive Orders are adjusted so that they benefit Black people.

IR: That's what I say about Booker T. Washington.

RP: What about Booker T. Washington?

IR: He did the same thing: supported the enfranchisement of Blacks behind the scenes.

IR: This is my last question. I am doing an anthology for Haki Madhubuti's *Third World Press* about Blacks in Hollywood emphasizing *Django Unchained*. So I did a little research. Black people started making movies around 1912. What broke them was their stars would go to Hollywood to make more money and the equipment became more expensive. Is that the same thing that happened in the newspaper industry? The Black Press was once very powerful and influential, but when Black militant groups demanded that only Black reporters cover them, the mainstream press, in order to get stories, grabbed the best Black reporters. Yet, now, according to your valuable site, *Journal-isms*, they're being fired or being bought out. Do you think that is a problem?

RP: I think the problem with the Black press to me is that they are not enough up to date. Every time there's a news event that affects Black people, I always go to the Black press first, and consult their websites to see whether they are on it, and a lot of times they aren't. They might make the excuse that they are weeklies, but that also goes for *The Village Voice*, but the *Village Voice* website is current. I wanted to check something in *Black Enterprise* magazine, recently—something about Black income or Blacks in business. Nothing! Here's another example: when Chuck Brown died, *The Washington Post* was all over it. They sent out reporters and even did a story in their style section. By the time the Black press caught up it was an old story.

IR: One more question. You have been writing as long as I can remember—at least the last five years about the disappearance of Black correspondents and executives from the media. What's behind that?

RP: Well, I think the media in general is shrinking, not just that the presence of Black people is shrinking. It's because of the economy and the Internet taking away their business, so in terms of who remained, why are more Black people being let go? I don't know.

IR: They say they like Asian women a lot.

RP: What's that?

IR: The White executives say that they like Asian women a lot. They're easier to get along with. They are not confrontational. They all wanted a Connie Chung until she went away mad after her interview with Newt Gingrich's mother got her into trouble; she made a defiant speech at a gathering of Asian American journalists.

RP: I'm not sure what the reason is. I guess may be some kind of institutional racism. It could be. I'm not saying that. Here's the reason. They don't recognize the value of diversity enough. Instead of saying, "We value diversity so much that we can't let these people go"—they're not saying that. They're saying, "The White people are going and you're going." Yvette Cabrera was the only Hispanic columnist in that city and then they let her go. They laid her off. That's an example of why they should value diversity. Given the Latino population of Orange County it would seem that of

all people, she should stay. She was a major value to that newspaper.
IR: Is that the old South way of saying, "We don't want your money, when forbidding Blacks from shopping in their stores?
RP: They can't afford that. Everybody needs money.
IR: MSNBC and CNN are trying to make that tea party Black guy David Webb a star.
RP: I don't know him.
IR: He's the one that said, "You don't need any outsiders in Sanford, Florida because the police are doing a good job." Tea Party—they have had him on both networks.
RP: I don't know about those guys.
IR: They had a preacher on saying that Trayvon Martin had it coming. This Black preacher.
RP: Are you talking about Jesse Lee Peterson?
IR: Yeah.
RP: I don't know where they get these people from. I remember him. They even brought him to the NABJ convention at one point and he got into a fight with somebody. It was a mess.
IR: Okay, Richard, thank you.
RP: Thank you.

JERRY RATCH

Unemployment

The line of the unemployed
wrapped back on itself
like an accordion pleat
and extended all the way across
a great hall
You could see the faces
of them, bluish and drawn
under the dim florescent
lighting

First in line were laid-off
bees
weeping with their wings
hanging down
dragging on the ground

Next came the bankers
on their knees
beaten and bruised
after being pummeled
by a crowd at the door

And scattered all around them
were little yellow and rust-colored
piles of iron will
along with shredded bundles
of abandoned nerves of steel

You only looked forward
No one could afford to look back
anymore, and you saw what
lay ahead

On either side of the line
were two tables
and you were given one
of three choices

Some walked straight into
the unending labyrinth of the
government. Or you turned
to the table on the right
into the waiting arms of the Army

Or you could drift to the left
into the Church
and we knew instantly
what that meant

But then I woke up
with a start
and realized it had all
been a bad dream
Only a dream

And happily stepped out the door
into the street
where I waited at the curb
for the flow of blood
to let up

ISHMAEL REED

Why I Will Never Write A Sonnet

The draw of the form I fail to see
The fourteen lines, which poets have groped
Too many birds, too many trees
Too many Hallmark "How do I Love Thees"
(An exception might be Milton's poke
At "the bloody Piedmontese")

Employed by men with too much time
Of noble birth and cousins of Kings
Whose toil was thoughts about the
Nature of Things
Who never had their hands touch grime
Whose Sonnets were roses, were soft
Lacked spine

Claude McKay made a Sonnet fight
So students of verse give
The Jamaican his props
His Sonnet like hard bop had some spunk
Like Silver's left hand on Opus De Funk
But even with this I can't get on it

So take this critics as a bee in your bonnet
You are reading a man who will never
Write a Sonnet

TENNESSEE REED

The Mid-Afternoon Brain Freeze

It is June of 2011 on a Tuesday afternoon
I go to the Starbucks at City Center Plaza in Oakland
with the former American, United and Delta ticket office
turned into a AAA Insurance Office,
Top Dog's, Wells Fargo, Dress Barn, Jamba Juice
and Panda Express
Down at the bottom is 12th Street BART
I go purchase a double espresso for Dad
It is 3:00 on the dot
There is a long line
even though it is a hot day
The line is filled with young people
dressed for work in suits, high heels or dress shoes
talking on their bluetooth devices
to short stocky girls in their teens or early twenties
in short shorts, t-strap sandals and graphic tee shirts
with a group of three or four friends
There are a lot of people sitting at tables
reading books, working on a laptop or tablet,
or listening to an mp3 player
The place is packed with the sounds
of customers having conversations,
the baristas shouting orders
the machines filling up cups with coffee and whipped cream
and the music blasting from the monitor to my right
describing the title, artist and album
I notice one young woman over by a window
working on her silver MacBook Pro
and sipping on an iced mocha frappuccino
It is mixed with espresso, sugar, cocoa, and low fat milk
inside of a clear plastic cup with the Starbucks logo on it
She sips on it through a green straw

I finally get to the front and order the double espresso,
wait for it for five minutes
and then head back through rotunda of the Federal Building
consisting of two twin towers
to the Victorian homes
turned into offices at Preservation Park
with white picket fences and climbing roses
shaded by trees
and people sitting on the grass in front of the gazebo
to hand Dad his double espresso
He is sitting on a wrought iron bench
behind the Persian fountain
underneath an old fashioned street lamp
"There was a long line," I said
"Everyone was having their mid-afternoon brain freeze."

FRED REISS

Fightin' Cancer: Space Walking in the Outer Big C Galaxy

I'm on a space walk. There is nothing I can do to heal myself. I'm submitting to the comets and science fireballs. The Chemo Galaxy has me in its weightlessness. I collapse in bed, shivering through the flu-like chill under a pile of blankets and defensively curled in womb position and realize at this moment, I'm too weak to get rid of the cancer. I have to drift through the gravity pull of chemo treatment. Sometimes things register. I'm just floating about grabbing at whatever is loose in the air—music, books, movies, food that tastes like nothing, cold juices that sooth my sore throat. I bump into objects I can't see in the darkness. The bumps are asteroids. I'm space walking. My cord is no longer attached to a capsule. I can see the capsule. Its door is open but I can't get back inside to return to Earth. And I'm getting pinged between the space debris and spinning upside down. I cling to the surface of a passing asteroid, catching my breath and watching the planets spin around the sun, Because really, all I can do is drift and heal from the ray gun blasts taking whatever is inside me out.

I'm floating in a space odyssey with complete vulnerability. Who needs the unforgiving invincible when you're lost in space? I see others like me. Spinning, some are limp, coughing, or sleeping. Everyone's tumbling, looking at each other with hurt burnt-out eyes and drawn faces and cracked smiles. Some give up and allow themselves to helplessly drift. They burn upon re-entry in the earth's atmosphere or get sucked down black holes. I can't follow them. I jump from the asteroid trying to get back to the capsule where I can get control again, lightly touching the fingers of passing walkers amid the cosmic debris.

So we all float and drift, partially dethroned kings and queens of the universe. The sun is amazing. I spread my arms outward and its heat gives me a tan and dries out my tears.

DOREN ROBBINS

Vet Ode

Tried to help his father out retrieving a car he didn't own.
They were in a city he returned to after the war but they never
lived in together. Metal, rust brown, the Kaiser car memory-color.
He knew the street he meant he would find it on, by a stand of jacarandas.
"Why didn't you drive the car I loaned you? If you could see the
propeller in the tail of your father's sperm you wouldn't
find that car, and it's okay," he said.
"If it tastes like water or it tastes like mud,
if you get the proportions right
if you understand the refinement,
the kind of intelligence, the rhythm
of associations you need—you're still going
to be tasting, still deciding between water and mud.
And it's okay. You can't find the street
that leads to the car, that metal rust, mental rust, brown.
You want to call it a quest, that's fine, no one's going
to start chanting or ringing bells because you
came out of the wreck, most of it's a wreck."
My father was a vet.
"You'll go to Canada," he said,
"I have a cousin in Windsor, Ontario; you'll never go to war.
Find that car will'ya? You'll need that car some day,
you'll never go to war, you'll never see the two years I spent
my mind sucked-out in the VA, you'll never know
that guy I boarded with over there, his face, flame thrower
burned to the bones of his eyes and mouth; when they
changed his gauze, when ever they
touched him—the sounds in his throat made me sweat
down my crack. You'll never go to war.
Forget about the streetcar that doesn't go to the street
you see the car parked on
in your mind. Roll me closer
to the channel so we can see the rowers
and the women's legs. I want to look at those two pregnant women,
I want to know what they are laughing about, they laugh from
the pelvis outward, look at them, they're so ripe—no wonder
they're pregnant, no wonder we study them.
You're daydreaming again, you'll know the place where the car is
when you get there, I'll remember where I left it—I want to hear them,
wheel me closer. What're you daydreaming about, writing an ode or something?
To pregnant women or someone?
If I was going to write an ode, and look at me,
it would be a real truck pull for me to write an ode,
but if I had one in me, what it was like to hear my room mate's wife
on the phone—he'd never let her up to the room,
some kids' voices in the phone conversation background,
I'd always be telling her after a few minutes, 'I'm sorry, Rita, I can't talk
more, it's the medicine,'—'Robby,' he'd say, handing me back the receiver,
'it's her,'—I'd write an ode, to that.' "

TONY R. RODRIGUEZ

"I'd Rather Smile With You"

I heard apathy ooze from your insecure lips.

Sure—
I can't prove His existence,
But—
You can't disprove it either.

Yet . . .

even though you don't believe,
I'm quite sure He still believes in you.

No more debates.

You've set your mind closed.

[But how great it would be to smile as one.]

With arms in the air and heads bent back in sacred veneration,
many pray for your salvation and hopeful enlightenment.

But . . .

I don't anymore: Those who want to be Saved—get Saved.
                                   Those who don't—don't.

You make your own choices.
You make your own belief a reality.

I just sit back and examine my own consciousness—
smiling all the while.

ANDY ROSS

Becoming a Bookseller

I became a bookseller because I had a passion for books. This is not a particularly good reason to make a life choice. But my decision (if one could call it that) to enter the book business was disorderly. In 1971, I was a graduate student at the University of Oregon in Eugene on a Ph.D. track studying German cultural and intellectual history. I was writing a master's thesis on the nineteenth century precursors of existentialism and spending a lot of time thinking about such timely subjects as Kierkegaard's concept of the teleological suspension of the ethical.

Most of the people with whom I associated outside of the History Department were hippies or some variation thereof. I suppose I was too, although spending one's waking hours reading the philosophy of Johan Gottlieb Fichte created some real cognitive dissonance in my countercultural consciousness and lifestyle.

In my other life outside of the university, there was a lot of talk amongst my friends about freedom, spontaneity, communal living, feminism, the Maharishi Mahesh Yogi, psychedelic drugs, astrology, free love, vegetarianism, gestalt therapy, natural childbirth and that sort of thing. Marxism was very popular too. But the Marxism being bandied about was what we superior intellectuals in the History Department would call "vulgar Marxism", by which we meant people who actually wanted to change the world, not just pontificate about it. Among the vulgar Marxists, there was a lot of waving of Chairman Mao's *Little Red Book* and some vicious disputes over matters that were of no consequence to anyone other than the vulgar Marxists. There was also a war going on, and Kierkegaard didn't have much to say about that. Oh, yes. And there was a girl. There always is, isn't there? Things weren't going too well with us, as is often the case. One day she walked out on me and joined a free love commune called Earth's Rising Family. I kept going out there trying to get her back. The communards were pretty nice people. They graciously put me up in the teepee down the hill from the privy while they were in the farmhouse having orgies (or so I imagined). Fichte and Kierkegaard didn't have much to say about that either.

Somehow all this led me to the decision to leave academics and start a bookstore. As I said, I had a passion for books. I don't remember much about what kind of thought went into the decision. Not very much at all, I believe. Maybe 5 minutes of thought. Maybe it happened in my sleep. Maybe it happened in the teepee. It was dumb luck, but it probably set me in the right direction for the next 40 years and counting.

I was tired of the rain and depressed about rushing back and forth to and from the teepee at Earth's Rising Commune. So I moved down to the San Francisco Bay Area.

I found a bookshop for sale in Cotati, a small college town in Sonoma County about 50 miles north of San Francisco. It was a very modest store, Eeyore Books. The entire space was 600 square feet, about as big as my living room where I'm writing this. The store wasn't worth much money, because it didn't have many books and did even less business. But I still managed to drive a very bad bargain. It is a flaw that I fortunately overcame before becoming a literary agent. I paid them $15,000. And the store was mine.

I put in some new shelves, ordered up some books and opened for business a week later. On my first day of business I did $32 in sales. Later I learned that was the same amount of sales that Cody's had done on its first day of business in 1956. The old Cody's shop on the north side of campus was about the same size too.

A lot of people say that the quality of books has gone downhill in the last 40 years, that literary values have been replaced by commercial values and that American reading has been seduced by the dark forces of a hegemonic mass media with a fetish for celebrity. Actually most people in the book business don't talk that way, except maybe me, and then only at pretentious literary cocktail parties. Nowadays when I argue the point I like to recite the great line from Yeats' poem, "The Second Coming:" "The best lack all conviction, while the worst are filled with passionate intensity." And most people agree. (Although there are some who are not familiar with that poem and have to slouch off toward Wikipedia to find the reference).

Eeyore's was a one person operation. We did grow over the years. By the time I left Cotati in 1977 to take over Cody's, I think it had become a two person operation. I'm still pretty proud of that store. I think it had a kind of perfection, just right for its time and place.

CLIFTON ROSS

Night in the New World Order

Under the streetlights I'm three shadows
converging in a fist as the night
deepens in darkness and grief.
I follow home a smokeless flame the size of a thumb,
the size of a star in the sky,
disappeared by the lights of an empire reaching to rule the stars —
but in vain.
The traffic signals flash commands at empty streets and avenues
I wander in search of answers to cruelty
but it is all in me.
An enemy of all orders,
I'll find my own way home.
I'll take the long way around,
defying the lines laid out to define me,
my guide only the stars of my soul's constellation.

The Proud Sinner's Prayer

O God forgive me for having loved you more than life itself
and correct me in my ways;
make my way crooked so I might delight in the curves of the road.
Give me more tasks and less success
that I may always be occupied with work but never with fame.
And this daily bread may I gain with the work of my own hands.
Withhold from me the love you bestow on prophets and lead me not
in the way of saviors, that I might have a long life unblessed by your rewards for the just.
May I never again fall into belief, nor tarry long in the way of doctrine,
but rather live by my own experience, guided only by the light of my soul.
Deliver me not from evil, for in evil have I found the good;
and lead me not, for I have found my own way, straying
from the narrow path to the open field, a realm that is your infinite loving heart,
where there is neither power, nor glory, nor kingdom,
forever and ever.
Amen.

Once It's All Lost

Once it's all lost, everything,
down to the last button and crumb
all tumbling back to earth,
remember the earth.
We were never the gods we thought ourselves to be,
one step beneath the winged angels,
we, always just another creature
recently risen from the wild sea
or the muck or dust.
May that wisdom lost in all our knowledge
then be recalled when all is lost;
may we save the wisdom
that saves us as we fall:
this earth hungrily embraces
even its wayward children,
we who had forgotten
and thought ourselves lost.

SUHAYL SAADI

The Oracle Of Easter Monday: For Murdered Writers

Listen to the oracle, Kuru, listen, where there is no sound!
Though we never met, my friend, yet perhaps
Through the sorceress's gin charms
In the song of the weaver-bird
One day, we shall meet
But now is the night of fire - listen!

Beyond the cliff's ninth edge, by the smile of the big, black river
They tossed you into a lizard's grave,
To lie beneath the hooves of goat and antelope, the sting of alligator peppercorns
For a thousand years the stars will fall into your tomb of concrete and lime
How dare they? They, who raped their mothers
And gave their souls, all seven, to darkness
They have many names, a hundred, turning heads
Like chameleons, they change their skins,
Black, white, green, blue, yellow
But their names, deeds, thoughts all
Rhyme only with Hell

Listen to the oracle, Kuru, listen, where there is no sound!
On the day before the end of time
When the yams will sprout seven leaves
And the harvest will yield only yoori
The lizards, grown fat, will slip from their holes
And will dance at midnight around the iroko tree
And will speak through their noses:
> We will sear the land black like the tortoise-back
> We will burn eyes into bone, one-by-one,
> We will take over your homes!

Listen, then, to the oracle, Kuru, listen, where there is no sound!
Hear the whisper of the mangrove swamp
At the river's mouth, cup in your palms
The blood of the rocks, the bones of wafered creatures
Cast back your singing head and drink full of the Black King's breath
Mould the paste of the pear tree into the form of a human being
Feed her light and set her dancing like the First One, the Queen of the Moon
And in her dance the fish will rise from the rivers,
Imo, Orashi, Dijla
And will drink kegs of palm wine
And with red mouths shall they sing!

Listen to the oracle, Kuru, listen, where there is no sound!
One day, my friend, together, our bodies glistening with raw cocoyam,
We will brush the lands between the rivers
Free of bush rats and lizards
And we will make the music of drum, horn and gere-gere
And day and night we shall sip wine from raffia palm

Until from the land shall rise magical trees, dragonflies, a thousand golden insects
And the tassles of the maize cobs will dance with a joy that flies higher and higher
Even unto the streams of the moon

Listen to the oracle, Kuru, listen, where there is no sound!
Deezian, Deebom, Deemura, Deekor, Deesan,
On that dawn, my friend Kuru, at second cockcrow
Your spirit shall rise from your people, no tomb shall hold them
And all the lizards will lower their brows in humility, in respect
For the children, the land, the dreams
On that day, my friend,
The people of fish, farm and forest, of port, village, metropolis
From Ramallah to Harcourt, from Wounded Knee to Chiapas Mountain
Will rejoice and breathe again,
In Khana, Gokana, Eleme, in all tongues
And their songs shall fill the sky!

Listen to the oracle, Kuru, listen, where there is no sound!
From the shell of your death, arise, O murdered Wise One
Lift your arms above your head, stretch your fingers beyond the bone
Rise up into the river of rivers, the sky's burning mantle,
Tear your face into the skin of a crazy man
Ascend, dear friend, ascend...
Your spirit is our spirit, the ink of our pens flows from your dreams
Take us high into the river of light! Let us see!
Then, at last, through the pebbles of your stories
Like the stars, like the moon, like the living dust
We all will be free

FLOYD SALAS

The Politics of Poetry

After a while they disconnected the wire from my finger
and connected it to my ear
They immediately gave a high dose of electricity
My whole body shook in a terrible way
My front teeth started breaking
At the same time my torturers would hold a mirror to my face and say:
'Look what is happening to your lovely green eyes
Soon you will not be able to see at all.
You will lose your mind.
You see you have already started bleeding in your mouth.'

Torture tactics in Turkey
an urgent appeal on behalf of hundreds of thousands of innocent victims
now suffering the tortures of the damned.
Amnesty International USA

But there is more to torture than the cell
There is a different kind of Hell:
Secret hush of the police sighing
over the snail trails of bookworms
sticking to the leaves of the library
those fakes in pipe and tweeds
just as hard as the street dudes
only wearing a sheepskin over the weeds
or the lines of your smiling face
the sense of the lie behind your grinning teeth
Take them out and dip them in a glass swimming with solvent
murky clouds of lime that will dissolve them in time
Dark sores on the calcium—can't you see it?

Think of never being able to say a word
for fear it will be heard
and transmuted and computed and filed in the appropriate place
deep underground with leaden walls to shrink your balls
catch even your cocktail chatter or the privacy of your bedroom
where you grimace at the mirror and cry in your secret heart

Caught in the web
gossamer traces of it brush your face when you enter a doorway
whispers that still hang in the air
faint fluttering of skirts and hum of static
the pretty girls with robes on beckoning beckoning

You like the animal come home from the hunt in a heat, the battle fought
needing love and the musky smell of sex
carrying your offering wrapped in puffs of cotton with a red silk ribbon and a bow
the selfish beast caged down inside and the angel let loose with beating wings so hard
it makes you thirst
Cushion the force of my lust with your lips
the surge up the middle, the love like bone

holding my head up and my dick
But she doesn't love you
Secret Agent of the Police State set out to warm your heart

Listen. There is more to torture than the coffin of the cell of that Hell
There is more to torture than the blow
the kick in the nuts, the knee in the groin
the smash in the face, the broken nose, the blood in the pee,
the stiff bones and the puffing muscles, the cattle prod, and the bottle up the snatch

Dear poet, how would you like to wake up in your own windowless room
with your heart's blood wetting the bed around you?
the mattress seeping through to the springs with your guts?
blank wall above you? Stone brick around you?
sunk in a concrete hole to keep the worms out
with only the dampness to decompose you?
skin a dull yellow in the cold air?

Waxy odor
The Ghoul has a painted face
With powder and rouge like an actor
he lays in the bed without flowers, without sniffling mothers
and suffering fathers with hands on their hearts
Without family the poet lies. The Holy Days click by
Soon his time will be up, fold him into a drawer
some marks of his name and number, the day he died
just his scratch on the wall, and the unread poem under the bed

There is more to torture than a cell, there is a worse kind of Hell
Still
a brown horse shivers his glossy sides!
twitches his mane!
swishes his tail!

Look!
I can see my shadow!
It gathers at my feet!
moves when I do!
jumps! steps! stops!
trots a little!
turns with me!
as if my toe were the axis of the sun!
and all things good!
and all things true!
turned with it!

MONA LISA SALOY

September 2005, New Orleans

They said, only businesses could come into the city,
first, then residents by zip code. New Orleans is all
of our business, so I went by rent-a-car with the
good husband—Rich—of my dear colleague at DU.
No traffic from Baton Rouge for many miles,
riding along swamp, and southern evergreens
still standing, like tall pines, a few magnolias.

Traffic slowed stacked, like toys, past Causeway
at the 610 split. G.I. Joes in Army fatigues asked:
"State your business."

Once in the neighborhood, the smell of death
laced the streets, covered in debris along the sides,
enough room to pass, with some live wires popping,
no sign of anything alive, no birds chirping, no
'skitoes buzzing, no cats crossing, no dogs running,
no people here, downtown, no cars either, just empty
silence, so loud, like the dead ghost towns of the old west.

New Orleans, a Neighborhood Nation

Possums sleep, middle of the road sometimes,
Invade soggy walls after hurricanes dump heavy rains,
Hide in clothes closets and eat through canvas book bags
Must taste like peanut butter and strawberry jam, the
Pages of wisdom spread like confetti on the floor.

10,000 spiders live in my neighborhood.
What grows wild sticks like thorns
What crawls will bite you red and blue
Roaches spread wings past dusk, invade door jams
We grow, eat, and love okra; there
Ain't no proper gravy without a little slime
Veggie Slimes are us Black folks on this planet

We know folks backwards and forwards
Translate to every little thing, nothing forgotten

Y'all is singular, plural, and a sweet sound in our ears
Festivals are us: shrimp, tomato, rice, crawfish, Blues & Jazz

We throw hissy fits in a heartbeat
Find cayenne, salt, onion, celery, parsley, & thyme on
Yard bird baked, fried, or stewed, even on the other
White meat, anything that swims in a bayou, lake or river:
Catfish, Grouper, Red fish, Crab, Sheephead, Cawain.

Out of bread, whip Galait or fritters deep fried with
Ripe bananas or plantains in season; syrup to taste.

When weather dips below 70, it's gumbo time
Okra, seafood, or beans de jour
Red beans, white beans, butter beans, crowder peas
Plus Black-eyed peas, the eyes of God on us

We still make hucklebucks in summer
Cook suppers to raise bucks for folks stuck between a
Rock & a hard place, and pass potato salad over a
Fence for a backyard barbeque with hot beer and
Hurricane cocktails at sunset in yards or on
Galleries glad for time measured in minutes.

When I saw bodies in Post-Katrina New Orleans

When I saw bodies bent to fold on cars
When I smell death across the lines of fence
Bodies rot soft so left to stink on bars
Whole families broken no recompense
A car's antenna so straight and stuck
On men on boys to fit a shirt so stretched
To keep bodies I see in place just lost
You see their trunks so arched as made to freeze
I would prefer to wake or have them smile
A frame for families such loss to grieve
No one stood straight but limp to snatch a dream
Upward to God for true just grief to scream

RICHARD SILBERG

George Hackett Simpson and the Three Sad Cigarettes

"I'm too old—
I'm too old for this shit!"
as if he could step off the street
his face like gutted flame
into a school for accountancy
limps close on a bad knee
to hit me up for change
and stays to embroider his life
Nam   an improbable
Ph.D. in Physics
rambles in Japanese honor families
"wouldn't back down to no one"
and blurs to a glow
the coming of The Hero
He hits on a street dude for three cigarettes
then refuses one to a pockmarked black man
who begs him to buy it
with some pennies in a cup
pops back at me
ferret intense
"Fuckin' cops" he says
"fuckin' cops"
red dime on his cheek
the size of a bullet hole
"keep telling us to split—
they don't even know what
reality is"
With fawning eyes
he arrogates reality to us
him and me
dreaming atolls
We beat for a while
together in the street lights
the silent night air

LESLIE SIMON

Authorship

I am writing this poem because people have started to call us Nazis

I am writing this poem because, though this is not true, it moves closer to the truth with each child buried beside another child and their mother

I am writing this poem so that I do not forget the fear that manipulates some and the power that drives others

I am writing this poem because I have heard too much and don't know enough

I am writing this poem because ordinary people—the ones who still hate Jews and admit it, the ones who hate Jews but don't admit it, and the ones who struggle with their hatred of Jews, including other Jews—all of these ordinary people, all of them, all of us, do not understand how the starving of a people of food and medicine and then bombing their homes and hospitals and schools will end in anything but the end of these people, the Palestinian people, the cousins of the Jews, who many people still hate

I am writing this poem because I know there are others like me, Jews who grow sick in their dreams at night over the death done in our name

I am writing this poem so that I don't start to call Jews Nazis

I am writing this poem so that anyone who has claimed the name of victim can see the worst that can become of us, the anger that can pull us to pieces as we dismember another one of us

We are all of us writing this poem

JARMILA MARIE SKALNA

Laura

Laura understood beginning writers so well that she served as a judge in many short story competitions. She advised me to read poetry even if I was writing something else. One evening, she opened *Lady of Miracles* by the Romanian poet Nina Cassian. On page twelve she crossed out the word rotting and wrote below it the word stinking.

"Now I prefer the word stinking," she said decidedly and read to me a verse aloud, "No, there's just your cruelty circling my head like a bright stinking halo."

I took her word for it because she could do whatever she wanted with her translation.

"You might think that a poet knows his mother tongue perfectly," she said seriously. "Meanwhile, he's walking in and out of bookstores, making corrections in his book with a pen."

I laughed and asked, "Why didn't I hear much about Romanian literature when I was living in the Czech Republic?"

"I don't know," she responded. "I've heard that Romanians eat breakfast with an open book of poetry, and the poetry of Nina Cassian is a rich breakfast indeed."

On Saint Valentine's Day, I received a card from her. On the bottom, there was an invitation for an evening of poetry and music at Foothill College. I was glad to go there. When Laura recited her poem about how she peeled off leaf after leaf of lettuce and revealed the mystery of love to its very bareness, I realized what nakedness is. It is not difficult to expose one's body. Another time, I sat quietly in the corner of Laura's classroom and listened as she advised the beginning writers, "Wherever you go, remember three things and write them together in your stories like pieces of a puzzle."

Once when I was in Bear Valley, so much snow fell that I almost believed in Santa Claus. I walked with my friends on a white road with white banks reaching up to our waists. Under faint stars, I recalled that I should remember three pieces of a puzzle. Then slow, kind hands caught my attention from a distance. Outstretched hands in the window of a cottage were hanging Christmas ornaments on a lit tree. I didn't know if the hands belonged to a woman or a man. I saw only outstretched hands.

So I asked myself, "What would Laura have said to that?"

The next morning, I saw, between crystals of tender snow, the only imperfection on that mountain—a row of tiny footprints. It must have been a very tiny mouse if those tracks belonged to her. Or they might be from the Mountain Chickadees, hardly two inches tall, who, as the only audible inhabitants on that sunny morning, chirped merrily on spruces ten meters high. Then it occurred to me what they really were.

"Spider!" I shouted.

Everyone laughed on their cross-country skis, but only until they saw a black spider trotting across the snow toward our cabin.

A woman named Erica accidentally fell in the snow and yelled in joy, "It's cold! I didn't know snow was so cold!"

I also fell on the ground, so that I could recall how cold snow feels. But to my surprise, the button on my ski pants suddenly opened at the waist, and the slick pants slid down my legs all the way to my knees. This happened several times that day. My companions saw no humor in it at all, but were only angry at me for slowing them down. I felt ridiculous until that evening, when I found some suspenders.

What would Laura say about my three words—hands, spider, pants—that I put together like a puzzle? As a reward for always thinking of Laura, she invited me to a concert at the Freight & Salvage Coffeehouse in Berkeley, where a Czech musician named Radim Zenkl was playing the mandolin. All evening I held my breath. How quickly and gracefully he played! Especially his own composition *Faraway Over the Mountains*.

"Where did you learn to play so well?" I asked him after the concert.

"In Moravia," he replied, and then threw back a beautiful, long, curly head of hair, of which no horse would be ashamed.

I confided in him that a professor with the same name had taught me music at the University of Ostrava.

He stared at me a minute and said, "That was my father."

Laura said, "It's a small world."

Soon after, she called from the hospital with the hope that her class at Foothill College would resume soon. I bought a big red heart on a card in the Museum of Modern Art in San Francisco and sent it with my love to the Alta Bates Hospital in Berkeley, where only her daughter could read it to her. By then Laura was speaking only in Hungarian.

She died peacefully on December 10, 1993. I opened *Lady of Miracles* to page fifty and read quietly to myself:

My root is gone.
A butterfly pinned to the wall.
We all die, sweet mother,
Hand in hand.

REBECCA SOLNIT

Oakland's Beautiful Nonviolence

Now that we're done remembering the major violence, let's talk about Occupy Oakland. A great deal of fuss has been made about two incidents in which mostly young people affiliated with Occupy Oakland damaged some property and raised some hell.

The mainstream media and some faraway pundits weighed in on those Bay Area incidents as though they determined the meaning and future of the transnational Occupy phenomenon. Perhaps some of them even hoped, consciously or otherwise, that harped on enough these might divide or destroy the movement. So it's important to recall that the initial impact of Occupy Oakland was the very opposite of violent, stunningly so, in ways that were intentionally suppressed.

Occupy Oakland began in early October as a vibrant, multiracial gathering. A camp was built at Oscar Grant/Frank Ogawa Plaza, and thousands received much-needed meals and healthcare for free from well-organized volunteers. Sometimes called the Oakland Commune, it was consciously descended from some of the finer aspects of an earlier movement born in Oakland, the Black Panthers, whose free breakfast programs should perhaps be as well-remembered and more admired than their macho posturing.

A compelling and generous-spirited General Assembly took place nightly and then biweekly in which the most important things on Earth were discussed by wildly different participants. Once, for instance, I was in a breakout discussion group that included Native American, white, Latino, and able-bodied and disabled Occupiers, and in which I was likely the eldest participant; another time, a bunch of peacenik grandmothers dominated my group. This country is segregated in so many terrible ways—and then it wasn't for those glorious weeks when civil society awoke and fell in love with itself. Everyone showed up; everyone talked to everyone else; and in little tastes, in fleeting moments, the old divides no longer divided us and we felt like we could imagine ourselves as one society. This was the dream of the promised land—this land, that is, without its bitter divides. Honey never tasted sweeter, and power never felt better.

Now here's something astonishing. While the camp was in existence, crime went down 19% in Oakland, a statistic the city was careful to conceal. "It may be counter to our statement that the Occupy movement is negatively impacting crime in Oakland" the police chief wrote to the mayor in an email that local news station KTVU later obtained and released to little fanfare.

Pay attention: Occupy was so powerful a force for nonviolence that it was already solving Oakland's chronic crime and violence problems just by giving people hope and meals and solidarity and conversation.

The police attacking the camp knew what the rest of us didn't: Occupy was abating crime, including violent crime, in this gritty, crime-ridden city. "You gotta give them hope," said an elected official across the bay once upon a time—a city supervisor named Harvey Milk. Occupy was hope we gave ourselves, the dream come true. The city did its best to take the hope away violently at 5 a.m. on October 25th. The sleepers were assaulted; their belongings confiscated and trashed. Then, Occupy Oakland rose again. Many thousands of nonviolent marchers shut down the Port of Oakland in a stunning display of popular power on November 2nd 2012.

That night, some kids did the smashy-smashy stuff that everyone gets really excited about. (They even spray-painted "smashy" on a Rite Aid drugstore in giant letters.) When we talk about people who spray-paint and break windows and start bonfires in the street and shove people and scream and run around, making a demonstration into something way too much like the punk rock shows of my youth, let's keep one thing in mind: they didn't send anyone to the hospital, drive any seniors from their homes, spread despair and debt among the young, snatch food and medicine from the desperate, or destroy the global economy.

That said, they are still a problem. They are the bait the police take and the media go to town with. They create a situation a whole lot of us don't like and that drives away many who might otherwise participate or sympathize. They are, that is, incredibly bad for a movement, and represent a form of segregation by intimidation.

But don't confuse the pro-vandalism Occupiers with the vampire squid or the up-armored robocops who have gone after us almost everywhere. Though their means are deeply flawed, their ends are not so different than yours. There's no question that they should improve their tactics or maybe just act tactically, let alone strategically, and there's no question that a lot of other people should stop being so apocalyptic about it.

Those who advocate for nonviolence at Occupy should remember that nonviolence is at best a great spirit of love and generosity, not a prissy enforcement squad. After all, the Reverend Martin Luther King, Jr., who gets invoked all the time when such issues come up, didn't go around saying grumpy things about Malcolm X and the Black Panthers.

BARRY SPECTOR

What Will the New Myths Be? How Will We Create Them?

Interviewers often ask me, "What will the New Myths be? How will we create them?"

These questions imply a characteristic American impatience with "being" in favor of "doing." We are a practical, "can-do" people who prefer the heights of spirit to the depths of soul. But the impulse to move quickly toward solutions may reveal an unwillingness to acknowledge the suffering in our midst, the diminishment of our imagination, the darkness that surrounds us, the massive grief that lies just below the surface.

So I suggest: stop, consider just how rough our predicament *really* is; sit quietly, listen to the soul's lament. Be, in Theodore Roethke's words, "...a god of nature weeping to a tree." Perhaps the proper response to a great ending, of a myth, of a national dream, of the collapse of the environment, is to enter into rituals of mourning, even while continuing to act for healing and renewal. Then, new language may arise, and new visions may come not from us but through us. The paradox grows deeper when we consider Wendell Berry's words: "Be joyful even though you've considered all the facts."

Joseph Campbell said that we can't predict what the new myths will be any more than we can know what we'll dream tonight. But he also said that they won't be local or tribal. Rather, they will express the metamorphoses of all living beings and our interconnectedness with the natural world. And we've had the image for those stories since 1968: the picture of the Whole Earth.

What affects one part of an ecosystem affects the whole system. When one strand in the web of life breaks, the web begins to unravel. Such thinking brings us back to old notions like the anima mundi—the soul of the world—that address us through the unconscious images of dreams and art.

Myths change exceedingly slowly. After all, it took perhaps 5,000 years for the myth of patriarchy to become fully constellated across the planet. And yet, this story has begun to crack in our lifetimes. The growth of feminism (and *spiritual* feminism, and the men's movement that arose in response to it) speaks of the return of the Goddess. This narrative is already approaching mythic proportions not simply because millions entertain its images of female (and black, brown, red, yellow and gay) empowerment, but because it pulls us away from linear history, towards the cyclic processes of nature. This story of times when the genders lived in partnership invites us to imagine our own myth of return (and the return of myth). If it happened once, why can't it happen again?

We all understand the bumper sticker: "She's back, and she's pissed!" Is She utterly inconsolable, or can we welcome Her by remembering things deep in our bones, what the land itself knows, and how our ancestors remembered?

We can invoke her in two ways. First, by restoring the creative imagination. To Lorca, imagination "...fixes and gives clear life to fragments of the invisible reality...." We can replicate the original processes of myth making, by telling as many alternative stories, as often as possible, until, perhaps, they coalesce into world stories.

Secondly, we must engage in the rituals, and do the arts, that bypass what I call the predatory and paranoid imaginations. We must use sacred language, in the subjunctive mode: *let's pretend, what if, perhaps, suppose, make believe, may it be so,* and *play.* Then, says Lorca, we move from dreaming to desiring.

Now, all creative acts have political implications. Dianne Di Prima writes, "The only war that matters is the war against the imagination."

Can we imagine a society like Bali, where people practice all the arts so universally that they have no word for "art?" There, creativity balances the worlds of the living and the unseen. Much healing comes through memory, in creatively reframing one's story. Memory herself,

Mnemosyne, mated with Zeus and birthed the Muses, who reverse the work of Father Time, *Kronos*, the god that eats his children.

The Greek word *xenos* (root of xenophobia) means "stranger," but it also means "guest." We can choose to welcome the demonized Other and invite everything that America has forced outside the gates of the city back inside. When the Stranger becomes the Guest, the darkness that we have required him to hold becomes our blessing. The Muses collected the scattered limbs of dismembered bodies; it was they—art—who reassemble what the madness of the world rips apart.

Ultimately, we heal ourselves and the culture by remembering what we came here to do. This is how we dream new myths. The old knowledge has never completely left us. The spirits could meet us halfway, but they need to know that we're willing. Indeed, the point may not be the content of the new stories, but how we arrive at it.

There is a great hunger, *and* a great opportunity. Long ago, the Persian poet Hafiz wrote:

> *The great religions are ships; poets are the lifeboats.*
> *Every sane person I know has jumped overboard.*
> *This is good for business, isn't it, Hafiz?*

JAYNE LYN STAHL

Did Somebody Order Fireworks?

A homeless guy on
the train
called me classy
last night
The landlord raised
my rent 8%
he must think I'm classy, too.
My insurance company calls me
a "long distance driver"
though I drive
less than 5,000 miles a year and
the ATM says "no funds are
available at this time."
Whose idea of Independence
Day is this anyway?
Even the birds are chirping on
credit
a vendor in front of
Bank of America swears
he's smoking J. Edgar Hoover's
ashes, but where are the fireworks?
no fireworks either when
billions disappear from state
coffers in Iraq and
trillions from the Federal Reserve
where are the fireworks
when one in five children
goes to bed hungry?
The Domino's pizza guy
says they're out of
deep dish
by the time he shows up
I have no appetite.
Heat rises under my feet like
the universe is having hot flashes.
A mechanic vows to find me
new shocks, ones that
can hold up to all these potholes.
I want to believe him.

DOREEN STOCK

The Oil Poem

The hand that holds the pen holds the pump poem.
The stick it in first, second, third, fourth, reverse, taker 'er
out for a spin poem, the over hill over dale we will hit the
dusty trail to Afghanistan, Iraq, bases around the world poem,
the Sky Alliance poem, the Detroit in collapse poem, the lipstick
on big plump lips on the edge of a plastic cup poem, the Mongolian
shaman throat singing save the earth poem, the oil rig and
eleven men blown to Kingdom come poem, the we have to fight
the war to get the oil to fight the war to get the oil to fight the war
to get the oil to fight the war poem.
The anti violence pro peace poem. The anti British Petroleum in cahoots
with US government agencies against the ordinary US citizen poem! This
is the oil poem. The dead bird in the hand of the whole world
that pumps the oil poem. The we need the oil to get off the airstrip poem,
because we all, all of us, how long have we forgotten how to fly?

SUSAN SUNTREE

Lineage

When violence drives its steel points
    through the flesh and wrenches bone from bone,
When lurid greed's harrowing grip
    and the grip of hatred seem to strangle
        any body it chooses
      and rage sounds like the clock ticking
          the heart beating, someone refuses orders
   someone pulls the wounded
        to the side of the road
                  to protect them.

What is love but a vapor, ever present, that we breathe
    that our lives depend upon
        whether we know it or not
      and those whose bodies absorb its grace, act
  and the act is love.

When the count is taken in history books,
                in hindsight,
   a lineage of love
      marks the bloody pages
           like a streak of light.

SUSAN TERRIS

Bald Eagle on Potato Lake

Like the U.S. symbol, the boy whispers between
his kayak and mine, only real and bigger.

From looking-glass water twelve feet away, we
watch the full-grown male, his head achingly white.

While pivoting past a fallen birch, we'd spotted him
poised on rocky ground. Despite the sunfish in his talons,

he seemed, for a moment, an over-large chicken.
Then, wingtips half-spread just like our nation's seal—

yes, that one now bloodied—he twitched his head,
scissored his beak, and singed us with one hot eye.

Though every predator knows the urge to kill,
this eagle kills only to eat. Yet the sunfish,

wedge of turquoise-gold neon in the noonday sun,
is fanning its gills, desperate to survive.

Do something, the boy urges. Scare
him away. Or say that death prayer you know.

For the fish? For all the lost ones? I'm sorry, the boy
calls out to the dying fish. I am sorry!

And the eagle, alerted by the high thin boy-tone,
opens his wings and, still gripping the sunfish,

streaks white and black and murderous just above
our heads. Nature red in beak and talon. Nature

true to its dark nature. And I am sorry, too, I tell the boy.

CLIFFORD E. TRAFZER

Never Enough

Old Chief Joseph agreed to sign the first Nez Perce Treaty in 1855 by which the Nimipu secured for themselves a good portion of traditional lands. In 1861, a few white men found gold on the Nez Perce Reservation, which triggered an unauthorized rush onto Indian land. Neither the Indian Office nor the Army prevented hundreds of miners from invading and remaining on the Nez Perce Reservation. Finally, in 1863, a federal commission proposed to remove the miners from the reservation. Agents offered to remove miners by creating a new treaty and shrink the reservation to one-tenth its original size. When Young Chief Joseph and the recognized chiefs heard this proposal, they left Fort Lapwai without signing. But one Nez Perce leader, appropriately named Lawyer, remained on the council ground and concluded a treaty, with the support of other members of his band—not one of whom was a chief. Government officials quickly sent the new treaty to the Senate for ratification, and President Abraham Lincoln signed it into law. Under the terms of the treaty, the Nez Perce lost 6,932,270 acres for 8 cents per acre, and they called the agreement, The Thief Treaty.

The Thief Treaty and forced removal ultimately caused the famous Nez Perce War of 1877 that killed and wounded many people. The Nimipu made a conditional surrender at the Bear Paw Mountains of Montana, an agreement General Sherman reversed, forcing the prisoners of war to Eekish Pah, the Hot Country of Kansas and Indian Territory where they remained until 1885. The Nez Perce fighters and their Palouse and Cayuse allies never returned to their own homeland but were forced onto reservations. State and federal officials as well as citizens took former Indian land and resources worth billions of dollars. That was not enough. Through the Dawes Severalty Act, the government withdrew more Indian land and resources, and they broke up families, sending Nez Perce children to boarding schools designed to destroy their history, culture, and language. Tuberculosis, pneumonia, and gastro-intestinal disorders killed infants, children, and young adults on the reservations and in the schools. Congresses and Presidents did not support budgets needed by the Medical Division of the Office of Indian Affairs to fight infectious disease or malnutrition.

In the nineteenth century, the state of California stole the land of the Chemehuevi Indians of the Oasis of Mara. In 1875, after claiming the Oasis as state land, state politicians sold Chemehuevi land at the Oasis to the Southern Pacific Railroad. The railroad claimed Indian land and resources, including the water at the Oasis. In the early twentieth century, Indian agents urged the Chemehuevi to move out of the Mojave Desert into an area around Palm Springs, California. When Agent Clara True tried to file a reservation for the Chemehuevi at the Oasis of Mara, she learned Southern Pacific owned the land. A tragic murder and manhunt brought the Chemehuevi into the national spotlight, and in 1910, the Chemehuevi moved several miles to the Cabazon Indian Reservation in Indio, California. Actions of the state, nation, and Southern Pacific Railroad cost the Chemehuevi dearly. They lost their Oasis, resources, and freedom. The Chemehuevi once knew and used thousands of acres in the desert and along the Colorado River where miners took millions in gold, silver, and other precious metals while ranchers grazed herds of cattle and horses. The Chemehuevi ended up with 200 acres in Indio and 120 acres in Twenty-nine Palms. They lost lands and resources, but in 1994, the Twenty-Nine Palms Tribe began high-stakes gaming. Federal agents confiscated two semi-truck loads of slot machines. Chair Dean Mike explained the tribe's response to the loss of these slots was, "We ordered two more truck loads of slots." The Chemehuevi fought their way back from removal and poverty to become a leader of their successful business of Indian gaming. Schwarzenegger sparked a controversy with his fighting words that Indians should pay their fair share, but he had no knowledge or little interest in the history of California's first nations or the theft of their lands and resources.

The Nez Perce and Chemehuevi share a common history with thousands of other Native Americans throughout the Americas that have faced opposition from local, state, and national governments that generally ignore Indian rights to their land and resources. The theft of

Indian land and resources is a re-occurring theme in American history. During the 1990s, I researched a history of American Indians, and in 2000 Harcourt published *As Long as the Grass Shall Grow and Rivers Flow: A History of Native Americans.* Later, Harcourt sold the book to Thompson, and it remains in print. Research for the book led to many discoveries, including overt and destructive racism, bigotry, and theft. Throughout the work, I contemplated a title, "Never Enough," because it became clear that whatever American Indians had, non-Indians wanted. Little has changed. Ignorance prevails, and politicians and corporations want a portion of that which Indians own and earn.

ALMA LUZ VILLANUEVA

Breathing While Brown

*A la gente, to the people, of Arizona, and all those
breathing while brown, black, the human rainbow
—and to my son, Jules Villanueva-Castano
(who works with the dispossessed daily, my hero).*

To the beautiful, brave
young who have always
sat at lunch counters,
racists spitting on them, pulling

their hair, calling them nigger,
killing the brave, young white
students who joined them—the
insane dogs, taking bites of their

tender skin, the insane police who
hose them down, killing pressure
to their knees, take them to hot,
filthy jails, the ones meant

for colored—the beautiful, young
Black Panthers, Brown Berets,
hunted into extinction, AIM at
Wounded Knee, Leonard Peltier in

jail over twenty years, a wise man,
a shaman, after all these years,
knowing the Spirit is always, yes,
always free—Malcolm X,

Mandela knew this, every pregnant
woman knows this, Gandhi
knew this, Aung San Suu Kyi knows
this, the Spirit is always, yes,

always free. I remember my
youngest son followed home
daily in Santa Cruz, Califas, breathing
while brown, I went to the cop

station and had a fucking fit—
what do we do when an entire
state makes it perfectly legal
to punish humans for breathing

while brown—nine young, beautiful,
brown warriors chained themselves
to the Capitol's entrance, that's what
we do, the beautiful, brave

young. Cesar Chavez would be
proud. Martin Luther King would be
proud. Gandhi would be
proud. Dolores Huerta is

proud, of the beautiful,
brave young. And my son
continues to breathe while brown,
always free.

GERALD VIZENOR

Blue Ravens: Native American Indians in the First World War

Aloysius Hudon Beaulieu created marvelous blue ravens that stormy summer. He painted blue ravens over the mission church, blue ravens in the clouds, celestial blue ravens with tousled manes perched on the crossbeams of the new telegraph poles near the post office, and two grotesque blue ravens cocked as mighty sentries on the stone gateway to the hospital on the White Earth Reservation.

My brother was twelve years old when he first painted the visionary blue ravens on flimsy newsprint. Aloysius was truly an inspired artist, not a student painter. He enfolded the ethereal blue ravens in newsprint and printed his first saintly name and surname on the corner of the creased paper. Aloysius Beaulieu, or beau lieu, means a beautiful place in French. That fur trade surname became our union of ironic stories, necessary art, and our native liberty. Henri Matisse painted the Nu Bleu, Souvenir de Biskra, or the Blue Nude, that same humid and gusty summer in France.

The blue ravens were visionary traces and original abstract totems, the chance associations of native memories in the natural world. Aloysius was teased and admired at the same time for his distinctive images of ravens. Frances Densmore, for instance, the renowned ethnomusicologist, attended the annual native celebration and must have seen the blue ravens that summer on the White Earth Reservation. Her academic interests were more dedicated, however, to the mature traditions and practiced presentations of music than the inspirations of a precocious native artist.

President Theodore Roosevelt, that same year, proposed the Hague Convention. The international limitation of armaments was not sustained by the great powers because several nations united with Germany and vetoed the convention on military arms. The First World War started seven years later, and that wicked crusade would change our world forever.

Marc Chagall and my brother would be celebrated for their blue scenes and visionary portrayals. Chagall painted blue dreams, lovers, angels, violinists, donkeys, cities, and circus scenes. He was six years older than my brother, and they both created blue visionary creatures and communal scenes. Chagall declared his vision as an artist in Vitebsk on the Pale of Settlement in Imperial Russia. Aloysius created his glorious blue ravens about the same time on the Pale of White Earth in Minnesota. He painted blue ravens and new reservation scenes, perched over the government school, the mission, hospital, cemetery, and icehouses. Many years later he blued the bloody and desolate battlefields of the First World War in France. Chagall and my brother were the saints of blues.

Aloysius was commended for his godly native talents and artistic portrayals by Father Aloysius Hermanutz, his namesake and the resident priest at Saint Benedict's Mission. Nonetheless the priest provided my brother with black paint to correct the primary color of the blue ravens. The priest was constrained by holy black and white, the monastic and melancholy scenes and stories of the saints. Black was an absence, austere and tragic. Blues were a rush of presence. The solemn chase of black has no tease or sentiment. Black absorbed the spirit of natives, the light and motion of shadows. Ravens are blue, the lush sheen of blues in a rainbow, and the transparent blues that shimmer on a spider web in the morning rain. Blues are ironic, the tease of natural light. The night is blue not black.

Augustus Hudon Beaulieu, our cunning and ambitious uncle, overly praised my brother and provided more blue paint to encourage his artistry. Our determined uncle would have painted blue the entire mission, the face of the priest, earnest sisters, the government school and agents. He has provoked the arbitrary authority of federal agents from the very start of the reservation, and continued his denunciations in every conversation. Our uncle easily provided the newsprint for the blue ravens because he was the independent publisher of the *Tomahawk*, a weekly newspaper on the White Earth Reservation.

Aloysius never painted any images for the priest, black or blue, or for the mission, and he bravely declined the invitation to decorate the newspaper building with totemic portrayals of blue bears, cranes, and ravens. He understood by intuition that our uncle and the priest would exact familiar representations of creatures, and that would dishearten the natural inspiration of any artist who created the visionary sense of native presence. My brother would never paint to promote newspapers or the papacy.

Blue ravens roost on the fusty monuments.

Aloysius was actually a family stray, but he was never an orphan or outcast in the community. He had been abandoned at birth, a newborn ditched at the black mission gate with no name, note, or trace of paternity. My mother secretly raised us as natural brothers because we were born on the same day, October 22, 1895.

We were born in a world of crucial missions unaware of the Mauve Decade and the Gilded Age and yet we created our own era of Blue Ravens on the White Earth Reservation. That same year of our birth Captain Alfred Dreyfus was unjustly convicted of treason and dishonored as an artillery officer in France, and Auguste and Louis Lumière set in motion the cinematograph and screened films for the first time at Le Salon Indien du Grand Café at the Place de l'Opéra in Paris. . . .

MICHAEL WARR

Hallucinating at the Velvet Lounge

To Malachi Thompson (Chicago, April 25, 2004).

When Malachi blew his horn
I dreamed of cornbread, yellow
mounds with burnt edges
on the Velvet's culinary altar.
His sharp cut riffs morphed
into squares of cornbread islands,
floating in streams of warm butter,
clinging to the ribs of my memory.
Speaking in trumpet tongues
of passages and uprisings,
ancient pain and "Good Times" jiving,
sacred beats and blues timing,
drive-by crying and signifying,
an opiate inside of oppression:
a cratered chunk of bacon-infused,
sweet potato, chicken-smothered,
maple-pecan, custard-filled,
smackin' cracklin', jalapeno
enflamed, cornbread—the crepe
of the slaves, now sold
at Whole Foods, in this
jazz-drenched town, built
of golden bricks, and smoke
stacks billowing fumes of corn
on the cob and catfish.
My mind lost in music
and metaphysics, reminiscing
the Sunday manna served
beside my Mother's succotash.

HARRIET A. WASHINGTON

Thalidomide Redux: Prudence and the Pill

A momentous act of prudence stands out as the US Food and Drug Administration's shining hour. In 1962, doubts about its safety testing led Dr. Frances Oldham Kelsey to recommend against approving the German drug thalidomide for the prevention of insomnia and morning sickness in pregnant US women, even though it had been distributed in Europe since 1957. Its marketer, Merrell-Richardson, threatened a lawsuit in response.

Kelsey was correct. Thalidomide is a teratogen, that is, a drug that causes birth defects which it triggered in at least 10,000 children in 46 countries. These children were born with phocomelia, which is characterized by internal organ damage and missing or dramatically shortened limbs.

But only 16 American children were affected, and the FDA takes justified pride in having saved Americans from sharing in this global tragedy.

Unfortunately, today's largely overwhelmed FDA lacks the effectiveness and independence of the agency Kelsey knew, according to a 2006 report by the Institute of Medicine entitled "The Future of Drug Safety: Promoting and Protecting the Health of the Public." The report found major deficiencies in the FDA's system for ensuring that medications on the US market are safe.

Moreover, the agency now depends upon the very drug makers whose products it evaluates for approximately 40 percent of testing costs, presenting a conflict of interest that seems to have upset the balance of power between the agency and the industry it regulates.

Even Dr. David Graham, Associate Director of the FDA's Office of Drug Safety, told the Senate Finance Committee in 2005 that "the scientific standards CDER [The FDA's Center for Drug Evaluation and Research] applies to drug safety guarantee that unsafe and deadly drugs will remain on the U.S. market."

Worst of all, evidence is rife of a "Cassandra effect" as the US has been bedeviled by a recent spate of FDA-approved bad drugs. Initially decried by their FDA evaluators, medications such as the diabetes drugs Rezulin and Avandia as well as the COX-2 pain relievers Celebrex, Vioxx and Bextra were approved, widely marketed, and then ignominiously withdrawn from the market in the wake of injuries, deaths and reports of unacceptable medical side effects and risks.

In 1998, the FDA approved thalidomide for the lesions of Hansen's disease, or leprosy, and its close analogue lenalidomide, was approved for the blood cancer multiple myeloma. Today the maligned drug graces pharmacists' shelves in Europe and the US and occupies center stage in at least 36 ongoing research studies in the developing world—with the FDA's blessing.

How could this be? Partly because Westerners' memory of the tragedy fades with each succeeding generation and because people in Third World test sites have no previous experience with thalidomide. The drug's identity is further blurred as it marketed under unfamiliar names such as Synovir and lenalidomide and it is being tested on research subjects in Brazil, Nigeria and other countries of the developing world.

Despite the staggering emotional impact of its side effects, its risks must be weighed against the drug's potential benefits. The risk of birth defects is clearly unacceptable in the 1950s usage to stem vomiting and sleeplessness.

But today, thalidomide is prescribed for life-threatening conditions and the risk of birth defects can be minimized by mandating that fertile women use two contraceptive methods while taking the drug. So in the industrialized West, where robust ethical protections, monitoring and multiple forms of contraception are widely available, the risks seem manageable.

But in the developing world, the risks are not manageable. A November 2009 The New England Journal of Medicine study revealed that one in three US clinical-study sites is abroad, most of these in developing countries. Women in the thalidomide studies often are not adequately warned of the need for contraceptives, and poor women in developing nations lack the funds, access and the power to negotiate their use.

Medical monitoring is scarce. The World Health Organization "did not set up any advisory body to monitor the side-effects, or even to record how many patients were being treated," accuses Dr. Colin Crawford, a leprologist at London's Imperial College School of Medicine.

As a result, a 1994 Brazilian study found 61 people born after 1965 with birth defects ascribed to thalidomide and a 2011 *Public Library of Science* paper validated these concerns.

Although some researchers cited Brazil's high rate of leprosy as a rationale for conducting trials there, the research will not benefit Brazilians and Nigerians who, as a rule, cannot afford expensive branded Western medications and therefore constitute neglected pharmaceutical markets. Of the 1,233 drugs licensed globally between 1975 and 1997, pharmaceutical companies developed only four new medications to treat human diseases of the tropics. Countries like Nigeria and Brazil bear the risks of thalidomide without reaping its benefits.

This inequitable distribution of risks and benefits means that thalidomide trials should be suspended in poor developing nations and be confined to the US, UK, Europe and nations whose citizens can benefit and where its hazards can be better controlled.

ERIC MILES WILLIAMSON

Back to Oakland

Last month I went back to Oakland, my hometown, the town I was raised in, and my father before me, and his father before him. I hadn't been back for over 20 years, since my father died. I've been trying to escape that town ever since I can remember.

The reason I went back was to receive the PEN Oakland Josephine Miles Literary Award for my most recent book of fiction. PEN is an international writers organization, and Oakland is a local branch. Norman Mailer won the award once, and the *New York Times* called it "the blue collar PEN," probably not in a flattering context. I'm proud of it, though, winning the "blue collar PEN." I've got my laborer's card, Local 304, Oakland, California, in my pocket as I write this. All my novels are set in the Bay Area, and my characters are the workers I grew up with and toiled with and bled with and drank with, the men and women who reared me. When I got off the plane and into the arc-welded ozone air where I could smoke a cigarette, the first person I saw was a shirtless man with hippie hair and an Oakland Raiders logo tattooed beneath his chest fur. I made my way to the Alamo car rental booth ($9.00 a day—it's Oakland, after all), and behind the counter was a large black woman in a purple dress, fake pearl necklace and fingernails long as chisels and painted red. She asked for my license and my credit card, which I gave her, and to which she laid scrutiny. My driver's license is Texas, by the way, has been since 1986, my first tour down here.

I was dressed in my usual duds: a heavy flannel shirt, open, a white wife-beater undershirt, torn Levi's, beaten-up cowboy boots, my 30 year-old black Stetson fedora.

She gave me the up-down with her quick eyes. "You from here," she said, and she cut me a look.

"What?" I said. "What's the deal? What gives me away?"

"It's in your blood," she said. She didn't laugh. She looked at me hard, a chastisement, an accusation, a look that condemned me for abandoning my home.

I walked toward my rental car in shame.

My last night in Oakland I walked from my hotel along Hegenberger, which was under construction, a train line being built to the airport. Homeless people huddled in corners under makeshift shelters of construction debris. At the convenience store an old black man wearing layers of shirts and jackets stood outside shivering.

"You okay?" I said.

"No," he said. "Man won't let me in the store to buy some food." His hands, buffed slick from toil, shone like weathered chrome.

"What you need? You need a beer?"

"No. I need food and a soda," he said. "Food," he said. "And a soda."

I walked to the bullet-proof glass and the attendant talked to me through the slit in the window. "What do you want," he said.

"Beer and food," I said. "And a soda."

He buzzed the door and let me in. He had a foreign accent. "You're not from Oakland," I said.

"Algeria."

I started talking to him in French. I said, "You of all people should know that just because someone's black and not white doesn't make him a thief. How they treat you folks in Paris?"

"I have never been to Paris," he said.

"You're in Oakland now. You're the foreigner, not him."

"I cannot tell here in America," he said. "I cannot tell who is a thief."

"That's not your job," I said. "It's your job to sell the man a sandwich."

Outside I gave the man his sandwich and his soda. "Know why he let me in and not you?" I said.

"Cause you white," he said.

"The fuckers," I said. "Want a beer?"

"Just soda," he said.

A police cruiser pulled into the parking lot and drove past us slow. I looked at him and nodded. He drove on.

"If I hadn't been here would that cop have run you off?" I said.

"Damn straight."

"You from here?" I said.

"Born and raised," he said. "Can't you tell?"

"Me too."

"I know," he said. "Ain't no white man not from Oakland buy me a sandwich and a soda."

When the cops, when the convenience store clerks, when the factory workers and cabbies and teachers realize that the great issue in working class America is not race, but class, only then will we have a better nation.

I had to catch my plane. I shook hands with my new friend. He got a look of serious. He said, "We all in this together. Oakland isn't a town, it's a race."

I was home.

A.D. WINANS

Dancing with Words

There are poets who like
To dance with words
Dance for favors and grants
But dancing for an audience
Isn't like moving
To the music on your own
Stirring the notes of the soul

Fame kills
Billie Holiday's ghost attests to this
Money pigeonholes
Power corrupts
The spiritual truth
The scriptures tell us this

The true poet knows this
Stands tall above
The dancing with word poets
Who are little more than
Instruments of a poem greater
Than themselves

Be like Walt Whitman
Walk blood stained battlefields
Real and imagined

Forsake the minds ego
Be like the people of Egypt
Risking life and limb
For their beliefs
Be like your sister and brother in Wisconsin
Fighting for worker rights
Love them become one with them
Take to the streets
Shout your poems from rooftops
In solidarity with them

Whitman was the champion of poetry
Going the full fifteen rounds
Standing tall and fearless
Among the enemy
Which is never really man
But the poison in his soul
Pride envy and lust

How can those afflicted with the disease
Of egomania jealousy
For fame and fortune
Write about and from the heart?

One column of media praise is of less value
Than a single tear drop on a poem
From a waitress in a greasy
Road stop diner

These dancing with word poets
Know nothing of genius
How can cockroaches evaluate eagles
The true poets' topic is people
Not the poet.

KOON WOON

The Phantom of the Opera

I can see hundreds of thousands of military boats
in the Peking Opera sung by a phantom chorus,

And in each boat, there is a tender nerve, sensitized to
each new-born cry, and maybe tonight music will turn to war,

and neither war nor newborn will be categorized.
The peaceful invasion of opium has been reversed.

In my little room with the window propped open by a stack
of poetry books, kitchenware and dish soap on the counter,

the bed unmade. I had slept with a cheaply dyed shirt
and my sweat made it seemed I was bleeding into the sheets,

and now I know, The Phantom is a wave that moves across
the crests of the Pacific waters, while in this little room,

I have picked up and lay my pen down each morning
for three years without any significant revelation except

the premonition that we are closer to war.

After each violent storm, knick-knacks from Asia litter our beaches,
and the undertow is still just as strong and violent

As you put your coins into the parking meter
you will spend the rest of your life shopping in China,

Where the credit is good and each village has its own Phantom

But even there the homeless man makes empty gestures
and an impotent curse; he says take your five dollars bills and your pennies,

The currencies with Lincoln's face and liberate your own slaves.

The high walls I cannot scale
(with apologies to Tu Fu)

Desolate in my Chinatown morning,
among the scraps and people sleeping in urine
doorways, I ache from the politics of the heart.

Pigeons flock together in Hing Hay Park,
no children to greet them.
I walk for my sanity, since alone in my room
before dawn, the mind constructs improbable things.

The city is humming for profits
and I wait for the porridge place to open.
A bowl of sampan porridge
adorned with a clump of watercress.

These Chinese and I are one, scattered
in the four corners of the globe.
I only have enough to pay for one bowl
and so sorry, my friend, I must dine alone.

A Smoke Break at the Nuclear Command

We multitask chop, grill, wok, and pickle.
They are fickle, can come all hours, drunk,
after sex, before meetings, during greetings;
hucksters, gangsters, no telling who wants what
stir-fried, steamed rock cod with its head and bulbous eyes.

My father at the meat block hacks spareribs, carves bone from chicken,
mince onions, six sons chow the mein, French-fry the sausage,
whip the gravy, beat the eggs until you can fool the young
into thinking that's sperm yanked from a calf.
Smoke signals say the pork chops are burnt,
the white sauce turning yellow and the waitresses ladle the soup.
Sounds like feeding at the zoo. Chopsticks tingle from a corner booth.

On and on motors start and stop, door open and shut, ice water
set down as menus are tossed. You need a minute? Mom is helping the girls to wash
glasses and tea pots. It would be sinful to run out of hot mustard during the rush.
My father drinks my coffee and I smoke his Marlboro,
Two cowboys in cattle drive fending off rustlers, and damn!
The waitress says that the women's toilet has overflowed!

We are going to go fishing as soon as our mental breakdowns are over with.
And we are going to take a smoke break from the nuclear command.
Just then a party of 12 comes in — well, put two tables together,
like a man joining a woman, the yin and yang, and kids with yo-yo's.
We are family doing family business, money for school books,
Mom's dentures.

SUE OWENS WRIGHT

Homed For The Holidays: A Christmas Wish for Homeless Pets

Elvis Presley sang a song about a Blue Christmas, but if you want to see a real blue Christmas, pay a visit to the dog pound on December 24, as I did last year. Following a tip from a friend about a stray female basset hound, I steeled myself to visit what had to be the saddest place on earth that foggy Christmas Eve.

What I found there was the antithesis of the charming childhood *Lady and the Tramp* tale of the adorable, curly-coated pup wrapped up in a beribboned box that would be opened on Christmas morning. A Disney-reared youth myself, I also grew up believing the myth of the puppy under the Christmas tree as the must-have gift, but that was a cartoon, of course. What I saw at the animal control facility that evening was the grim reality behind the fairy tale ending.

Many of these abandoned dogs were probably once adorable puppies given as gifts one Christmas, pups like Disney's Lady, who had the misfortune to grow into adult dogs that are no longer small and cute. Like her, they end up chained to a doghouse or caged in the city pound. It's doubtful their owners gave any thought beforehand to the physical and behavioral characteristics of the breed, how much food it would consume, the expenses associated with keeping a dog, and myriad other factors one should always carefully consider before embarking on the responsibility of dog ownership.

I had been to this place many times before, but this was a silent night like none I had ever witnessed at Christmastime. Usually when I visit the pound where I have adopted several of my dogs, I can hear the cacophony of barking and howling from the parking lot. When I entered the door, not a creature was stirring, and not even a whimper could be heard throughout the facility. I saw dogs curled up on the hard kennel floor, regarding me with the saddest eyes I have ever seen. Never before had I visited the pound at any time of day when the dogs did not eagerly approach every passerby with searching eyes, licking people's hands through the chain link, pleading for liberation from their fate.

This night there was an overwhelming air of sadness and resignation emanating from every kennel that haunted the place like Scrooge's ghosts. I'm certain the dogs understood that they were spending Christmas alone and forsaken instead of with their families, where they well knew they should be on this night.

According to a report by the County of Sacramento Municipal Services Agency, most people surrender their pets because they cannot afford to spay or neuter them. Over 50 percent of the pets surrendered will be euthanized because there are not enough homes for the number of pets being born. When you consider that the average female is capable of bearing 15 offspring per year, the numbers are staggering. As the report states, "To end the euthanasia of adoptable animals, spay and neuter services must be available to everyone within our community."

I didn't locate the stray basset I had come to find. I discovered that she was one of the lucky ones that had been adopted. Honestly, I was relieved because I knew that as much as I wanted to adopt her, I really couldn't accommodate one more dog in my home. I would have loved to rescue every dog at the shelter, but as much as you want to save them all, you know you can't.

Passing through the lobby, I saw a man and his two children, who held two squirming lab pups in their arms. They were in the process of surrendering the puppies, probably in the vain hope that someone would adopt them for a Christmas present at the zero hour.

As I left, I made a wish for all of the dogs and cats spending a lonely Christmas Eve in this pound and every pound or shelter across America. I wished that all of the people who are as lonely and forlorn at the holidays as the animals I saw, and those who are in need of a faithful friend who will never forsake them and who can provide a loving home for a homeless pet, would pay a visit to the pound and adopt one of them. If every person who was able to adopt a dog or a cat would do so, the pound would be silent on Christmas Eve because it would be empty—at least for a little while.

No, the dog wouldn't be discovered under the tree on Christmas morning wrapped in a fancy box with a big bow, as Lady was, because this dog's rescuer would understand before bringing her home for the holidays that a dog is not just for Christmas; it's for life.

AL YOUNG

Four Septembers

1
He'd been her lover, her tutor, her savior, her guide. Side by side they'd hugged the night before on the posh, new bed in a roomy, mostly still-empty Village flat she'd found for them to move in together. No more trading worlds. Now web exec and master chef could walk to work if they wished. Then sip by sip and puff by puff and pricey pill by pill, her biggest wish grew therapies and whopping doctor bills. She wanted time to stop and wind him back. On her little brother's tip, she acted fast. Flew west to land herself a sweet executive chef slot in foodie-rich L.A. She made new friends; they shared each others' blues. September sticks, refueling her with tears. But never enough to snuff the smell, the smoke, the tender catch at the throat; her migraine-deep desire to die just like her lover: in a slick, sick, go-for-broke, grand-slam hoodunit still stubbornly, heartbreakingly unsolved.

2
On wobbly tiers of black plastic trash bags, his ancient laptop leans. Chipped, funky, scarred and scratched—it's all he needs for now. Positioned outside a stark Gilroy McDonald's, he can pick up enough of a wi-fi wave, wake just enough with an any-size coffee, check enough email and Facebook and YouTube to still feel close enough to summer and its dawning sun to maybe reach fall half-full.

3
Her surrender to September, her sad back-to-school time, hadn't always spooked her out. Not from jump. From Head Start and K she could sing or even dance out her family's landline, mobile, and street numbers. By fifth grade they no longer had an address. She remembers a number of fun Septembers; some in the stuffy van when they all five would crash in the big box store lot, Richmond, where Mom still worked half-time. Camped out there, she and Briana cheered their father and Kevin's breeze-helped football throws. To sometimes keep warm, she and Briana would squeeze into the same dull sleeping-bag. Big Kevin had his own. Mom and Pops up under their comforter never really sounded comfortable. Let's don't even talk about a bathroom. When Costco up and painted a fat stoplight red all around the parking lot, overnighters like them had to haul ass fast. Hurt she'd just as soon forget. Weirdness September jump-starts.

4
In the fresh, gorgeous light of a Venice September, story-ready, both ear canals well cleansed, he walks the fabled boardwalk. He loves it for the sunny stage it sets; he knows its needy stars and acrobats. A few know him. He needs no monkey-do tattoo. He doesn't want his fortune read. A thrilling lunch—that's all he wants. He's old enough to recall when The Holy Barbarians hit, Lawrence Lipton's book about the Venice arts bohemia. Soon came San Francisco poet-chronicler Herb Caen, who called his city Baghdad By the Bay, who linked Beat to the Soviet Sputnik to come up smart with Beatnik. He knows about the tobacco tycoon who'd first set Venice up. He knows the years it suffered, nicknamed Slum By the Sea. Slum clearance melted into urban renewal and then came gentrification. He wonders what kids see when they look dead out at him? An oldster full of history and content they'd rather Google than hear him tell? Singing softly to himself, he lets September go.

One August Summary

The scents of summer, once so moist and vast,
now scorch your nose. O how your pricked eyes water!
This fire's going to last and last and last
until your in-laws, wife, two sons and daughter
collapse among the Pepsis, Cokes and chips.
The makeshift rescue center, where you've learned
some distant neighbors' names from their own lips,
fills still with losers just like you. Hurt. Burnt.

A dry La Niña winter, snow-melt, drought
(July: Colfax, June: Colorado Springs,
New Mexico) let heated winds strike out
across your parchment landscape with a zing
that flared up like a sulphurous safety match.
But here's the catch: Can this mean climate change
is real? Do savvy Californians watch
what happened back in 2009, the range
of wildfires: Santa Barbara, Santa Cruz
(their so-called Lockheed Fire), the Station Fire
near L.A? Half a million square miles. News.
You sweat. Your wife and family, they perspire.

Août! Août! Août! Août!—August, moaned in French,
needs no translation. You can smell and feel
the fall and peel of summer. Inch by inch
you sink into this smoky state. You reel.
You suddenly realize what really counts:
You're still alive. Don't underestimate
again how unseen danger creeps and mounts.

Ooo, ooo, ooo, ooo—August stops you at its gate!

ANDREA ZAWINSKI

What About a Fight?

What is it that balls a man's fists into sudden rage,
jabbing and blocking, body weaving and swaying—
a poker bet gone bad, tiff over a last shot and beer,
wrong song on the jukebox, something the other guy
said years ago to the woman he didn't marry anyway?

What is it, when the brawl tumbles into the street,
rubberneckers honking horns, grunting OohRah!
even when one face is already kissing the pavement?
No Sugar Ray or Ali, what drives the everyday Joe,
digs in so deep, courses across scarred knuckles,
the broken tooth, blackened eye, flattened nose?

They say my father liked a fight. Was it his old juvie record
trumping determination or hope, his annulled marriage
to a bigamist collecting veteran's checks, or layoffs at the mill
just before benefits kicked in, a monotony of existence?

What of those of us who years later toss and turn over
brutal thoughts that won't abate, still hearing the screech
of a police car hitting the curb, the smack of the body
slamming the asphalt? They say my father liked a fight.

And as they carted him off to jail again, what of the wife—
my mother behind the window's bent blind slat
who, as the cruiser takes off, she thinking I am not there
to hear her own wounded spirit sigh, says:
"Finally, maybe now I can get a good night's sleep."

APPENDIX A

The History of PEN Oakland

PEN Oakland, the brainchild of writer and activist Ishmael Reed, was launched in fall, 1989, at the Asmara Restaurant on Telegraph Avenue in Oakland at a lunch meeting hosted by Ishmael with soon-to-be co-founders Floyd Salas, Reginald Lockett and Claire Ortalda. Here Reed outlined the idea of forming a multicultural branch of PEN to, as Jack Foley would later write, "promote works of excellence by writers of all cultural and racial backgrounds and to educate both the public and the media as to the nature of multi-cultural work."

An organizational meeting was convened at the Before Columbus offices at Preservation Park in Oakland, with invitations going out to a wide range of Bay Area writers. From that well-attended and somewhat noisy meeting, a core group emerged. In addition to the original four at the lunch meeting, Jack Foley, John Curl, Adelle Foley, Kim McMillon, Gary Soto and Jesse Beagle began the hard work of fashioning an organization.

One of the first goals was achieving affiliation with PEN, the international organization of poets, essayists, and novelists. The fledgling group, with its potential to bring in significant new membership, was courted by both PEN Center USA West in Los Angeles and PEN American Center in New York. The group affiliated with PEN Center USA West in early 1990, billing itself as the "first multicultural chapter of PEN."

Within months, PEN Oakland had hosted a standing-room-only fundraiser featuring Isabel Allende and Maxine Hong Kingston, who donated their talents, and secured funding from the California Arts Council's Multicultural Entry Grant program. Vice President Reginald Lockett and member Jesse Beagle applied for —and received— a California Council for the Humanities grant for the PEN Oakland program, "Oakland Out Loud," a reading/symposium on historical Oakland writers. The name for PEN Oakland's first anthology and attendant reading series sponsored by the Oakland Public Library derived from that early program.

The group also launched their PEN Oakland Josephine Miles Literary Awards, named after poet Josephine Miles, the University of California professor famed for her encouragement of fledgling poets. National in scope, the PEN Oakland Josephine Miles Literary Awards represented "a new perception of multicultural literature that did not seek validation from the literary establishment, but created its own standards and models of literature" (Foley).

In 1997, the first annual Literary Censorship Awards were inaugurated to challenge censorship within the literary culture of the United States, including all aspects of the publishing process, as well as considerations of inclusion/exclusion as they pertained to distribution, reviews, library acquisition, and academic conferences. A noted recipient of the Censorship award was the late Gary Webb, for his daring expose in a series of articles in the *San Jose Mercury News* and later in his book, *Dark Alliance*, of the CIA/Contra/cocaine connection, which cost him his career and later his life.

In 1991, spearheaded by a number of well-placed articles by Ishmael Reed, PEN Oakland launched its most audacious and publicized event, a nationwide call for a thirty-day tune-out of prime time network news (ABC, CBS, NBC and CNN) to protest televised racism, including depiction of minorities, and to highlight the lack of a significant number of minority, women and alternate-voice journalists in major newsrooms. An Open Mic at Lakeside Garden Center in Oakland, attended by more than 400 people, kicked off a nationwide series of lectures and readings given around the country to discuss media abuses of women, people of different ethnic and religious backgrounds and sexual orientations. The media boycott received coverage in *The New York Times*, ABC-TV's San Francisco affiliate (Channel 7), *The Washington Post*, *Spin* magazine, *The Nation* and many other nationwide news forums.

Prior to this series of successes, Reed pressed for a more independent platform on which to both celebrate the work of multicultural writers and to lay bare the problems faced by marginalized peoples worldwide, as related to written expression, including media depictions and de facto censorship and suppression.

Floyd Salas, now elected president, and Claire Ortalda, secretary-treasurer, were dispatched to the PEN International conference in May, 1990, in Funchal, Madeira, Portugal, to petition the world-wide body for a third United States center. The bylaws of PEN International call for one center per country, except in countries with more than one official language, such as Switzerland, in which one center is allowed for each language, or in countries of large size and population, such as the United States, with its two centers. What Reed and Salas were proposing was a third center, based not on population or language but on ethnicity. PEN Oakland was to be that center, focusing on multicultural issues not just in the United States, but in the world at large.

"PEN Oakland represents multicultural writers in the United States who produce a different literature, written in the same language as the mainstream, commercial writers of America, just as the former colonies of European countries produce a different literature written in the same language as their former European masters," Salas stated in a speech at the conference. "Our literature is different because it gives a different perspective on the American social strata and its problems than the status quo writers…We feel the dissemination of these multi-ethnic literatures will go a long way toward promoting harmony between the races in our country in what continues to be an immigrant society."

Salas' motion, in the face of entrenched opinion and without benefit of being on the official agenda, was handily sidelined by the governing body of PEN International but it excited the attention of the exiled Eastern European writers (one year after the Berlin Wall had fallen and playwright, Solidarity leader and PEN member Vaclav Havel had been elected president of Czechoslovakia), key African writers, and attendees from PEN Center USA West.

The president of PEN Center USA West, Carolyn See, immediately invited Salas and Ortalda to lunch and the first chapter rights were hammered out there: a yearly stipend, a voting member on the PEN Center USA board, a column in the newsletter, use of the center's non-profit ID number for grants, and the promise to encourage the formation of other chapters.

At the same international conference, Salas introduced a media resolution, authored by Reed, which called for PEN to demand more equitable reporting of ethnic and racial minorities in the media. This, too, did not reach the floor, but it was re-introduced in November, 1991, by Gerald Nicosia, at the conference in Vienna. Nicosia strenuously fought for the resolution, with the support of the Nigerian delegate and a few others. The resolution, in watered-down form, stating that PEN should encourage fair reporting on minorities in the media, was passed the following year.

Locally, PEN Oakland continued to offer symposia on the written word and its societal impacts, with the support of such sponsors as the California Arts Council, the City of Oakland, the Lef Foundation, the Zellerbach Foundation, the East Bay Community Foundation, Before Columbus and the Oakland Public Library. In addition, PEN Oakland produced "An Evening of Dangerous Plays," at the Berkeley Repertory Theater, *Domestic Crusaders*, a play about a Muslim Pakistani-American family's efforts to deal with the aftermath of 9/11 at various venues, and "4x4 Plays: Staged Readings," and "Short Plays," the latter two at the Live Oak Theater in Berkeley. At the instigation of Kim McMillon, PEN Oakland's chief program manager, PEN Oakland sponsored the Oakland Literature Expo portion of the City of Oakland's Art & Soul Festival from 2001 through 2005.

PEN Oakland, an all-volunteer organization with limited funding, has, for the past twenty-five years, been a voice for the issues of marginalized peoples through a series of hard-hitting forums in which important issues often ignored by the mainstream media are aired and debated. At the same time, we have brought national attention to multicultural literature through our awards program.

- Claire Ortalda, Treasurer, PEN Oakland

APPENDIX B

The United States Needs a New PEN Center

Since the 1960s, new American writing communities have arisen which include multi-cultural writers, those who know the cultures of Latin America, African-America, Asian-America, as well as European culture. The multi-cultural writer views the European tradition as one among many of the world's traditions.

Though the names of these writers, black, Hispanic, and Asian-American, are well known in African, Asian, European, British and Irish universities, in the Unites States, the multi-cultural writers have been met with either a condescending acceptance of a few, or silence, or even resistance. These few are usually assimilationists, who preach the acceptance of "mainstream" American values, and in the United States "mainstream" is a code name for "white."

The multi-cultural writers are considered "ethnic" and "narrow" in American literary publications that would be considered, on a global scale, to be provincial.

Reflecting the growing dissatisfaction of a number of American writers with the country club American literary organizations and their all-white leadership, PEN Oakland was organized in 1989 to actively recruit, not only Asian American and African American and Hispanic writers, but American European writers as well. Currently, we are a chapter of PEN Center USA West, located in Los Angeles. To better serve working class and multi-cultural writers, we recently petitioned PEN International in London for Center status.

Instead of being welcomed, our request for center status, made to PEN secretary Elizabeth Patterson, was met with unfriendly letters. She sought to discourage us on the grounds that we are recruiting members on the basis of race, when our organization includes more European American writers than the other PEN organizations, including blacks, Hispanics and Asian Americans. In a second letter, she suggested that we are violating the PEN charter. She suggests that we attempt to reform the other PEN organizations, one of which was criticized by American writers, including E.L. Doctorow, for having the image of a club patronized by the rich.

We disagree with Ms. Patterson. We feel that we can better use our energies to create a new American PEN center that would extend from Northern California to the North Pole. We want to put our energies to fight against censorship, not only when it occurs abroad, but to fight the subtle forms that American censorship takes, the inability of minority writers to respond to a corporate media which daily batters minority groups in a manner reminiscent of a propaganda bureau for a nation at war. We would better serve the American cultural community by fighting the repression of black and Latin music lyrics, which American legislatures are attempting to ban. Already, record store clerks have been arrested for selling lyrics written by black writers. We feel that the well-heeled writers of the other PENs couldn't possibly understand the grievances of the working class American writers—writers who can't possibly afford to attend their banquets with the rich.

While South Africa seems to be making progress toward the ending of apartheid, even according to its severest critics like Jesse Jackson, the leading literary organizations in the United States still maintain an all white leadership.

Hispanic-American Floyd Salas, president of PEN Oakland, the only multi-cultural PEN in the United States, and Italian-American Claire Ortalda, secretary-treasurer, were refused delegate status, and though we pay dues to PEN Center USA West, its President didn't even return my letter and phone calls requesting delegate status for Mr. Salas and Ms. Ortalda.

The composition of the American delegation to this congress does not reflect contemporary American writing, nor does it reflect the American future. It's time for a change in our literary structures. For how can our country preach diversity to the world, when its cultural and intellectual organizations don't practice diversity at home? As Martin Luther King, Jr. once said:

"If not now, when?"

We are requesting that this congress do the right thing and reflect the democratic changes that are sweeping the world by passing the resolution granting PEN Oakland center status, and by doing so, admit other points of view to the American discourse.

-Ishmael Reed, Chairman of the Board, PEN Oakland

Note: *This appeal to the 55th World Congress of International PEN for the creation of a third United States PEN Center dedicated to multicultural writers was formally denied on Thursday, May 10, 1990, by Interim President Per Wastberg. [See Appendix C.]*

APPENDIX C

PEN 55th World Congress - Funchal, Madeira, Portugal

The stand of PEN Oakland, now a branch of PEN Center USA west, is based upon Principle Number 4 of the PEN Charter, which states that PEN stands for the principle of unhampered transmission of thought within each nation and between all nations. It states that members pledge themselves to oppose any form of suppression of freedom of expression in the country and community to which they belong as well as throughout the world, whenever this is possible. It further states that "a free criticism of governments, administrations and institutions is imperative."

PEN Oakland represents multicultural writers in the United States who produce a different, literature, written in the same language as the mainstream, commercial writers of America, just like the former colonies of the European countries produce a different literature written in the same language as their former European masters. Our literature is different because it gives a different perspective on the American social strata and its problems than the status quo writers.

We, the multicultural, non-commercial writers of America, are like a colony within America because we are suppressed by corporate fascism which only chooses writers for publication, media attention and fame who give the corporate image of a falsely idyllic America back to the corporation which publishes them. We are suppressed by these right-wing attitudes of selfishness based upon the commercial, profit-motivated interests of the mercantile powers, the business conglomerates which now control publishing. Only writing that has no important social, moral or critical point to make gets published, unless the writer is already famous and can earn the conglomerates a healthy profit, in which case, the critical view is then acceptable. The conglomerates are not institutions to stand on principle.

We can't express our views of our experience truthfully and succeed in the publishing world in the United States. We remain unpublished and unread in our own country. As Per Wastberg, PEN Interim president, said in his opening speech, "the writer's freedom is endangered by the high-tech, economic propaganda of the industrialized countries because he depicts Hell rather than Paradise, because he is basically antisocial and has no superior to account to. He needs not only the freedom from but the freedom to write freely." Which I interpret to mean that commercial art is economic propaganda of the corporate state. Our American society is wanting and we see it and write about it. Its problems become our plots. Because we write about these problems from our view as victims, because of our critical perspective, literary acceptance and publication is withheld, regardless of the merit of our writing. In turn, the American public and the world suffer from non-publication of ethnic and minority writing which depict a non-stereotyped view of contemporary America. We feel the dissemination of these multi-ethnic literatures will go a long way toward promoting harmony between the races in our country in what continues to be an immigrant society, and in the world community of nations.

We as writers are denied the rights of writers as surely as if we were put in prison. Because our view is critical, we are denied publication and the attention of the mass media. We suffer from pre-publication censorship and need a voice, a way to be heard, and international PEN is our best opportunity to remedy this.

We ask all the delegates and members of PEN, including the officers, to live up to their words and ideals and grant us the status of a PEN center so we can represent ourselves, so our voice can be heard, so that PEN can recognize we are a colony within the mother country just like the former colonies of the Third World. We need the help of the other members of PEN to establish our own center.

Thank you very much for the opportunity to speak.

-Floyd Salas, President, PEN Oakland

Note: *This speech was given by Floyd Salas on Friday, May 11, 1990 at the literary session, "Rights and Freedoms of the Writer" one day after PEN Oakland was denied the right to establish a third center in the United States by Interim President Per Wastberg on the grounds that only two PEN centers per country were allowed, and the U.S. already had two centers in New York City and Los Angeles.*

ACKNOWLEDGEMENTS

Elmaz Abinader. "Poetry, Politics and How Tyranny Changes the P to a p and the p to a P," previously entered in the author's blog at: *www.redroom.com/member/Elmaz-Abinader/Blog*, May 10, 2010.

Francisco X. Alarcón. "Poetic Manifesto," previously published in Entering: *The Davis Poetry Anthology, 2011*, edited by Allegra Jostad Silberstein as Poet Laureate of the City of Davis, California. Reprinted by permission of the author. "In Ixtli In Yollotl," previously published in *Snake Poems: An Aztec Invocation*, Chronicle Books, 1992. Reprinted by permission of the author.

Karla Andersdatter. "A Poet in the Third World" from *Diary of a Poet: An Imaginary Life, New and Selected Works*, In Between Books, Limited Edition edition (2006)

Avotcja. "Cosmic Soul Mates" and "Blue To The Bone," previously published in *With Every Step I Take*, with artwork by Eliza Shefler, Taurean Horn Press, 2013.

Carla Blank. "A New New Deal for the Arts," previously published in the *San Francisco Chronicle* Op-Ed section, February 6, 2009. Reprinted in *CounterPunch*, February 16, 2009. Reprinted by permission of the author.

Cecil Brown. "MC Cyrano" is an excerpt from the beat-box play of the same name.

Judith Cody. "Truth. All of it at Once." previously published in *The Montreal Review*, Montreal, Quebec, Canada, 2011; "Did You Shoot Anyone, Daddy?" previously published in *Limestone – Obscura Legacy*, University of Kentucky, Lexington, KY, 2009; "Going Home," previously published in *Nimrod International Journal, Vietnam Revisited issue*, University of Tulsa, OK, 2004; also in *The Cumberland Poetry Review*, Final Issue, Nashville, TN, Spring 2004.

Gillian Conoley. "occupied," previously published in *Occupied Writers*, The 99 Percent, 2013. Reprinted by permission of the author.

Lucha Corpi. "Berkeley Blues," original written in Spanish and translated into English by Catherine Rodríguez-Nieto. Published by permission of the translator and the author.

John Curl. "O Columbia," previously published in *Amerus #1*, Amerus Press, 1977, reprinted in *Revolutionary Alchemy*, Homeward Press, 2012. Reprinted by permission of Homeward Press.

Lucille Lang Day. "The People Versus Oscar Cole," previously published in *ForPoetry.com*, 2007, and *The Curvature of Blue*, Cervena Barva Press, 2009. Reprinted by permission of Cervena Barva Press and the author.

Camille Dungy. "Daisy Cutter" previously published in *Smith Blue*, Carbondale: Southern Illinois University Press, June 2011. Reprinted by permission of Southern Illinois University Press.

Maria Espinosa. "Dying Unfinished," excerpt from *Dying Unfinished*, Wings Press, 2009. Reprinted by permission of Wings Press.

Adele Foley. "60 Years Later/After the Camps" previously published in *Along the Bloodline*, Pantograph Press/Goldfish Press, 2003. Reprinted by permission.

Jack Foley. "H.D. Moe (1937-2013): Fluxional, Vehicular and Transitive" is a revision of Foley's afterword to *Birth to Birth* by H.D. Moe, The Deserted X Press, 2002.

Jack Foley. "The Name is Popularly Interpreted to Mean 'Wanderer,'" Author's note: "This poem to Wanda Coleman is a mixture of her words and mine; it quotes two passages from her work; the first ("I've been thrown out…at home") is a prose passage I have lineated as verse; the second ("in cold grey morning…I will never leave here") is a poem, "Prisoner of Los Angeles (2)." Both passages appear in *California Poetry from the Gold Rush to the Present*, edited by Dana Gioia, Chryss Yost, and Jack Hicks, Heyday Books, 2004. Both passages also appear in Jack Foley, *Visions & Affiliations: A California Literary Time Line / Poetry 1940-2005* (Pantograph Press, 2011). Quoted by permission.

CB Follett. "Words to the Mother Whose Son Killed My Son" previously published in *Out of Line*, 2004. "The Jackdaws Come at Noon" previously published by *Natural Bridge*, Number 23, Spring 2010 and in *One Bird Falling*, Time Being Books, 2011. Copyright © 2011 by Time Being Books. Reprinted by permission of Time Being Books.

Joan Gelfand. "Good Morning America, Where Are You?" was previously published in the anthology *Continent of Light*, 2011, New Way Media, Albany, California. Reprinted by permission of New Way Media. It was also previously published in *NewverseNews.com, Occupoetry*, July 2012, *99 Poems for the 99 Percent*, 99 Press, and 99 Blog.

Nathalie Handal. "On the Way to Jerez de la Frontera" was previously published in *Poet in Andalucía*, University of Pittsburgh Press, 2012. Published by permission of University of Pittsburgh Press.

Mitch Horowitz. "Black Moses," adapted from *Occult America*, Bantam, 2009/2010. Used by permission of the author.

Kitty Kelley. "Unauthorized, But Not Untrue," excerpt from previous publication in *The American Scholar*, Winter 2011. Visit http://www.theamericanscholar.org/unauthorized-but-not-untrue Reprinted by permission of *The American Scholar*.

Vandana Khanna, "Echo," previously published in *Train to Agra*, Southern Illinois University Press, 2001. Reprinted by permission of Southern Illinois University Press.

Paul Krassner, "Remembering Kesey," excerpt from *Confessions of a Raving, Unconfined Nut: Misadventures in the Counterculture*, Touchstone, 1994. Reprinted by permission of the author.

Nhuan Xuan Le (Thanh-Thanh). "Just Cause," previously entered in the author's blog at *www.Thanh-Thanh.us* and the *Poem Hunter* website at http://www.poemhunter.com both in 1992; published in Poems by Selected Vietnamese, Alameda, CA: Xay-Dung, 2005; reprinted in *Vietnamese Choice Poems*, Bloomington, IN: Xlibris, 2013. Reprinted by permission of the author.

Leza Lowitz. "Stop the Bullet," from *Yoga Heart: Lines on the Six Perfections*, Berkeley, Stone Bridge Press, 2011. Reprinted by permission of Stone Bridge Press.

Mary Mackey. "Walking Upside Down on the Other Side of the World," previously published in *Sugar Zone*, Marsh Hawk Press, 2011. Reprinted by permission of Marsh Hawk Press.

Norman Mailer. "The Meaning of 'Western Defense,'" an excerpt from *Dissent Magazine:* Spring 1954. Reprinted by permission of the Norman Mailer Estate.

Clive Matson. "Thank You" was previously published in *The Crazy Child Scribbler*, Clive Matson, July 1990; *Exquisite Corpse*, Culture Shock Foundation, January-April, 1991; *We Speak for Peace*, Knowledge, Ideas, and Trends, Inc., 1993; and *Thus Spake the Corpse*, Black Sparrow Press, 1999.

devorah major. "political poem" previously published *where river meets ocean*, City Lights Press 2003. Reprinted by permission of City Lights Publishing.

Elizabeth Nunez. "Boundaries," excerpt from *Boundaries* by Elizabeth Nunez. New York: Akashic Books, 2011. Reprinted by permission of Akashic Books.

Peter Orner. "Plaza Revolución, Mexico City, 6 A.M." first appeared in *Witness*, August 2011. Reprinted by permission of Little, Brown and Company.

Claire Ortalda. "NO-Body," previously published in *Porter House Review*, 2013. http://www.cabrillo.edu/publications/portergulch/2013/Final%20Online%20PGR%202013%20.pdf

Sandra Park. Excerpt from "Black Hair, White Wings," from *If You Live in a Small House*. Honolulu: Mutual Publishing, 2010. Reprinted by permission of Mutual Publishing.

Jerry Ratch. "Unemployment," previously published by *www.public-republic.net*, 2009.

Clifton Ross. "Night in the New World Order" and "A Proud Sinner's Prayer" were previously published in *Translations from Silence*, Freedom Voices Publications, 2009. Reprinted by permission of the author.

Floyd Salas. "The Politics of Poetry," previously published in *Transfer Fifty*, Commemorative Issue, A Magazine of Creative Writing at San Francisco State University, San Francisco, Fall, 1985, *Stories and Poems from Close to Home*, ed. and with an introduction by Floyd Salas, Ortalda & Associates, Berkeley, 1986, and "The Politics of Poetry" (article and poem), *San Diego's Weekly Reader*, May 18, 1995.

Mona Lisa Saloy. "September 2005, New Orleans," "New Orleans, a Neighborhood Nation," and "When I saw bodies in Post-Katrina New Orleans," previously published in *Second Line Home, New Orleans Poems*, MO: Truman State University Press, 2014. Reprinted by permission of Truman State University Press.

Richard Silberg. "George Hackett Simpson and the Three Sad Cigarettes," previously published in *The Horses: New & Selected Poems* by Richard Silberg. Pasadena: Red Hen Press, September 2012. Reprinted by permission of Red Hen Press.

Rebecca Solnit. "Oakland's Beautiful Non-Violence," originally published at *Tomdispatch.com* as "Mad, Passionate Love–and Violence Occupy Heads into the Spring," February 21, 2012.

Doreen Stock. "The Oil Poem" was previously published in Solo Novo, v.1, *Wall Scrawls*, Solo Press, Carpinteria, CA, 2011. Reprinted by permission of Solo Press.

Susan Terris. "Bald Eagle on Potato Lake" was previously published in *Great River Review*, Fall 2009.

Sue Owens Wright. "Homed For The Holidays: A Christmas Wish for Homeless Pets," previously published in the "Pets and Their People" column in *Inside Publications*, Sacramento, California. December 2005.

Alma Luz Villanueva. "Breathing While Brown" is included in her poetry book, *Gracias*, Wings Press, 2014. Published with the permission of the author.

Gerald Vizenor. "Blue Ravens: Native American Indians in the First War" is a chapter from his novel, *Blue Ravens*, Wesleyan University Press, 2014. Published with the permission of the author.

Michael Warr. "Hallucinating at the Velvet Lounge" was previously published at *PoetrySpeaks.com* and recorded on *the space of in between* (Nefasha Ayer), 2009.

Harriet A. Washington. "Thalidomide Redux: Prudence and the Pill," is an adaptation of her work previously published in *Deadly Monopolies: The Shocking Corporate Takeover of Life Itself—and the Consequences for Your Health and Our Medical Future* and also at *http://www.biopoliticaltimes.org/article.php?id=5504,* December 13, 2010

Koon K. Woon. "The Phantom of the Opera," "The High Walls I Cannot Scale" and "A Smoke Break at the Nuclear Command" were previously published in *Water Chasing Water*, Kaya Press, 2013. Reprinted by permission of the author.

Andrena Zawinski. "What About a Fight?", previously published in *Arroyo Literary Review*, 2012.

CONTRIBUTORS

Elmaz Abinader is a writer from Oakland who has published a memoir, *Children of the Roojme*, and a collection of poems, *In the Country of My Dreams*. Abinader has written and performed several plays. Her forthcoming poetry collection, *This House, My Bones* is due out in fall 2014. She teaches at Mills College and is the co-founder of VONA/Voices at www.voicesatvona.org

Opal Palmer Adisa, Jamaican born, is a Caribbean writer who pens in all genres; she has fourteen published books and her poems, essays and stories have been anthologized in over 400 books, journals and magazines. A cultural activist, professor and traveler, Adisa uses her creative writing to illuminate her culture and to address socio-political issues that impact various communities. Her latest novel, *Painting Away Regrets*, explores the issue of divorce and forgiveness, and is available online. For more information about Adisa, visit her website at www.opalpalmeradisa.com

Francisco X. Alarcón, Chicano poet and educator, is the author of thirteen volumes of poetry, including, *Snake Poems: An Aztec Invocation*, Chronicle Books 1992, winner of a 1993 PEN Oakland Josephine Miles Literary Award and *From the Other Side of Night: Selected and New Poems*, University of Arizona Press 2002. His latest book is *Ce • Uno • One: Poems for the New Sun*, Swan Scythe Press 2010. His most recent book of bilingual poetry for children is *Animal Poems of the Iguazú*, Children's Book Press 2008. He teaches at the University of California, Davis. In response to Arizona's xenophobic laws, he created the Facebook page on Poets Responding to SB 1070: www.facebook.com/PoetryofResistance.

Mimi Albert, originally from New York, has lived, written, and taught creative writing in Northern California for many years, most recently in the UC Berkeley Post-baccalaureate program. Her published work includes the novels *Skirts* and *The Second Story Man,* and much short fiction and nonfiction published all over the world, including Scandinavia and the UK. She lives in Oakland.

Karla Andersdatter (April 9, 1938 - May 23, 2011) was an award winning author, poet, teacher, and storyteller. *A Poet in the Third World* was written in Tegucigalpa, Honduras in 1983 and finally published in 1986 in a chapbook edition of 150 copies which were subsequently mailed to every United States Senator in Congress. The University of California at Davis bought the only copy left with the exception of one remaining in the hands of the author. It was written during the U.S. involvement with the Contras and the revolutions in Nicaragua and Guatemala. Her *Diary of a Poet: An Imaginary Life* won a PEN Oakland Josephine Miles Literary Award in 2007.

Avotcja (pronounced Avacha) is a card carrying New York born Music fanatic/sound junkie & popular Bay Area Radio DeeJay & member of the award winning group Avotcja & Modúpue, which was The Bay Area Blues Society's Jazz Group of the Year in 2005 & 2010. She's a lifelong Musician/Writer/Educator/Storyteller & is on a shamelessly Spirit driven melodic mission to heal herself. Avotcja talks to the Trees & listens to the Wind against the concrete & when they answer it usually winds up in a Poem or Short Story. Avotcja has been published in English & Spanish in the USA, Mexico & Europe. She's an award winning Poet & multi-instrumentalist. Avotcja teaches Creative Writing & Drama & is an ASCAP recording artist. Her latest Book is *With Every Step I Take*, Taurean Horn Press, 2013 available at: www.spdbooks.org &/or Amazon.com

Devereaux Baker is a Pushcart Prize nominee and winner of the 2011 PEN Oakland Josephine Miles Literary Award for her book, *Red Willow People*. She is the recipient of the 2012 Hawaii Council of Humanities International Poetry Prize, and the Women's Global Leadership Initiative Poetry Award. Her poetry fellowships include a MacDowell Fellowship, the Hawthornden Castle International Fellowship, three California Arts Council Awards and the Helene Wurlitzer Foundation Fellowship. She has published three books of poetry, *Red Willow People, Beyond the Circumstance of Sight,* and *Light at the Edge,* and conducted poetry workshops in France and Mexico. She has taught poetry in the schools with the CPITS Program and produced the Voyagers Radio Program of original student writing for KZYX Public Radio.

Marsha Lee Berkman is coeditor of *Here I Am: Contemporary Jewish Stories From Around The World*. Her prize-winning short stories have appeared in many publications and anthologies, including *The Schocken Book of Contemporary Jewish Fiction; Writing Our Way Home; Mothers: Twenty Stories of Contemporary Motherhood; Shaking Eve's Tree; Feldspar Prize Stories 2; Jewish Woman's Literary Annual; Chicago Quarterly Review; REAL:Regarding Arts and Letters; The Long Story; Western Humanities Review; Lilith,* and many other publications. She holds graduate degrees in English, Creative Writing, and Jewish Studies and is completing a doctoral degree at Spertus College in Chicago. Marsha Lee Berkman lives and writes in the San Francisco Bay Area.

Christopher Bernard has published fiction, criticism, drama and film scenarios, essays, and poetry in numerous reviews, periodicals, and anthologies. In 1989 he founded *Caveat Lector* magazine. In 2005, Regent Press published his novel, *A Spy in the Ruins*. He has also published two other books: *The Rose Shipwreck: Poems and Photographs* and the short story collection, *In the American Night*. His novel *Voyage to a Phantom City* will appear in 2014. His poetry and fiction have been nominated for Pushcart Prizes, and he is a past winner of the Temple University Student Poetry Award.

Carla Blank is author and editor of *Rediscovering America, the Making of Multicultural America 1900-2000*, 2003, and co-author of *Live On Stage!*, 1997, 2000, which is a performing arts textbook for teachers and students, adopted by four states. With Ishmael Reed, she edited the anthology *POWWOW, Charting the Fault Lines in the American Experience—Short Fiction from Then to Now*, 2009. She is also a director, choreographer and dramaturge, having directed plays by Opal Palmer Adisa, Boadiba and Claire Ortalda for PEN Oakland's 2009 4x4 Playwright Series. Her multimedia collaboration with Robert Wilson titled KOOL premiered as a live performance at New York City's Guggenheim Museum in April 2009. In 2013 she directed Palestinian and Syrian actors in a Palestinian Arabic version of *Holiday* by Philip Barry at the Al-Kasaba Theater in Ramallah.)

Abby Lynn Bogomolny is originally from Brooklyn, New York, and she is the author of the poetry collection *People Who Do Not Exist*, as well as the editor of the anthology *New to North America: Writing by U.S. Immigrants, Their Children and Grandchildren*. She teaches English full-time at Santa Rosa Junior College and lives in Northern California.

Marek Breiger has published prose and poetry in six anthologies and over 100 magazines and newspapers. Anthologies include *Updating the Literary West*, Texas Christian University, *Where Coyotes Howl and The Wind Blows Free*, University of Nevada, *To Honor a Teacher* (Andrew McMeel), *The Coffee Mill Anthology, Through the Mill,* as well as a *S.F. Chronicle,* an essay on Robert Kennedy on the 20th anniversary of his death for *U.S. News* and *World Report,* Jewish Currents, the Alameday News group and many more. He has an M.A. in Creative Writing, San Francisco State University, 1977. He is the author of *The City and the Fields: Multicultural Themes in Modern California Literature*, Valley Memories Press, 2014. He teaches English and Language and Composition at Irvington High School in Hayward, CA.

Cecil Brown, novelist, essayist and playwright, is the author of *Coming Up Down; Dude, Where's My Black Studies Department?; The Life & Loves of Mr. Jiveass Nigger; Days Without Weather; Stagolee Shot Billy; I, Stagolee*, and *Journey's End*. Brown's PhD from University of California, Berkeley, is in narrative African-American literature and folklore.

Janine Canan lives in California in the Valley of the Moon. She studied at Stanford University *cum laude,* University of California at Berkeley, and New York University School of Medicine, and has been a psychiatrist for over thirty years. Her first book of poems received a National Endowment from the Arts grant. Since then, Janine has published 18 books of poetry, translations, anthologies, essays and stories, including major translations of Francis Jammes and Else Lasker-Schüler, and the award-winning anthologies *Messages from Amma* and *She Rises like the Sun*. Her latest book is *Ardor: Poems of Life,* Pilgrims Press, Varanasi, 2011. Visit www.JanineCanan.com for more information.

Neeli Cherkovski is an international figure in poetry. A recent volume of selected poems, *Falling Light,* was published in Austria and a limited edition of a hand-written notebook will appear from Viviani Edizione, Verona Italy in late winter, 2014. He is currently completing a memoir and a new book of poems, *Spent Shadow*.

Judith Cody, poet and composer, won national awards from Atlantic and Amelia magazines and a national award in music. Poetry, in Spanish and English editions, is in the Smithsonian Institution's permanent collection. Poems were quarter-finalists for the Pablo Neruda Prize, were put forward for the Lyric Recovery Award's Carnegie Hall reading, and won honorable mentions from the National League of American Pen Women. Poems are published in over 79 journals such as: *Stand, Nimrod, New York Quarterly, South Carolina Review, Texas Review, Fugue, Distillery, Cumberland Poetry Review, Fox Cry Review, Louisville Review, Madison Review, Phoebe, Primavera, Poet Lore, Poem, Caduceus*. Anthologies include: *Oakland Out Loud, Anthology of Monterey Bay Poets, Meridian Anthology of Contemporary Poetry.* Cody was Editor-in-Chief of the *Resource Guide on Women in Music,* co-sponsored by San Francisco State University. Books include: the internationally notable biography of composer, *Vivian Fine: A Bio-Bibliography*, Greenwood Press, and *Eight Frames Eight,* poems. She is the editor for a NASA division history. Visit www.judithcody.com and http://library.newmusicusa.org/judithcody

Gillian Conoley was born in Austin Texas, where, on its rural outskirts, her father and mother owned and operated a radio station. She is the author of seven collections of poetry, including Peace, just released with Omnidawn in spring 2014, *The Plot Genie, Profane Halo, Lovers in the Used World*, and *Tall Stranger,* a finalist for the National Book Critics Circle Award. Her work has received the Jerome J. Shestack Poetry Prize from *The American Poetry Review*, a National Endowment for the Arts grant, and a Fund for Poetry Award. Conoley's work is widely anthologized, most recently in W.W. Norton's new Postmodern American Poetry. Her translations of Henri Michaux, *A Thousand Times Broken: Three Books by Henri Michaux*, appearing in English for the first time, will be published by City Lights in 2014. Editor and founder of Volt magazine, she is Professor and Poet-in-Residence at Sonoma State University.

Lucha Corpi was born in Jáltipan, Veracruz, Mexico. She came to Berkeley as a student wife in 1964. Corpi is the author of two collections of poetry (Spanish, with English translations by Catherine Rodríguez Nieto), two bilingual children's books, and six novels, four of which feature Chicana detective Gloria Damasco. She has been the recipient of a National Endowment for the Arts fellowship in poetry, an Oakland Cultural Arts fellowship in fiction, a PEN Oakland Josephine Miles Literary Award, the Multicultural Publishers Exchange Literary Award, and two International Latino Book Awards for her mystery fiction. Her new book, *Confessions of a Book Burner: Personal Essays and Stories,* was published by Arte Publico in April, 2014. Until 2005, she was a tenured teacher in the Oakland Public Schools Neighborhood Centers. She lives in Oakland.

John Curl is the author of eight books of poetry, a memoir, and several volumes of history. His latest poetry volume is *Revolutionary Alchemy*, 2012. His book *Ancient American Poets*, 2005, contains the earliest Native American poetry in the original languages and his translations from Nahuatl, Yucatec Maya, and Quechia. He is vice president of PEN Oakland. He represented the USA at the World Poetry Festival of 2010 in Caracas, Venezuela. *Memories of Drop City,* 2008, is his memoir of the counterculture and communal movement of the 1960s. Curl's play, *The Trial of Christopher Columbus*, was produced by the Writers Theater in 2010. A second expanded edition of his historical study *For All The People: Uncovering the Hidden History of Cooperation, Cooperative Movements, and Communalism in America,* was published in 2012.

Steve Dalachinsky was born in Brooklyn, is a New York downtown poet active for several decades in the free-jazz scene. He has performed his poetry with many notable jazz musicians including William Parker, Matthew Shipp, and has written liner notes for many artists, including Anthony Braxton, James "Blood" Ulmer, and Rashied Ali. The author of several dozen books and chapbooks of poetry, Dalachinsky's book *The Final Nite & Other Poems: Complete Notes from a Charles Gayle Notebook* won a PEN Oakland Josephine Miles Literary Award in 2007. He lives in Manhattan with his wife, painter and poet Yuko Otomo.

J.P. Dancing Bear is editor for the *American Poetry Journal* and Dream Horse Press. Bear also hosts the weekly hour-long poetry show, *Out of Our Minds*, on public station, KKUP and available as podcasts. He is the author of twelve collections of poetry. His latest books are *Family of Marsupial Centaurs and other birthday poems* (Iris Press, 2012) and *The Abandoned Eye* (FutureCycle Press, 2012).

Lucille Lang Day is the author of eight poetry collections and chapbooks, most recently *The Curvature of Blue,* Cervena Barva, 2009. She has also published a children's book, *Chain Letter,* Heyday Books, 2005 and a memoir, *Married at Fourteen,* Heyday Books, 2012, which received a PEN Oakland Josephine Miles Literary Award.. Her poetry and prose have appeared widely in such magazines and anthologies as *Atlanta Review, The Hudson Review, The Threepenny Review,* and *New Poets of the American West, Many Voices,* 2010. She is the founder and director of a small press, Scarlet Tanager Books, and lives in Oakland. Her website is http://lucillelangday.com.

Kathleen de Azevedo's novel of Brazilian American immigrants, *Samba Dreamers*, University of Arizona Press, was nominated for the Northern California Book Award and won a 2007 PEN Oakland Josephine Miles Literary Award and the 2012 Latino Books into Movies Award. Her short stories and articles have appeared in many publications including the *Los Angeles Times, Américas, Boston Review, Michigan Quarterly Review, Greensboro Review, Cimarron Review, Gulf Coast, Gettysburg Review, TriQuarterly, 5Trope*, and the anthologies *New Stories of the Southwest,* and *Latinos in Lotus Land.* She was born in Rio de Janeiro but currently lives in San Francisco.

Wendy Doniger (O'Flaherty) graduated from Radcliffe College and received her Ph. D. from Harvard University and her D. Phil. from Oxford University. She is the Mircea Eliade Distinguished Service Professor of the History of Religions at the University of Chicago and the author of many books, most recently *The Bedtrick: Tales of Sex and Masquerade, The Woman Who Pretended to Be Who She Was, The Hindus: An Alternative History* and *On Hinduism.*

Sharon Doubiago's memoir, *My Father's Love/Portrait of the Poet as a Young Girl,* was a finalist in the Northern California Book Awards in Creative Non Fiction, 2010. Love on the Streets, Selected and New Poems, University of Pittsburgh, received the Glenna Luschei Distinguished Poet Award, and was a finalist in the Paterson NJ Poetry Prize. She's written two dozen books of poetry and prose, most notably the epic poem *Hard Country*, the book length poem South *America Mi Hija,* the poetry collection, *Body and Soul,* and the story collections, *El Niño,* and *The Book of Seeing With One's Own Eyes,* which was selected to the Oregon Culture Heritage list: *Literary Oregon, 100 Books, 1800-2000.* She holds three Pushcart Prizes for poetry and fiction and the Oregon Book Award for Poetry for *Psyche Drives the Coast* and a California Arts Council Award. *Naked To The Earth* is her new poetry manuscript.

Camille T. Dungy is the author of *Smith Blue, Suck on the Marrow,* and *What to Eat, What to Drink, What to Leave for Poison*. She edited *Black Nature: Four Centuries of African American Nature Poetry*, and co-edited the *From the Fishouse* poetry anthology. Her honors include an American Book Award, two Northern California Book Awards, a California Book Award silver medal, and a fellowship from the NEA.

Margarita Engle is the Cuban-American author of young adult novels in verse about the island's history. *The Surrender Tree* received the first Newbery Honor ever awarded to an author of Hispanic ancestry. Other honors for Engle's books include two Pura Belpré Medals, two Américas Awards, and a Jane Addams Award. Her most recent book is *Hurricane Dancers. The Wild Book*, Harcourt, 2012. Visit www.margaritaengle.com

Maria Espinosa is a novelist, poet, and translator as well as a teacher. She has published four novels: *Dark Plums, Longing*, which received an American Award and has been translated into Greek, *Incognito: Journey of a Secret Jew*, and *Dying Unfinished*, which received a PEN Oakland Josephine Miles Literary Award. Espinosa is the author of two poetry chapbooks, *Night Music and Love Feelings*. She also translated George Sand's novel, *Lelia*. Raised in Long Island, she has lived most of her adult life in northern California. Recently she moved to Albuquerque, New Mexico where she teaches English as a Second Language at Central Community College of New Mexico and leads creative writing workshops for the University of New México. Website links include: www.mariaespinosa.com, www.redroom.com, www.wingspress.com and www.wikipedia.com.

Adelle Foley is a retirement administrator, an arts activist, and a writer of haiku. She is on the board of *Poetry Flash*. Her column, "High Street Neighborhood News," appears monthly in *The MacArthur Metro*. Her poems have appeared in various magazines, in the textbooks, *An Introduction to Poetry and Literature: An Introduction to Fiction, Poetry, and Drama*, and in Columbia University Press's internet database, *the Columbia Granger's World of Poetry*. *Along the Bloodline* is her first book-length collection. Beat poet Michael McClure has said that "Adelle Foley's haikus show us humanity. Their vitality and imagination shine from her compassion; from seeing things as they truly are."

Jack Foley has published 12 books of poetry, 5 books of criticism, and *Visions and Affiliations*, a chronoencyclopedia of California poetry from 1940 to 2005. His radio show, Cover to Cover, airs on Berkeley, California radio station KPFA every Wednesday at 3; his column, "Foley's Books," appears in the online magazine *Alsop Review*. In 2010 Foley was awarded the Lifetime Achievement Award by the Berkeley Poetry Festival, and June 5, 2010 was proclaimed "Jack Foley Day" in Berkeley. The Fall 2012, vol. 5, no. 1 issue of the online *Tower Journal* is a Festschrift for Foley: www.towerjournal.com, go to Archive. *EYES*, Foley's selected poems, has appeared from Poetry Hotel Press. A chapbook, *LIFE*, is forthcoming from Word Palace Press. With his wife Adelle, Foley frequently performs in the San Francisco Bay Area. Performances can be found on YouTube. www.jack-adellefoley.com and also in a *Wikipedia* article: http://en.wikipedia.org/wiki/Jack_Foley_(poet)#Biography

CB Follett is widely published and awarded both nationally and internationally. She has nine books of poetry and several chapbooks. Her press, Arctos Press has published over 20 poetry books and with co-editor, Susan Terris, published the seven years of *RUNES, A Review of Poetry* (2001-2008). She is also a visual artist, and was the Poet Laureate of Marin County (2010-2013).

Joan Gelfand's poetry, fiction, reviews, essays and letters have appeared in national and international anthologies, literary journals and webzines. She teaches writing for Poetry Inside Out, coaches writers in San Francisco, is a member of the National Book Critics Circle, and a contributing Poetry Editor to the "J." She was also the Past President of the Women's National Book Association. Her work has been nominated for Pushcart and Carver Prizes. Joan blogs regularly for the *Huffington Post*. Her books are: *A Dreamer's Guide to Cities and Streams*, SF Bay Press, 2009, *Here & Abroad*, a chapbook of short fiction, which won the 2010 Cervena Barva Fiction Award, *Seeking Center*, Two Bridges Press, 2006 and *The Long Blue Room*, Benicia Literary Arts, 2014. *Transported*, a spoken word CD with original music can be found on iTunes® & reverbnation.com. Visit http:// joangelfand.com

Herbert Gold's most recent book is *Still Alive: A Temporary Condition* (reissued as *Not Dead Yet: A Feisty Bohemian Explores the Art of Growing Old*). His works of fiction include *The Man Who Was Not With It*, *Fathers* (which was translated into eight languages), *A Girl of Forty*, and *Lovers and Cohorts: Twenty-Seven Stories*. His non-fiction books include: *Haiti: Best Nightmare on Earth*. Forthcoming is a novel, *A Bad Man in Love*. He will long be remembered for his compassionate but judgmental yellow eyes. He has taught at Stanford, Harvard, Cornell and the University of California.

Rafael Jesús González, Professor Emeritus of literature and creative writing, was born (10/10/35) and raised biculturally/bilingually in El Paso, Texas/Cd. Juárez, Chihuahua, and taught at University of Oregon, Western State Collage of Colorado, Central Washington State University, University of Texas El Paso (Visiting Professor of Philosophy), and Laney College, Oakland, California where he founded the Dept. of Mexican & Latin-American Studies. Also a visual artist, he has exhibited in the Oakland Museum of California, the Mexican Museum of San Francisco, Charles Ellis Museum of Art, Milwaukee and others. His collection of poems *El Hacedor De Juegos/The Maker of Games* (1977-78) had two printings; his collection *La musa lunática/The Lunatic Muse* was published in 2009. Nominated thrice for a Pushcart price, he was honored by the National Council of Teachers of English and Annenberg CPB for his writing in 2003. In 2009 he was honored by the City of Berkeley for his writing, art, teaching, and activism for social justice and peace. He received the 2012 Dragonfly Press Award for Outstanding Literary Achievement. His work may be read at http://rjgonzalez.blogspot.com

Ray Gonzalez is the author of numerous books of poetry, including five from BOA Editions: *The Heat of Arrivals*, which received a 1997 PEN Oakland Josephine Miles Literary Award, *Cabato Sentora* a 2000 Minnesota Book Award Finalist, *The Hawk Temple at Tierra Grande,* winner of a 2003 Minnesota Book Award for Poetry, *Consideration of the Guitar: New and Selected Poems*, 2005, and *Cool Auditor: Prose Poems,* 2009. *Turtle Pictures*, University of Arizona Press, 2000, a mixed-genre text which received the 2001 Minnesota Book Award for Poetry. He authored three essay collections, one of which, *The Underground Heart: A Return to a Hidden Landscape,* Arizona, 2002, received numerous awards. His collection of short stories, *The Ghost of John Wayne*, Arizona, 2001, won a 2002 Western Heritage Award for Best Short Story and a 2002 Latino Heritage Award in Literature. He is the editor of twelve anthologies, most recently *Sudden Fiction Latino: Short Short Stories from the U.S. and Latin America,* W.W. Norton. He has served as Poetry Editor of *The Bloomsbury Review* for thirty years and founded *LUNA*, a poetry journal, in 1998. He is Full Professor and the Director of the MFA Creative Writing Program at The University of Minnesota in Minneapolis.

Nathalie Handal was raised in Latin America, France and the Arab world. She is the author of numerous books, most recently the critically acclaimed *Poet in Andalucía,* which Alice Walker lauds as "poems of depth and weight and the sorrowing song of longing and resolve," and *Love and Strange Horses*, winner of the 2011 Gold Medal Independent Publisher Book Award, which *The New York Times* says is "a book that trembles with belonging (and longing)." Handal is the editor of the groundbreaking classic *The Poetry of Arab Women: A Contemporary Anthology,* winner of the PEN Oakland Josephine Miles Literary Award, and co-editor of the W.W. Norton landmark anthology *Language for a New Century: Contemporary Poetry from* *the Middle East, Asia & Beyond* (http://languageforanewcentury.com/) both Academy of American Poets bestsellers.

Peter J. Harris, founder and Artistic Director of Inspiration House, has since the 1970s published his poetry, essays, and fiction in a wide range of national publications; worked as a publisher, journalist, editor and broadcaster, and been an educator and workshop leader for adults and adolescents. He is founding director of *The Black Man of Happiness Project,* a creative, intellectual and artistic exploration of Black men and joy, www.blackmanofhappiness.com and also author of the joyful e-book, *The Vampire Who Drinks Gospel Music,* which takes readers from darkened movie houses filled with enthusiastic narrators, to the Washington, D.C., campus of Howard University, to covens illuminated by masterful art and hidden in plain sight off the coast of Georgia and outside *Ile Ife* in West Africa. See Harris' work at Amazon's Kindle at www.amazon.com/dp/B0093N3BY2; also Barnes & Nobles' Nook; and Smashwords for Apple's iPad® at www.smashwords.com/books/view/230399

Gerald Haslam was born in Bakersfield, California. His many non-fiction books include: *In Thought and Action: The Enigmatic Life of S. I. Hayakawa,* with Janice Haslam, University of Nebraska Press, 2011; *Workin' Man Blues: Country Music in California,* with Richard Chon and Alexandra Haslam, University of California Press; 1999, and *The Great Central Valley: California's Heartland* with Stephen Johnson and Robert Dawson, University of California Press, 1993. Haslam's many award-winning fiction books include: *That Constant Coyote,* University of Nevada Press, 1990; *Straight White Male,* University of Nevada Press, 2000, and *Grace Period,* University of Nevada Press, 2006. He received a 2006 PEN Oakland Josephine Miles Literary Award for *Haslam's Valley,* Heyday Books, 2005; he has also received numerous other awards for his fiction and non-fiction books and literary achievements. His work is widely anthologized, and he has contributed to several hundred magazines and journals such as *The Nation, Los Angeles Times Magazine, This World, Sierra,* and *Poets & Writers.* Currently Haslam is Professor Emeritus, Sonoma State University, and Adjunct Professor, Fromm Institute, University of San Francisco. Visit www.geraldhaslam.com

Juan Felipe Herrera, son of farm workers, born in Fowler, California, was confirmed by Governor Brown as Poet Laureate of California in December of 2012. He has published 29 books in various genres of poetry. Recent awards include a PEN Oakland Josephine Miles Literary Award, PEN USA, the National Critics Circle Book Award, the Latino International Book Award and the Guggenheim Fellowship. Currently, he is encouraging young people to joint his "i-Promise Joanna/Te Prometo Joanna" 5th Grade Bullying Project across California schools. Juan Felipe is Professor of Creative Writing at the University of California - Riverside.

Jack Hirschman, the Emeritus 4th Poet Laureate of the City of San Francisco, is a member of the Revolutionary Poets Brigade, and the Poet-in-Residence with the Friends of the San Francisco Public Library. Hirschman was born in 1933 in The Bronx, has published more than 100 books and chapbooks including translations from 9 languages of poets like Mayakovski, Pasolini, Neruda, Kirsch, Artaud, Laraque, Gogou, Brugnaro and many others. He has translated more women poets than any poet in the United States. His own masterwork is *The Arcanes,* published in American by Multimedia Edizioni in Salerno, Italy in 2006.

Mitch Horowitz is vice-president and editor-in-chief at Tarcher/Penguin, the division of Penguin books dedicated to metaphysical literature. He is the author of *Occult America,* Bantam, which received the 2010 PEN Oakland Josephine Miles Literary Award. His latest book is *One Simple Idea: How Positive Thinking Reshaped Modern Life,* Crown, January 2014. Horowitz frequently writes about and discusses alternative spirituality in the national media. He is online at: www.MitchHorowitz.com.

Doug Metapoet Howerton was born in Philadelphia, PA and educated in the Catholic school tradition. He attended Community College of Philadelphia, majoring in English, and U.C. Riverside extension classes in Audio/Visual Technique. He is a poet and short story writer who has written for many homeless newspapers on both coasts. He worked in New York City at Gotham Book Mart, mid-town Manhattan.

Kitty Kelley is an internationally acclaimed writer. Her last five biographies have been number one on the New York Times best seller list. Her 2013 book, *Let Freedom Ring*, commemorates the 50th anniversary of the March on Washington. Kelley's awards include: the 2011 International Book Award for *Oprah: A Biography*, the 2005 PEN Oakland Censorship Award for *The Family: The Real Story of the Bush Dynasty*, an Outstanding Author Award from the American Society of Journalists and Authors for "courageous writing on popular culture" in *His Way: The Unauthorized Biography of Frank Sinatra*, and selection by *Vanity Fair* for its Hall of Fame. Kelley was named one of 100 of "The Most Famous, Fascinating and Influential Alumni of the Past 100 Years" by the University of Washington. Brandeis University National Women's committee established a major book collection in her honor. She has debated at Oxford University and she has spoken at the Kennedy School of Government at Harvard University on "Public Figures: Are Their Private Lives Fair Game for the Press?" Her articles have appeared in the *New York Times, The Washington Post, Wall Street Journal, The Los Angeles Times, The Chicago Tribune, USA Today, Newsweek, People, McCall's, The New Republic, Huffington Post,* and *The American Scholar*. Visit www.kittykelleywriter.com

Vandana Khanna was born in New Delhi, India and received her M.F.A. from Indiana University. Her collection of poetry, *Train to Agra*, won the Crab Orchard Review First Book Prize. Ms. Khanna's work has been nominated for a Pushcart Prize and has appeared in journals including *Crazyhorse, Callaloo* and *The Indiana Review*, as well as the anthologies *Homage to Vallejo, Asian American Poetry: The Next Generation* and *Indivisible: An Anthology of Contemporary South Asian American Poetry*. She lives in Los Angeles, California.

Paul Krassner edited the groundbreaking magazine, *The Realist*, from 1958-2001. He calls himself an "investigative satirist." When People named him "Father of the underground press," he immediately demanded a paternity test. The FBI labeled him "a raving, unconfined nut." George Carlin said, "The FBI was right. This man is dangerous–and funny, and necessary." Krassner is an award-winning stand-up comedian, he ran an abortion referral service when it was illegal, and was a co-founder of the Yippies (Youth International Party). Krassner has written for *Rolling Stone, Playboy,* the *Los Angeles Times,* the *San Francisco Chronicle, The Nation, Utne Reader, Alternet.org* and *Huffington Post*. Currently, he publishes *Mad* artist Wally Wood's infamous Disneyland Memorial Orgy poster and, the author of a dozen books, he is now working on his first novel, about a contemporary Lenny Bruce-type performer. In 2010, PEN Oakland honored him with a Lifetime Achievement Award.

Michael Lally is the author of twenty-seven books including *March 18, 2003* (with drawings by Alex Katz) Libellum/Charta, 2006; his several awards, include 1972 92nd St. Y Poetry Center's Discovery Award for *The South Orange Sonnets, Some Of Us*, 1972, two National Endowment for the Arts Poetry Grants, 1974, 1981 (the latter used by Republican Congressmen to attack the NEA for promoting "pornography" citing the poem "My Life"), the 1997 PEN Oakland Josephine Miles Literary Award for *Cant Be Wrong*, Coffee House Press,1996, and the 2000 American Book Award for *It's Not Nostalgia*, Black Sparrow Press, 1999. He has held many day (& night) jobs, including musician, editor, college teacher, night guard, book critic (for the *Washington Post* and *The Village Voice*), chauffeur, actor (in the films *White Fang* and *Cool World*, and the TV shows *NYPD Blue, Law & Order,* and *Deadwood*), script doctor (*Drugstore Cowboy, Pump Up the Volume*), and as screenwriter co-wrote Fogbound, "Best Feature Film" 2003 Thessalaski International Film Festival. Though now retired from most day (& night) jobs, Lally still writes poetry and prose every day, including his online blog *Lally's Alley*.

Nhuan Xuan Le (pseudonyms: Thanh-Thanh for poetry, Kieu-Ngoc for prose, Nguyet-Cam for drama, Nguoi Tho for critique, Le Chan-Nhan and Duc-Co Le for research, Tu Ngong for satire) was born in Vietnam in 1930. He leads the *"Xay-Dung"* literary group (recognized at the Vietnam 1957 National Cultural Festival as a main branch of Vietnam's Cultural Tree). He began writing in English when he settled as a political refugee in California, USA, in 1992. He has contributed works to more than 30 English poetry anthologies, including *Oakland Out Loud*, and published, besides many books in Vietnamese, *Poems by Selected Vietnamese*, verse translations of 101 pieces by 55 authors, and *Vietnamese Choice Poems*, verse translations of 146 pieces by 81 authors, all living in the United States, Canada, Australia, Belgium, France, Germany, Norway, and Vietnam. He is a US citizen, member of PEN Center USA, and now lives in Alameda, California.

Rabbi Michael Lerner is editor of *Tikkun*, a quarterly critique of politics, culture and society, (www.tikkun.org), chair of the interfaith (including atheists) Network of Spiritual Progressives, (www.spiritualprogressives.org) and rabbi of Beyt Tikkun Synagogue-Without-Walls in Berkeley, California. He is the editor of 11 books including two national best sellers: *Jewish Renewal: A Path to Healing and Transformation* and *The Left Hand of God: Taking Back our Country from the Religious Right*, as well as *The Politics of Meaning, Spirit Matters,* and *The Socialism of Fools: Anti-Semitism on the Left*. He welcomes your connecting with him at RabbiLerner.tikkun@gmail.com.

Leza Lowitz is an award-winning multi-genre writer and yoga instructor. Her work has appeared in *The New York Times online, The Huffington Post, Shambhala Sun* and *Best Buddhist Writing of 2011*. She has published over 17 books, most recently Yoga Heart: Lines on the Six Perfections. Her debut novel for young adults, *Jet Black and the Ninja Wind*, the first in a trilogy about a female ninja's fight to save her tribal lands, received the 2013-2014 APALA Award from the ALA. Her awards include a PEN Josephine Miles Literary Award, a PEN Syndicated Fiction Award, grants from the NEA and NEH, and the Japan-U.S. Friendship Commission Award for the translation of Japanese literature from Columbia University. Though she grew up in the Bay Area, she now lives in Tokyo with her husband, the writer Shogo Oketani, and their son. They own Sun and Moon Yoga.

Kirk Lumpkin has been an important part of the Bay Area and beyond poetry scene for years, hosting readings in San Francisco and Berkeley, helping to facilitate the Watershed Environmental Poetry Festival [with *Poetry Flash* & former U.S. Poet Laureate, Robert Hass], and hosting open mikes at Burning Man." -*Bay Area Poets Seasonal Review*. He's the author of two books of poems, *Co-Hearing* and *In Deep*. His poetry/music ensemble, The Word-Music Continuum has released two CDs, the first, self-titled and the second called, *Sound Poems*. He's done featured performances of his poetry all around the San Francisco Bay Area and Northern California, in Los Angeles, New York City, Colorado, Toronto, Canada and readings in England under the auspices of the Campaign for Nuclear Disarmament. He's been featured on KPFA radio's *Cover to Cover—Open Book*. He has now worked for the Ecology Center and its program the Berkeley Farmers' Market for over 20 years. Michael McClure wrote, "… solid real illumination …" and in Examiner.com, "No matter what, he will make sure the sidewalks are shaking before you go home."

Alison Luterman has written three books of poetry, *The Largest Possible Life*, Cleveland State University Press, *See How We Almost Fly*, Pearl Edition, and Desire Zoo, Tia Chucha Press. She lives in an old neighborhood in Oakland with her husband, two cats, a fig tree, two peach trees, a lemon and a guava. She is a sidewalk-loiterer, an eavesdropper, and a story curator. In addition to poetry, she writes plays and personal essays. She has taught at The Writing Salon in Berkeley, at Esalen Institute and Rowe Camp and Conference center, at Omega institute, Santa Barbara Writer's Conference, and elsewhere. Visit www.alisonluterman.com

Mary Mackey is the author of 13 novels and 6 collections of poetry including *Sugar Zone*, winner of the 2012 PEN Oakland Josephine Miles Literary Award. Her poems have been praised by Wendell Berry, Jane Hirshfield, Dennis Nurkse, Ron Hansen, Dennis Schmitz and Marge Piercy for their beauty, precision, originality, and extraordinary range. Four times Garrison Keillor has featured her poetry on his program *The Writer's Almanac*. Her novels, which have recently become available as e-books, have made *The New York Times* and *San Francisco Chronicle* bestseller lists, been translated into twelve languages, and sold over a million and a half copies. To learn more, you are invited to visit www.marymackey.com, and www.facebook.com/marymackeywriter

Mike Madison lives in the Sacramento Valley where his vocation (farming) supports his avocation (writing). His essays have appeared on the Op-Ed pages of the *L.A. Times* and the *N. Y. Times*, as well as in numerous magazines. He is the author of four books; his book *Blithe Tomato* was awarded a PEN Oakland Josephine Miles Literary Award in 2006.

Norman Mailer (January 31, 1923 -November 10, 2007) was an American novelist, journalist, essayist, playwright, filmmaker, actor, and a political candidate for the mayor of New York City in 1969. As a writer, Mailer was awarded two Pulitzer Prizes and the National Book Award, among other prominent literary recognitions. Along with the likes of Truman Capote, Hunter S. Thompson, and Tom Wolfe, Mailer is considered a pioneer and respected innovator of creative nonfiction, a genre sometimes called New Journalism. He stands as an iconic force in American literature.

devorah major, a California-born granddaughter of immigrants, documented and undocumented, served as San Francisco's third Poet Laureate (2002-2006). In addition to her poetry books, she has two novels, two biographies, and a host of short stories, essays, and individual poems published. She performs her work nationally and internationally with and without musicians. Her passion for writing and performing her work is almost equaled by her delight in teaching poetry to people of all ages from young readers to seasoned elders, in community organizations, as poet in residence at San Francisco Fine Arts Museums and as a part-time adjunct professor at California College of the Arts. She is also an iterant member of the international Revolutionary Poets Brigade.

Clive Matson, MFA Columbia University, was drafted as *Chalcedony's* (kal-SAID-'n-ease) astonished scribe in 2004. His early teachers were Beats in New York City and, amazingly, his seventh book was placed in John Wieners' coffin. He became immersed in the stream of passionate intensity that runs through us all and has finally stopped trying to go anywhere else. That delights his students, and it's old hat, according to *Let the Crazy Child Write!,* 1998, the text he uses to make his living. He and Alan Cohen edited *An Eye for an Eye Makes the Whole World Blind - Poets on 911,* which won a PEN Oakland Josephine Miles Literary Award in 2003. He recently began a blog, *Writing Occupy Workshop*, and has been working double-time to keep up ever since. He enjoys playing basketball, table tennis, and collecting minerals in the field. He lives in Oakland, where he helps bring up his teenage son, Ezra. Visit Clive at www.matsonpoet.com.

Michael McClure's recent books are *Of Indigo and Saffron: Selected and New Poems*, and *Mysteriosos*. McClure is the recipient of awards including a PEN Oakland Josephine Miles Literary Award, a Guggenheim, an Obie Award, a Rockefeller grant, and the Alfred Jarry Award. His play *The Beard* was central in the battles against censorship and went on to win international praise and awards. McClure sometimes performs poetry with Ray Manzarek. Composer Terry Riley's and McClure's recent album is titled *I Like Your Eyes Liberty*. McClure wrote the pop song *Mercedes Benz* with Janis Joplin. He lives with the sculptor Amy Evans McClure.

Colleen J. McElroy lives in Seattle, Washington where she a Professor Emeritus at the University of Washington. McElroy's last collection of poems, *Sleeping with the Moon,* 2007, received a 2008 PEN Oakland Josephine Miles Literary Award. Many of her poems have been translated into Russian, Italian,

Arabic, Greek, French, German, Malay, and Serbo-Croatian. Her ninth collection of poetry is, *Here I Throw Down My Heart*, University of Pittsburgh Press, 2012.

Kim McMillon has over 20 years of experience producing theatre in the San Francisco Bay Area. In 1987, Ms. McMillon wrote, produced, and directed *Voyages, A Multi-Media Excursion Into Reincarnation* at UC Berkeley's Zellerbach Playhouse. In 2000, Ms. McMillon wrote, and produced *Confessions Of A Thespian: When Spirit & Theatre Collide* at the Julia Morgan Theatre in Berkeley. From 2001 – 2005, Ms. McMillon produced the Oakland Literature Expo with PEN Oakland as part of the City of Oakland's Art & Soul Festival. She is currently enrolled in a doctoral program at UC Merced's School of Social Sciences, Humanities and Art.

Adam David Miller has served the Northern California arts community for five decades as teacher, writer and publisher, radio and television programmer and producer, and theater actor, writer and director. As co-owner of Mina Press, he published *Japanese American Women, Three Generations*, a seminal work. His most recent publications are *Ticket to Exile*, a memoir and *The Sky Is A Page*, new and selected poems. adamdavidmillerpoet@yahoo.com

E. Ethelbert Miller is a literary activist. He is the director of the African American Resource Center at Howard University and the board chair of the Institute for Policy Studies, a progressive think tank located in Washington, D.C. His most recent book is *The 5th Inning*, a second memoir.

Yasmin Mogul was born in Bombay (Mumbai), India. She graduated from Elphinstone College in Mumbai with an Honours degree in Economics. At Temple University, Philadelphia where she moved after her move to America in 1969, she studied and received a graduate M.A. degree in Economics. After teaching for a number of years both at the University and high school level, she was chosen as a Fulbright Exchange Teacher to represent the State in the U.K. She studied at the Iowa Writers Workshop in 1979 to 1980 where she met and married Vance Bourjaily. She has an MFA in Creative Writing from the University of Arizona.

Jefferson Morley, editor of JFK Facts Web site (jfkfacts.org), won the 2009 PEN Oakland Censorship Award for his original reporting on JFK's assassination. His most recent book is *Snow-Storm in August: Washington City, Francis Scott Key and the Forgotten Race Riot of 1835*, published by Doubleday in 2012. He is also the author of *Our Man in Mexico: Winston Scott and the Hidden History of the CIA*. Links to his journalism can be found at JeffersonMorley.com.

Jill Nelson is a journalist, essayist, novelist, and author of six books, among them the memoir *Volunteer Slavery*, the novel *Sexual Healing*, and the anthology Police Brutality. She lives in Harlem with her husband, Flores Alexander Forbes, an urban planner and author of the memoir, *Will You Die With Me? My Life and the Black Panther Party*.

Gerald Nicosia is the author of the award-winning books *Memory Babe: A Critical Biography Of Jack Kerouac* and *Home To War: A History Of The Vietnam Veterans' Movement*. He has published three books of poetry, and was a close friend and supporter of Jack Kerouac's daughter, the novelist Jan Kerouac. He has lectured extensively about the Beats around the world, at such places as Cambridge University in England, the Dylan Thomas Centre in Swansea, Wales, and Sichuan University in Chengdu, China.

A.L. Nielsen's volumes of poetry include *Heat Strings, Evacuation Routes, Stepping Razor, VEXT, Mixage* and *Mantic Semantic*. He is currently the George and Barbara Kelly Professor of American Literature at Pennsylvania State University. His awards include the SAMLA Studies Prize, The

Kayden Award and the Gertrude Stein Award. PEN Oakland presented his critical study *Integral Music* with the Josephine Miles Literary Award. His edition of Lorenzo Thomas's posthumous book, *Don't Deny My Name,* was the recipient of an American Book Award.

Elizabeth Nunez is co-founder of the National Black Writers Conference and the author of eight novels: *Boundaries* nominated for the 2012 NAACP Image Award for Outstanding Literary Fiction, *Anna In-Between,* winner of a 2010 PEN Oakland Josephine Miles Literary Award for literary excellence; *Prospero's Daughter,* which was named the 2006 Novel of the Year for *Black Issues Book Review*; *Bruised Hibiscus,* winner of an American Book Award; *Discretion,* short-listed for the Hurston/Wright Legacy Award; *Grace*; *Beyond the Limbo Silence,* winner of an Independent Publishers Book Award in the Multicultural Fiction category; and *When Rocks Dance.*

Peter Orner is the author of four books of fiction including *The Second Coming of Mavala Shikongo,* a novel set in Namibia and a finalist for the Los Angeles Times Book Prize; Esther Stories, winner of the Rome Prize from the American Academy of Arts and Letters; Love and Shame and Love, winner of a California Book Award, and most recently, Last Car Over the Sagamore Bridge, a New York Times Edit'rs Choice Book. Orner is also the editor of two books of oral history, *Underground America: Narratives of Undocumented Lives* and *Hope Deferred: Narratives of Zimbabwean Lives,* both published by Voice of Witness/ McSweeney's. Orner's newest novel is *Love and Shame and Love* (Back Bay Books, 2012.) A 2006 Guggenheim Fellowship recipient, Orner is Professor at San Francisco State University.

Claire Ortalda, treasurer and co-founder of PEN Oakland, is an award-winning fiction writer and poet, whose work has been published in numerous literary journals. Her short story, "A Village Dog," was winner of the Georgia State University Fiction Prize. A poem, "Iowa," was nominated for a Pushcart Prize. Other awards and mentions include national Hackney Literary Award, Fugue Fiction Award and the Chesterfield Writers Film Project, Paramount Pictures. Her children's book, *The Stair in the Wall,* is available on Kindle. She is an editor for *Narrative Magazine,* and also served as editor for *The Other Side of the Closet,* IBS Press, and *Financial Sanity,* Doubleday. Visit www.claireortalda.com

Sandra Park was born and raised in Hawai'i and teaches in the San Francisco Bay Area. Her novella, *If You Live in a Small House* (Mutual Publishing 2010)—a runner-up for the Iowa Fiction Award—takes place in 1950s Hawai'i. Her poetry and fiction have appeared in the *St. Petersburg Review, The Iowa Review, New American Writing, Five Fingers Review, Fourteen Hills, Cordite, CrossBRONX, Airplane Reading* and anthologized in *Honolulu Stories.* Her stage play, *Red Money Bag,* was a finalist for the Aurora Theatre Global Age Project. She received fellowships abroad to Prague and St. Petersburg. Recent teaching and writing projects are posted at www.sandratpark.com.

Margo Perin is the contributing editor of *Only the Dead Can Kill*, CommunityWorks/West, 2006, and *How I Learned to Cook, Tarcher/*Penguin, 2004. Awarded two San Francisco Arts Commission Cultural Equity Grants, a Creative Work Fund grant, and a nomination for the Pushcart Prize, Perin's most recent project is the poetic text for the *Spiral of Gratitude* memorial for survivors of police officers fallen in the line of duty, a Shimon Attie/San Francisco Arts Commission/BALEAF collaboration. She has taught at San Francisco County Jail and San Quentin State Prison for more than a decade and, most recently, with California Poets in the Schools. Margo Perin has been featured in the *San Francisco Chronicle Sunday Magazine, O Magazine, the Washington Post, Dallas Morning News, SF Weekly, BUST, Ellegirl, Seventeen, Psychology Today, Mexico's El Petit Journal, Holland's Psychologie,* and on KRON 4 TV, NPR *Talk of the Nation,* KALW, KPFA, WAMC, MAXIM Radio, WMMT Thousand Kites, and other public media. Visit www.margoperin.com

Richard Prince, noted writer and journalist, is the author of Richard Prince's Journal-isms at the Maynard Institute for Journalism Education. It also appears on TheRoot.com. He has been a reporter and copy editor at the *Washington Post* and editorial writer and columnist at the *Rochester Democrat & Chronicle* in Rochester, N.Y. He is a member of the Trotter Group and chairs the Diversity Committee of the Association of Opinion Journalists. Prince received the 2013 Ida B. Wells Award from the National Association of Black Journalists, the 2010 Robert C. McGruder Award for Media Diversity, Kent State University, as well as the 2010 PEN Oakland Censorship Award. Visit http://mije.org/richardprince

Jerry Ratch has published twelve books of poetry, and the novel, *Wild Dreams of Reality*, as well as the memoir, *A Body Divided*, the story of a one-armed boy growing up in a two-fisted world. His poems have been published in: *Accents Publishing anthology, Antioch Review, AppleValleyReview.com, Avec, Bap Quarterly, Beatitude, Carolina Quarterly, COE Review, Contact II, Faithful Fools Anthology, flashparty.weebly.com, fwrictionreview.com, Ironwood, kaffeinkatmandu.com, languageandculture.net, Louisville Review, MarylandLiteraryReview.org, Milvia Street Journal, Negative Capability, Nerve Cowboy, negativesuck.com, Voices, Seems, Public-Republic.net, Slant, TonopahReview.org, verdadmagazine.org,* and elsewhere. His work can be purchased through the author's website, jerryratch.com or email jerryratch@yahoo.com as well as through Amazon.com.

Ishmael Reed is author of twenty-nine books, including his tenth non-fiction work, *Going Too Far: Essays About America's Nervous Breakdown* (2012); his tenth novel, *Juice!* (2011); six collected plays in Ishmael Reed, *THE PLAYS* (2009); and *New and Collected Poems, 1964-2007* (2007). In addition he has edited numerous magazines and thirteen anthologies, of which the most recent is *POWWOW, Charting the Fault Lines in the American Experience-Short Fiction from Then to Now* (2009), and he is a publisher, songwriter, public media commentator, and lecturer. Founder of the Before Columbus Foundation and PEN Oakland, non-profit organizations run by writers for writers, he now teaches at California College of the Arts and taught at the University of California, Berkeley for over thirty years, retiring in 2005. He is a MacArthur Fellow, and among his other honors are National Book Award and Pulitzer Prize nominations, a Lila Wallace-Reader's Digest Award, San Francisco LitQuake's 2011 Barbary Coast Award, and the 2008 Blues Songwriter of the Year from the West Coast Blues Hall of Fame. He currently serves as San Francisco Jazz Center's first poet laureate, having collaborated with jazz musicians for over thirty years, and three new songs with Reed's lyrics will soon be released by Macy Gray and David Murray. His online international literary magazine, *Konch,* can be found at www.ishmaelreedpub.com. His author website is located at www.ishmaelreedpub.org.

Tennessee Reed is the author of six poetry collections and a memoir. *Adventures Among the X Challenged* is her first published novel. Ms. Reed has read around the Continental United States, Alaska, Hawaii, England, the Netherlands, Germany, Israel, Palestine and Japan. She has received her B.A. from the University of California at Berkeley and her M.F.A from Mills College. Ms. Reed is the managing editor of *Konch Magazine* and the secretary of PEN Oakland.

Fred Reiss wrote *Today Cancer Tomorrow The World* to show how to use the power of your life, your influences, dreams and the love of others to fight cancer as well as help cancer patients reduce their pain during treatment. *Today Cancer* is also available for 99-cents as a Kindle book for financially stressed people going through chemo. So far his health is strong, and he is working on another book, and doing volunteer work for the American Cancer Society. He wants you to live forever as long as you can. He won a PEN Oakland Josephine Miles Literary Award for his novel, *Surf.Com*. *Today Cancer* as well as his other books, *Gidget Must Die, Surf.Com, Blind Guys Break 80, Aliens! Surf! Santa Cruz!* are available at www.fredforyourhead.com. Reiss's blog is http://fredforyourhead.wordpress.com.

Doren Robbins' poems and prose poems have appeared in *5AM, American Poetry Review, Cimarron Review, Exquisite Corpse, Hotel Amerika, Indiana Review, Kayak, Nimrod, North Dakota Quarterly, Sulfur,* and other periodicals. His recent collections of poetry include *Driving Face Down*, awarded the Blue Lynx Poetry Award, 2000, and *My Piece of the Puzzle*, awarded the 2008 PEN Oakland Josephine Miles Literary Award. In 2011 Lost Horse Press published his collection of poems, Amnesty Muse. Robbins is also the author of the prose poem-sequence, *Parking Lot Mood Swing: Autobiographical Monologues and Prose Poetry*, Cedar Hill Press, 2004. His position as the editor of 5 Trope, an online literary journal, will begin with issue #27. His chapbook, *Title to Pussy Riot*, was just released from Imaginary Friend Press (2014). He teaches at Foothill College in Los Altos Hills, California.

Tony R. Rodriguez is a San Francisco Bay Area native who has written four books, including *When I Followed the Elephant*. Since 2008, Rodriguez has written for Examiner.com, where he composes the column *San Francisco Literary Examiner*. In his column he has covered various literary beats that have captured his fancy. Namely, Rodriguez has been fortunate to review dozens of books and interviews with celebrities, authors, and public figures such as Anne Rice, Paul Krassner, Rachel Kramer Bussel, Lisa Lutz, Eric Drooker, Carolyn Cassady and many more. He's also a board member of PEN Oakland. Please visit his website at: tony-r-rodriguez.com.

Andy Ross was the owner of the legendary Cody's Books in Berkeley from 1977-2007. In 2008 he started the Andy Ross Literary Agency. Andy represents books in a wide range of genres including: narrative non-fiction, journalism, history, current events, literary and commercial fiction, and teen fiction. Authors include: Daniel Ellsberg, Jeffrey Moussaieff Masson, Mary Jo McConahay, and Paul Krassner. Andy has a popular blog, "Ask the Agent," where he talks about writing, and book publishing and reminisces about his life as a bookseller. You can find Andy's website at www.andyrossagency.com.

Clifton Ross is the author, translator or editor of a half dozen books and one movie, *Venezuela: Revolution from the Inside Out*, 2008, PM Press, which he directed, filmed and wrote. Ross represented the U.S. in the World Poetry Festival of Venezuela in 2005 and his book of poetry *Translations from Silence*, 2009, Freedom Voices won a PEN Oakland Josephine Miles Literary Award in 2010. A version of the collection, *Traducciones del Silencio*, was published in Spanish in 2011 by Editorial Perro y Rana (Caracas, Venezuela) in the series, *Poetas del Mundo*. The first two poems published here were taken from that collection.

Suhayl Saadi is a novelist, poet and stage and radio dramatist based in Glasgow, Scotland. His hallucinatory realist novel, *Psychoraag* (Black and White Publishing, 2004) won a PEN Oakland Josephine Miles Literary Award, was short-listed for the James Tait Black Memorial Prize and the Pakistan National Literary Award and was nominated for the Dublin-based IMPAC Prize and was published in French by the Paris-based Editions Métailié. *Psychoraag* was acclaimed by the Scottish Book Trust as one of the 'Top 100' Scottish books of all time. Saadi's eclectic short story collection, *The Burning Mirror* (Polygon, 2001) was shortlisted for the Saltire First Book Prize. His first novel, the literary erotic fiction, The Snake (Creation Books, 1997) was penned under the pseudonym, Melanie Desmoulins. Saadi wrote the libretto for a mini-opera (music composed by Nigel Osborne and Wajahat Khan) which received its London premiere, courtesy of Scottish Opera, at the Riverside Studios, Hammersmith, London in August 2008. His new novel, Joseph's Box, set across various parts of Europe and Asia, was published by Two Ravens Press in October 2009 and was longlisted for the IMPAC Prize.

Floyd Salas, president and co-founder of PEN Oakland, is the author of eight books, including the novels *What Now My Love, Lay My Body on the Line,* and *State of Emergency,* and two books of poetry, *Color of My Living Heart and Love Bites: Poetry in Celebration of Dogs and Cats*. His award-winning first novel, *Tattoo the Wicked Cross* along with his memoir *Buffalo Nickel* are featured in Masterpieces of Hispanic Literature (HarperCollins 1994). His first historical novel, *Widow's Weeds,* is now available on Kindle. He was 2002-2003 Regent's Lecturer at University of California, Berkeley, staff writer for the NBC drama series, *Kingpin* and the recipient of NEA, California Arts Council, Rockefeller Foundation, and other fellowships and awards. *Tattoo the Wicked Cross* earned a place on the San Francisco Chronicle's Western 100 List of Best 20th Century Fiction. His work is archived in the Floyd Salas collection in the Bancroft Library, UC Berkeley. www.floydsalas.com

Dr. Mona Lisa Saloy, Author and Folklorist, is currently Professor of English at Dillard University. See her poems and scholarly articles in *The Southern Poetry Anthology, Louisiana Folklore Miscellany, Children's Folklore Review,* Forward to *Night Sessions: Poems by David S. Cho* (published by CavanKerry Press in 2011), and *Pan African Literary Journal.* Some of Dr. Saloy's articles on *Toasts,* and *The Lore of Black Kids* are available online at the Louisiana Division of the Arts Folklife website. Also, her completed screenplay entitled *Rocking for a Risen Savior* is in production negotiations. Dr. Saloy's book, *Red Beans and Ricely Yours: Poems* (Truman State University, 2005), won a PEN Oakland Josephine Miles Literary Award (2006) and the T. S. Eliot Prize in poetry. Saloy's second collection of verse: *Second Line Home, New Orleans Poems* was published by Truman State University Press in 2014. She writes for those who don't or can't tell Creole cultural stories.

Richard Silberg is a poet, critic, translator, and Associate Editor of *Poetry Flash.* His poetry book, *Deconstruction of the Blues,* received a PEN Oakland Josephine Miles Literary Award in 2006, and was nominated for a Northern California Book Award. He is author of *Reading the Sphere: A Geography of Contemporary American Poetry,* essays, and several co-translations, among them *The Three Way Tavern,* by South Korean poet Ko Un, co-translated by Clare You, which won the 2007 Northern California Book Award, and *This Side of Time,* poems by Ko Un, White Pine Press, 2012. His most recent book is *The Horses: New & Selected Poems* (Red Hen Press, 2012).

Leslie Simon, born and raised on the South Side of Chicago, lives in San Francisco, where her children and grandchildren live nearby. She is the author of *Collisions and Transformations* (Coffee House Press), *High Desire* (Wingbow Press), *i rise/you riz/we born* (Artaud's Elbow) and *Jazz/ is for white girls, too* (Poetry for the People) and co-author (with Jan Johnson Drantell) of *A Music I No Longer Heard: The Early Death of a Parent* (Simon and Schuster). Simon founded Poetry for the People, a class and publishing collective at City College of San Francisco in 1975, and currently teaches Women's Studies at the college. She believes that Occupy re-awakened a consciousness that will manifest itself through visible and invisible channels as the century continues to unfold.

Jarmila Marie Skalna has always enhanced her teaching and educational career with creative interests. As a longtime editor of the county magazine for children and youth in the Czech Republic, she was encouraged to write short pieces for children produced on the radio in Ostrava. The year 1984 was a turning point in her life. She followed her husband to the United States and settled in California. As a representative on the P.E.N. Center USA West and the Society of Czech Writers she participated in several writers' conferences in Europe and Australia. She wrote six books. Three books written in Czech and broadcast over Czech radio, *Walking Stick, Blue Cowboy and a Yellow Cow,* and *You Should Remain Special,* are also about her observations of Ernest Hemingway and Willa Cather. Two books in English, *Striding into the Sun,* and *Who Needs Dreams?* contain the writer's journey. One would be wrong to expect this to be a book of travels. It is more like a topography of fantasy in confrontation with realistic impression and the nostalgic memories of childhood places in Moravia.

Rebecca Solnit is a San Francisco writer, historian, and activist and the author of fifteen books about environment, landscape, community, art, politics, hope, and memory, including *The Faraway Nearby; A Paradise Built in Hell: The Extraordinary Communities that Arise in Disaster; A Field Guide to Getting Lost; Wanderlust: A History of Walking;* and *Hope in the Dark: Untold Histories, Wild Possibilities.* A product of the California public education system from kindergarten to graduate school, she is a frequent contributor to the political site Tomdispatch.com.

Barry Spector writes about American history, culture and politics from the perspectives of myth, indigenous traditions and archetypal psychology. His book *Madness At The Gates Of The City: The Myth Of American Innocence* (2010, Regent Press) received a PEN Oakland Josephine Miles Literary award in 2011. Barry contributed the introductory essay for the anthology *Uncivil Liberties: Deconstructing*

Libertarianism (2013, Praxis Peace Institute). He has published three articles in *Jung Journal: Culture and Psyche* and writes for several online journals including *Mythic Passages, Inroads Online* and the *Depth Psychology Alliance*. Barry has served as a guest lecturer at Meridian University, Sophia University, California Institute of Integral Studies, the Depth Psychology program at Sonoma State University and the Osher Lifelong Learning Institutes at the University of California at Davis and California State University, East Bay. He serves on the planning committee of the Redwood Men's Center, which presents an annual men's conference in Mendocino, CA.

Jayne Lyn Stahl is a widely published poet whose work has appeared in numerous anthologies, and little magazines, over the years. She was short listed for PEN American Center's prestigious Joyce Osterweil Award for Poetry in 2006. Her recent book, *Riding with Destiny*, was published by NYQ Books. Stahl is also a screenwriter, playwright, essayist, and *Huffington Post* blogger.

Doreen Stock is a poet, essayist, and memoir practitioner who has been exploring creative nonfiction for forty years from the feminine point of view as a wife, mother of three, single human, and grandmother of eleven. Her first book of poems, *The Politics of Splendor*, Alcatraz Editions, Santa Cruz, 1984, was part of a New American Writers exhibit at the Frankfurt Book Fair that year. It combined her own poetry and prose poems with her translation from the work of Marina Tsvetaeva and Anna Akhmatova. Recent publications include *Before There is Nowhere to Stand, Palestine/Israel: Poets Responding to the Struggle*, Lost Horse Press, 2011; *Occupy SF/poems from the movement*, Jambu Press, San Francisco, 2012; *Wall Scrawls, Solo Novo*, Solo Press, Carpinteria, CA, 2011. The Oil Poem was written for a street demonstration during the last oil spill and was read in San Francisco in front of British Petroleum offices while the demonstrators were being arrested.

Susan Suntree is a poet, performer, essayist, and environmental activist who has presented her poetry and performances nationally and internationally. She has published books of poetry, biography, and creative nonfiction, as well as translations, essays, reviews, and book chapters. Her best-selling book, *Sacred Sites: The Secret History of Southern California*, won the Southern California Independent Booksellers Award for Nonfiction and a PEN Oakland Josephine Miles Literary Award. Her adaptation into a poem of the Universal Declaration of Human Rights has been set to music as a choral work by composer Adrienne Albert (*A Choral Quilt of Hope: The Universal Declaration of Human Rights*). Her book of poetry *Eye of the Womb* was published in Madrid as a bilingual edition, *El Ojo de la Matriz*. Her other books include: *Tulips*, a bilingual chapbook of translations of poetry by Ana Rossetti; *Rita Moreno* (young adult biography); and *Wisdom of the East: Stories of Compassion, Inspiration, and Love* (editor), with a foreword by the Dalai Lama.

Susan Terris' poetry books include *The Homelessness of Self, Contrariwise, Natural Defenses, Fire is Favorable to the Dreamer, Poetic License*, and *Eye of the Holocaust*. Her work has appeared in many publications including: *The Iowa Review, Field, The Journal, Colorado Review, Prairie Schooner, Spillway, The Southern Review, Volt, Denver Quarterly*, and *Ploughshares*. For seven years, with CB Follett, she edited, *Runes, A Review Of Poetry*. She is now editor of *Spillway* and a poetry editor for *Pedestal Magazine* and *In Posse Review*. She had a poem from *Field* published in Pushcart Prize XXXI.

Clifford E. Trafzer is Professor of History, Rupert Costo Chair in American Indian Affairs, and Director of the California Center for Native Nations at the University of California, Riverside. He is of Wyandot heritage and served on the Native American Heritage Commission for twenty-two years. His most recent books include *River Song* and *A Chemehuevi Song: A History of the Twenty-Nine Palms Tribe*. Trafzer won a PEN Oakland Josephine Miles Literary Award for *Earth Song, Sky Spirit*.

Alma Luz Villanueva is the author of seven books of poetry, most recently, *Soft Chaos, Desire* with poetry chosen for Best American Poetry. Three novels, *The Ultraviolet Sky* winner of the American Book Award,

Naked Ladies winner of a PEN Oakland Josephine Miles Literary Award, *Luna's California Poppies* recently excerpted in *Califlora, A Literary Field Guide, Weeping Woman, La Llorona and Other Stories* recently anthologized in *Flash Fiction Latino* and *Coming of Age in the 20th Century*. Villanueva grew up in San Francisco's Mission District, and now lives in San Miguel de Allende, Mexico. She has taught at Antioch University's MFA in Creative Writing program for fourteen years, so now journeys back and forth to teach and visit family and friends. www.almaluzvillanueva.com

Gerald Vizenor is a Distinguished Professor of American Studies at the University of New Mexico. He has published more than thirty books, narrative histories, literary studies, novels, essays, short stories, and poetry. *Native Liberty: Natural Reason and Cultural Survivance, Father Meme, Hiroshima Bugi: Atomu 57,* and *Chair of Tears* are his most recent books. He received the American Book Award for *Griever: An American Monkey King in China,* and the Western Literature Association Distinguished Achievement Award.

Michael Warr's books of poetry include *The Armageddon of Funk, 2011, We Are All The Black Boy*,1991, and as a co-editor, *Power Lines: A Decade of Poetry From Chicago's Guild Complex,* 1999, all published by Tia Chucha Press. His awards include a 2012 PEN Oakland Josephine Miles Literary Award, 2012 Poetry Honor Award from the Black Caucus of the American Library Association (BCALA), the Gwendolyn Brooks Significant Illinois Poets Award, a National Endowment of the Arts Creative Writing Fellowship, and others. The BCALA described *The Armageddon of Funk* as "A poetic soundtrack to black life." *The Crisis Magazine,* founded by W.E.B. DuBois, refers to Warr as a "literary long-distance runner," and "poet-traveler." A frequent collaborator with musicians, visual and performing artists, Michael's poems have been dramatized on stage, depicted on canvas, and set to original music. His writing, recordings and videos can be found at Armageddonoffunk.com.

Harriet A. Washington is the author of half a dozen books, including *Medical Apartheid: The Dark History of Medical Experimentation on Black Americans from Colonial Times to the Present,* and *Deadly Monopolies: The Shocking Corporate Takeover of Life Itself,* Doubleday, 2011. John le Carré said of *Monopolies*: "Harriet Washington shines her relentless torch into the darkest corners of Big Pharma with courage, dedication and accuracy." Marcia Angell, M.D., author and former editor of the *New England Journal of Medicine,* said of *Monopolies*: "Harriet Washington has written an important and compelling book." The *Kirkus Reviews* wrote (starred review): "A gripping, revelatory account." The book also received starred reviews from Booklist and ALA Library Journal. Washington's *Medical Apartheid: The Dark History of Medical Experimentation on Black Americans from Colonial Times to the Present* won the National Book Critics Circle Award for Nonfiction, a PEN Oakland Josephine Miles Literary Award, the BCALA Nonfiction Award, and the Gustavus Meyers Award.

Eric Miles Williamson is the author of three novels, two books of criticism, and a short story collection. A native of Oakland, as was his father and his father before him, Williamson was named by France's *Transfuge* magazine one of the 12 Great Authors of the World.

A.D. Winans is an award winning San Francisco poet and writer. He edited and published the *Second Coming Press* for seventeen years. He worked for the San Francisco Art Commission from 1975-80, during which time he produced the 1980 Poets and Music Festival, honoring the poet Josephine Miles and the blues legend John Lee Hooker. His work has been published in over 1500 poetry magazines and anthologies, including the *Outlaw Bible of American Poetry*. He is the author of over sixty books of poetry and prose, including *North Beach Poems* and *Drowning Like Li Po in a River of Red Wine: Selected Poems 1970-2010*. In 2014, Punk Hostage Press will publish a collection of his literary essays and Pedestrian Press, his first collection of short stories. In 2002 a song poem of his was set to music and performed at New York's Alice Tully Hall. In 2006 he won a PEN Oakland Josephine Miles Literary Award. In 2009 PEN Oakland awarded him a Lifetime Achievement Award.

Koon Woon is a China-born poet living in Seattle where he edits the online journal E-Chrysanthemum. He is the founder of Chrysanthemum Literary Society (a nonprofit charitable organization for the advancement of literature, education and world peace) and the founding editor of Chrysanthemum Publications and Goldfish Press. His two full-length books of poetry were published by Kaya Press. His first book, *The Truth in Rented Rooms* (1998), was a winner of a PEN Oakland Josephine Miles Literary Award and a finalist of the Norma Farber First Book Award from the Poetry Society of America. His second book, *Water Chasing Water* was published in 2013. His poetry appears in many venues in small magazines and has been anthologized internationally.

Sue Owens Wright is a pet columnist and award-winning author of both fiction and nonfiction about dogs. An eleven-time nominee for the Maxwell, awarded annually by the Dog Writers Association of America for the best writing on the subject of dogs, she has twice won the Maxwell Award and earned special recognition from the Humane Society of the United States for her writing on animal welfare issues. She also rescues homeless pets. She is a graduate of California State University, Sacramento and studied fiction writing at Trinity College in Dublin, Ireland and University College London, England. She is the author of the Beanie and Cruiser Mystery Series for dog lovers. Her books include: *Howling Bloody Murder, Sirius about Murder, Embarking on Murder, Braced for Murder, What's Your Dog's IQ?, 150 Activities for Bored Dogs*, and *People's Guide to Pets*. Visit www.sueowenswright.com.

Al Young's literary works are widely translated; his many books include poetry, fiction, essays, anthologies, and musical memoirs. From 2005 through 2008 he served as California's poet laureate. Other honors include NEA, Fulbright, Guggenheim Fellowships, The Richard Wright Award for Literary Excellence and, most recently, the 2011 Thomas Wolfe Award. On the first Friday of each month he broadcasts an original poem at KQED Radio's The California Report Magazine. He currently teaches imaginative writing and creativity at California College of the Arts, San Francisco. Detailed information about this versatile Berkeley-based author and his work may be found at www.AlYoung.org

Andrena Zawinski's book of poetry, *Something About,* from Blue Light Press in San Francisco, received a PEN Oakland Josephine Miles Literary Award. Her *Traveling in Reflected Light* from Pig Iron Press in Youngstown, won a Kenneth Patchen Prize in Poetry. She is editor of the anthology, *Turning a Train of Thought Upside Down: An Anthology of Women's Poetry* from Scarlet Tanager Books in Oakland, California. Her work has appeared in *Progressive Magazine, Blue Collar Review, Rattle, Pacific Review, Nimrod, Quarterly West*, and elsewhere. Zawinski teaches writing at Laney College and is Features Editor at PoetryMagazine.com. Her poem in this collection was a Pushcart Prize Nominee. http://andrenazawinski.wordpress.com/category/poetry

Our Thanks

Fightin' Words: 25 Years of Provocative Poetry and Prose from "The Blue Collar PEN" could not have been published without the generous support of the Zellerbach Family Foundation, PEN Center USA, Heyday Books, and the Oakland Public Library.

PEN Oakland wishes to acknowledge the assistance of the following people: Linda Howe of the Zellerbach Family Foundation; Adam Somers of PEN Center USA; Patricia Lichter of the Oakland Public Library; Malcolm Margolin, Gayle Wattawa, Diane Lee, Mariko Conner, and Mary Bisbee-Beek of Heyday Books; Gregory Berger of Pomegranate Design; Susan Yannello, Pat McCurdy-Crescimanno, and Tatyana Eckstrand of The Donohue Group, Inc., PEN Oakland board members John Curl, Sharon Doubiago, Tony Rodriguez, Floyd Salas, Ishmael Reed, Tennessee Reed, Lucha Corpi, Kirk Lumpkin, and the late Reginald Lockett; Eugene B. Redmond, Nina Serrano, Genny Lim, Gerald Nicosia, Eileen Herrmann, Nicole Corrales, Jack Foley, Adele Foley, the late Josephine Miles, Maxine Hong Kingston, Isabel Allende, Emily Stuart, Susan Anderson, Margo Perin, and Mimi Albert. Special thanks to PEN Oakland Vice President John Curl for initiating a series of interviews of founding members, a portion of which inspired Ishmael Reed's Introduction to this volume. Without the contributions of all of these people, this book would not have been possible.

We would also like to give thanks to all the authors who have recently passed on for the gift of their powerful writings, including Maya Angelou, Amiri Baraka, Wanda Coleman, and Jayne Cortez, in acknowledgement of their fighting spirits that made the difference to writers everywhere by their commitment to social justice for all.

PEN Oakland
www.penoakland.com